Systemic Functional Translation Studies

Key Concepts in Systemic Functional Linguistics

Series Editors
Gerard O'Grady, Cardiff University
Rebekah Wegener, University of Salzburg
Tom Bartlett, University of Glasgow

Books in this series provide monographic treatments of core theoretical concepts within Systemic Functional Linguistics, together with coverage of more recent concerns in Systemic Functional Linguistic theory and important areas of application and trans-disciplinary collaboration.

Each monograph is organised around a description of the historical factors that led to the emergence of the concept within Systemic Functional Linguistics and a detailed theoretical description of the concept within the overall architecture of the theory.

Published
Neo-Firthian Approaches to Linguistic Typology
William B. McGregor

Forthcoming
Verbal Art and Systemic Functional Linguistics
Donna R. Miller

Systemic Functional Translation Studies
Theoretical Insights and New Directions

Bo Wang & Yuanyi Ma

UNIVERSITY OF TORONTO PRESS
Toronto Buffalo London

Reprinted 2025 by University of Toronto Press
Toronto Buffalo London
utppublishing.com

First published 2021 by Equinox Publishing Ltd.

© Bo Wang & Yuanyi Ma 2021

All rights reserved. No part of this publication may be reproduced or transmitted in any form or by any means, electronic or mechanical, including photocopying, recording or any information storage or retrieval system, without prior permission in writing from the publishers.

ISBN-13 978 1 80050 031 0 (hardback)
         978 1 78179 831 7 (paperback)
         978 1 78179 832 4 (ePDF)
         978 1 80050 042 6 (ePub)

British Library Cataloguing-in-Publication Data

A catalogue record for this book is available from the British Library.

Library of Congress Cataloging-in-Publication Data

Names: Wang, Bo, (Researcher of translation studies), author. | Ma, Yuanyi, author.
Title: Systemic functional translation studies : theoretical insights and new directions / Bo Wang and Yuanyi Ma.
Description: Sheffield, South Yorkshire ; Bristol, CT : Equinox Publishing Ltd, 2021. | Series: Key concepts in systemic functional linguistics | Includes bibliographical references. | Summary: "This book offers a comprehensive account of Systemic Functional Translation Studies (SFTS)—a research area that applies Systemic Functional Linguistics (SFL) to study translation, and to relate researches by scholars in the community of both SFL and translation studies"—Provided by publisher.
Identifiers: LCCN 2020053823 (print) | LCCN 2020053824 (ebook) | ISBN 9781800500310 (hardback) | ISBN 9781781798317 (paperback) | ISBN 9781781798324 (pdf) | ISBN 9781800500426 (epub)
Subjects: LCSH: Translating and interpreting. | Functionalism (Linguistics) | Systemic grammar.
Classification: LCC P306.97.F86 W36 2021 (print) | LCC P306.97.F86 (ebook) | DDC 418/.020721—dc23
LC record available at https://lccn.loc.gov/2020053823
LC ebook record available at https://lccn.loc.gov/2020053824

Typeset by JS Typesetting Ltd, Porthcawl, Mid Glamorgan

Cover design: Mark Lee / hisandhers.design
Printed and bound by CPI Group (UK) Ltd, Croydon, CR0 4YY

For Christian M.I.M. Matthiessen

Contents

List of Tables	ix
List of Figures	xi
Abbreviations and Symbols	xiii
Abbreviations for Interlinear Glossing	xv
Acknowledgements	xvii
Foreword by Erich Steiner	xix

	Introduction	1
1	What is Systemic Functional Translation Studies?	3
2	The Environments of Translation	29
3	Systemic Functional Translation Studies and the Metafunctional Modes of Meaning	59
4	Register and Systemic Functional Translation Studies	79
5	Technology-based Approaches in Systemic Functional Translation Studies	105
6	Current Situation and Future Direction of Systemic Functional Translation Studies	133
	Notes	149
	Bibliography	151
	Sources of Some Examples	175
	Index	177

List of Tables

Table 1.1	Bühler's functions and Halliday's metafunctions	8
Table 2.1	Three lines of meaning in the clause	41
Table 2.2	Example 2.8	43
Table 2.3	Example 2.9	43
Table 2.4	Example 2.10	44
Table 2.5	Example 2.12	46
Table 2.6	Example 2.13	46
Table 2.7	Example 2.26	57
Table 3.1	Example 3.1	61
Table 3.2	Example 3.17	73
Table 3.3	Example 3.18	74
Table 3.4	Example 3.19	74
Table 3.5	Example 3.20	75
Table 3.6	Example 3.21	76
Table 4.1	Text types and their translation methods according to Reiss's text typology	80
Table 4.2	Mode and number of publication in the database	86
Table 5.1	Operationalizing explicitation as linguistic features according to metafunctions	115
Table 5.2	The cohesive categories being annotated in GECCo	117
Table 5.3	Comparisons between English and German original popular scientific texts seen from the frequency of selected linguistic items	123
Table 5.4	Shining-through and contact-induced changes in translated and non-translated German popular science texts	123
Table 6.1	Areas of multilingual studies in relation to the cline of instantiation and the hierarchy of stratification	140
Table 6.2	Properties and organizational features of the four orders of system	146

List of Tables

List of Figures

Figure 1.1	Holmes's map of translation studies	6
Figure 1.2	Halliday's (2001) categorization of imperative and indicative translation theories	7
Figure 1.3	The domain of language studies	10
Figure 1.4	A timeline of the chronological development of SFTS	12
Figure 1.5	House's model of translation quality assessment	15
Figure 1.6	The cline from 'translation equivalence' to 'translation shift' as degree of congruence between source and target texts in terms of all four metafunctional modes of meaning	20
Figure 1.7	Matrix of metafunctional translation shifts	20
Figure 1.8	Dimensions relevant for contrastive-linguistic descriptions of translations	21
Figure 1.9	Locating translation methods in the matrix of stratification and instantiation	22
Figure 1.10	Order of importance of metafunctional equivalence	25
Figure 2.1	The environments of translation	29
Figure 2.2	The environments and nature of translation	31
Figure 2.3	Stratification	33
Figure 2.4	The cline of instantiation	38
Figure 2.5	Halliday's stratification-instantiation matrix	39
Figure 2.6	Example 2.7	42
Figure 2.7	The strata of context and language and their internal composition in terms of rank	49
Figure 2.8	Multilingual correspondence and rank	49
Figure 2.9	Matrix of translation shifts characterized in terms of rank	52
Figure 2.10	Delicacy in the interpersonal system of MOOD	53
Figure 2.11	Example 2.24	55
Figure 2.12	The systemic (paradigmatic) axis realized by the structural (syntagmatic) axis	55
Figure 2.13	Basic choices in the system of THEME	57
Figure 2.14	Differences in the system of MOOD between English and Chinese	58
Figure 3.1	Modes of meaning in text revealed by the metafunctional part of discourse analysis	60
Figure 4.1	Reiss's (1971) text types and text varieties	81

Figure 4.2	The eight primary fields of activity and their sub-types	83
Figure 4.3	Frequency of the studies characterized according to the field of activity involved	87
Figure 5.1	Bidirectional translation corpus in the CroCo Project	113
Figure 5.2	The design of CroCo corpus and the different types of contrast	114
Figure 5.3	A revised scheme for analysis and comparing originals and translation texts	119
Figure 5.4	Translation corpus and comparable corpus in the 'Verdecktes Übersetzen – Covert Translation' project	121
Figure 5.5	Four areas of analysis in Munday's systemic model for descriptive translation studies	124
Figure 5.6	Illustration of micro translation unit giving rise to a macro translation unit during the translation process of the second translator	129
Figure 5.7	Eye fixations by the second translator while translating 'sich widersprechen' in the drafting phase	130
Figure 6.1	Relationship between comprehensiveness of analysis and volume of text analysed	133
Figure 6.2	Analytical framework in Wang and Ma (2020)	135
Figure 6.3	Martin's stratified model of context	137
Figure 6.4	The 'Hallidayan' model in Munday's (e.g. 2016) book	138
Figure 6.5	Phenomenal realm explored in multilingual studies differentiated in terms of the number of languages in focus and in terms of the cline of instantiation	139

Abbreviations and Symbols

BT	back translation
CDA	critical discourse analysis
CroCo	Cross-linguistic Corpus for the Study of Translation
DTS	descriptive translation studies
GECCo	German–English Contrasts in Cohesion
IG	interlinear glossing
PY	pinyin
RST	rhetorical structure theory
SFL	systemic functional linguistics
SFTS	systemic functional translation studies
ST	source text
TT	target text
TU	translation unit
↘	realization
╱	conflation
^	ordering (followed by)
< >	enclosed group/phrase
<< >>	enclosed clause
<<< >>>	enclosed clause complex
ø	ellipsis
|||	clause complex, boundary markers
||	clause (not rankshifted), boundary markers
		phrase or group, boundary markers
[[[ ]]]	rankshifted (embedded) clause complex, boundary markers
[[ ]]	rankshifted (embedded) clause, boundary markers
[]	rankshifted group/phrase, boundary markers
α	and other small Greek letters: elements of hypotactic interdependency structure
1	and other Arabic numerals: elements of paratactic interdependency structure
+	logico-semantic relation of extension
=	logico-semantic relation of elaboration
×	logico-semantic relation of enhancement

Abbreviations for Interlinear Glossing

ACC	accusative
APART	adverbial particle
ASP	clause particle: aspectual
CV	coverb
DAT	dative
DISP	voice coverb: dispositive
EMPH	emphatic
GEN	genitive
HON	honorific
MEAS	measurer
MOD	verbal particle: modal
NEG	verbal particle: negative
NOM	nominative
PV	postverb
SUB	subordinating
VADV	verbal adverb
VPART	verbal particle

Acknowledgements

First and foremost, our heartfelt thanks go to Professor Christian M.I.M. Matthiessen, who inspires us to write this book, and who continues to enrich our understanding of SFL and translation.

We thank Professor Erich Steiner for his enduring support and encouragement, and for kindly writing a foreword for our book and warmly recommending it.

We also extend our thanks to Professor Juliane House, Professor Chu Chi-yu, Dr Chris Shei, Professor Huang Guowen, Professor Chang Chenguang, Professor Wendy Bowcher, and Dr Isaac Mwinlaaru for their valuable personal exchanges and academic guidance during the previous years.

Our thanks also go to the editors of the book series – Dr Tom Bartlett, Professor Gerard O'Grady, and Dr Rebekah Wegener for their continued support and for their time and efforts in revising the book manuscript.

We thank Dr Mark Nartey for proofreading our draft, and Equinox Publishing for permission to reproduce the quotation originally published in Matthiessen and Teruya (2016). We are grateful to Valerie Hall, Sarah Lee, and Cheryl Merritt for their assistance in the production of the book.

Foreword

Erich Steiner

I am honoured and delighted to welcome readers to *Systemic Functional Translation Studies: Theoretical Insights and New Directions* by Bo Wang and Yuanyi Ma. There is currently no monograph available in English that would attempt an up-to-date outline and a conceptual map of Systemic Functional Translation Studies on the one hand, and that would do so with particular acknowledgement of recent contributions by scholars from China on the other, where Beijing, Guangzhou, Shanghai, and Hong Kong are among lively centres of activity for systemic-functionally based work on translation. After a first historical and conceptual chapter, we find coverage of some of the distinctive concepts of systemic functional translation theory: categories and scales of the theoretical architecture, metafunctional modes of meaning, register, context, and text types, relationship of systemic-functional work to translation-oriented language technology and to empirical work both in product- and process-based form. The book is rounded off with a productively critical discussion of the potential of systemic functional linguistics as a theoretical framework for translation.

Bo Wang and Yuanyi Ma are scholars with backgrounds in Chinese linguistics and translation studies, but also, and importantly, with expertise in translating and in translation evaluation. Their book is primarily aimed at researchers and students, but I am sure that translators looking for some methodological underpinnings of their professional practice will find much that is of interest to them.

Introduction

This book is written for researchers and students who wish to apply systemic functional linguistics (SFL) to study translation. To read this book, you do not have to be experts of SFL and translation studies. Instead, we hope you will be well acquainted with the area after reading it. The book covers a sketch of the area, the basic concepts, and some trends for future research. As we have rather limited space in the book, we cannot discuss all important publications in detail, but we have tried our best to create some links to them. We hope you can explore the area on your own after reading this book.

We try to include examples in different languages, including English, Chinese, German, French, Spanish, Portuguese, Hungarian, and Kalam. However, due to our language backgrounds, most examples are in English and Chinese. As for the examples in languages other than English, we provide interlinear glossing and back translation for your careful examination and comparison.

This book includes six chapters, whose major ideas can be summarized as follows:

Chapter 1 orients the book with a general introduction to systemic functional translation studies (SFTS). We first explain the relationship between translation and linguistics. Then, we define SFTS, differentiate SFTS from other functional approaches to translation, and locate SFTS in the map of translation studies. Towards the end of this chapter, we present a brief history of SFTS by highlighting various important works, models, and frameworks.

Chapter 2 outlines Matthiessen's (2001) environments of translation, providing accounts of the six dimensions of the environments, i.e. stratification, instantiation, metafunction, rank, delicacy, and axis. Examples are given to illustrate how these dimensions work in the process of translation. We also relate translation equivalence and translation shift to the dimensions.

Chapter 3 views SFTS through the lens of metafunction. Translation is understood as the recreation of the four metafunctional modes of meaning through choice. The four modes of meaning include ideational meanings of the logical kind, ideational meanings of the experiential kind, interpersonal meanings, and textual meanings. Various studies in the literature are introduced from the perspective of the four metafunctions.

Chapter 4 explores the relationship between register, text type, and translation. Besides the work by German functionalist scholars, we introduce Matthiessen's context-based functional text typology that characterizes texts according to the eight primary fields of activity. Based on Matthiessen's classification, we conduct a survey of the text types studied in the literature.

Chapter 5 focuses on the approaches in SFTS that are closely associated with the development of translation-oriented language technology. We address three research areas, including machine translation, corpus-based approaches, and the tools for investigating translation process.

Chapter 6 concludes the book by discussing some limitations in SFTS and giving some suggestions of future studies.

Chapter 1

What is Systemic Functional Translation Studies?

1.1 Approaching Translation from a Linguistic Perspective

The phenomenon of translation is always around us and has a huge effect on our lives. We may all have the experience of reading a translation, learning to translate, working as a translator, or seeing how others translate. The English term 'translation', which comes from the particle of the verb 'transferre' (to carry over), was first attested in around 1340. The word 'translation' now carries different meanings, as summarized by Munday (2016: 8):

- the general subject field or phenomenon ('I studied translation at university')
- the product – that is, the text that has been translated ('they published the Arabic translation of the report')
- the process of producing the translation, otherwise known as translating ('translation service').

As an activity with a long history in human society, translation is a 'many-splendored' phenomenon (as the title of a film – *Love Is a Many-Splendored Thing* – suggests). It can be defined and viewed from different perspectives – as art, science, product, process, etc. When a translator translates, he/she operates within a typology of four orders of systems in different phenomenal realms (Halliday 1996, 2005). The systems, including physical, biological [physical systems + 'life'], social [biological systems + 'value'], and semiotic ones [social systems + 'meaning'], are ordered with an increasing complexity. According to Matthiessen (2021), as translators, we can be aware of or trained to be sensitive to these systems (original emphasis):

- The physical environment plays a role, both enabling and constraining us; for example, enabling us by providing a physical **workspace** including a workbench providing electronic translation resources and tools (e.g. to support example-based translation and to provide technical glossaries) and constraining us through limitations imposed by these features.

- We inhabit this physical workspace as human **organisms**, drawing on certain key organ systems to carry out the process of translation as a biological activity. As we continue to translate texts over a period of time, we may become increasingly aware of our own bodies growing tired, failing to remember, or making more mistakes, so needing cups of tea or coffee, fresh air.

- At the same time, we are not just biological organisms; we are **persons** actively involved in different social networks, in each network in a different role, e.g. as professional translator in relation to colleagues in a team, possibly including editors, as translation service provider in relation to clients.

- But our primary experience is, naturally, as **multi-lingual meaners** who have mastered multilingual meaning potentials ranging over two or more languages, and who draw on these potentials to recreate meanings in context as we interpret the meanings of source texts instantiated in the meaning potential of one language and recreate them by instantiating the meaning potential of another language.

The study of translation as a discipline has a very long history, which dates back to discussions by Cicero and Horace and the translation of Buddhist sutras in the first century AD in China. Since the late 18th century, translation has also been regarded as a method of language teaching and learning (Cook 2010). In our time, translation is embraced by different theories and approaches, such as cultural theories, literary theories, and sociological theories (Steiner et al. 2018a, 2018b). Among the many approaches, the linguistic-oriented approach to translation is important, as it highlights the importance of language, which is the primary and the most difficult phenomenon in translation. **Systemic functional linguistics** (**SFL**) is a linguistic theory. It is **appliable**, which means it is designed to be applied and remains in constant dialogue with application (Halliday 1985a, 2007, 2008; Matthiessen 2014a). This book is concerned with applying SFL to translation.

From a linguistic perspective, translation can be defined as a procedure whereby a source text (hereafter ST, also called the original text) is replaced by a target text in a different language or language variety (House 2018). Similarly, Catford (1965: 20) defines translation as 'the replacement of textual material in one language [source language] by equivalent textual material in another language [target language]'. Drawing on the metafunctions in SFL, which are the highly generalized functions that determine the way language has evolved (including the ideational, the interpersonal, and the textual metafunctions), Matthiessen (2014b: 272) considers translation as 'recreation of meaning in context through choice'. In all the above definitions, both the written mode and the spoken mode (interpreting) are considered as translation. In this book, however, we mainly focus on the written mode, with very brief discussions on the spoken mode.

The history of translation studies shows that there has been a strong linguistic input in translation studies in the 1950s and the 1960s, marked especially by the works by Eugene Nida (1964) and J.C. Catford (1965). On the one hand, Nida's works (e.g. Nida 1964; Nida & Taber 1969) are influenced by Chomsky's transformational-generative grammar, and are located particularly in the context of Bible translation. Catford's (1965) monograph – *A Linguistic Theory of Translation*, on the other hand, is based on linguistic analysis carried out at different ranks and levels, and is written in a more general sense by conceiving translation as one aspect of typological comparative linguistics and general linguistics. The relationship between translation and linguistics is so close that some scholars even regard translation as part of linguistics. For instance, in *Towards a General Comparative Linguistics*, Ellis (1966) locates translation as a domain within comparative linguistics. Also, House (2016) considers translation as a sub-branch of applied linguistics, and gives suggestions like modelling and theorizing translation in relation to the structure of language.

The linguistic approach to translation tends to involve text analysis, thus highlighting the specific relation between the source text and the target text. For translators, such a relationship is rather complex. When translating, translators find themselves in a paradox where they act as both speaker and non-speaker. On the one hand, the target text is the translators' production. On the other hand, the target text is not exactly the translators' production or utterance, as they may need to be invisible under certain circumstances (cf. Venuti 2008). Therefore, translators are not really autonomous in making their choices. They are not only constrained by the source text, but are also limited by the convention and lexicogrammatical resources of the target language. As classic studies on translation from the linguistic approach, Nida (e.g. 1964) and Catford's (1965) works both emphasize the specific role that the source texts play in translation. In Section 1.3, we will find out how this linguistic tradition has been passed down throughout the decades when we examine the studies that apply SFL to translation.

There were several reactions against the linguistic orientation towards translation, marked especially by the various 'turns' in translation studies, such as the cultural turn and the sociological turn. The cultural turn, initiated by Bassnett and Lefevere (1990), emphasizes the bicultural nature of translation, and pays close attention to the mind-shifting in translation from one linguacultural model of the world to another (Katan 2009). In SFTS, the cultural perspective is included in the contextual analysis, notably the analysis of the context of culture (see Sections 2.2 and 2.3). For another example, the sociological approach theorizes the social nature of translation studies and is characterized by the ideas taken from Bourdieu (e.g. 1984) – a French social theorist. Some central concepts include *habitus*, field, capital, and *illusio* (e.g. Simeoni 1998; Wolf & Furaki 2007). The relationship between the sociological approach and SFTS is not clear-cut. One link to them is the position of Bernstein's (e.g. 1971, 1973) code theory in SFL. On the one hand, Bourdieu (1984) emphasizes how social classes are mirrored in cultural and linguistic preferences, which can be understood as Bernstein's code theory in a different sense; on the other hand, SFL is closely related to Bernstein's theory, which is about how the socialized individual constructs or develops a social identity in the sense of codes by placing us in the social semiotic structure that we are living in (see Steiner 2015a; cf. Steiner et al. 2018a).

Without denying the value and insights of various approaches to translation, we try to show in this book the importance of viewing translation through the lens of linguistics. Our aim is informed by two reasons: first, there is still so much that needs to be explored as far as translation from a linguistic perspective is concerned (cf. Matthiessen, Wang, & Ma 2017a); second, we argue that the various discussions made under the heading of culture or translation competence can be incorporated into the linguistic approach to translation on condition that there is a holistic and powerful linguistic theory engaging with language in context, and offering comprehensive descriptions of the source language and the target language involved in the translation activity. Halliday's SFL is such a theory.

The institutionalization of the discipline of translation studies began with **James S. Holmes**'s vision in the 1970s. Figure 1.1 is a widely known representation of Holmes's (e.g. 1988) map based on Toury's (1995) interpretation (cf. Lambert 2013; Malmkjær 2013).

As shown in Figure 1.1, translation studies is first divided into pure and applied branches. The pure branch is then divided into theoretical and descriptive sub-sections. The descriptive branch is further differentiated as product-oriented, process-oriented, and function-oriented; while the theoretical branch could be general or partial, with the partial branch being further divided into sub-branches that are restricted to medium, area, rank, text type, time, and problem. In contrast with the pure branch, the applied branch is marked by three strands of studies that deal with translator training, translation aids, and translation criticism. A fourth strand, namely, translation policy, has been added by Malmkjær (2013).

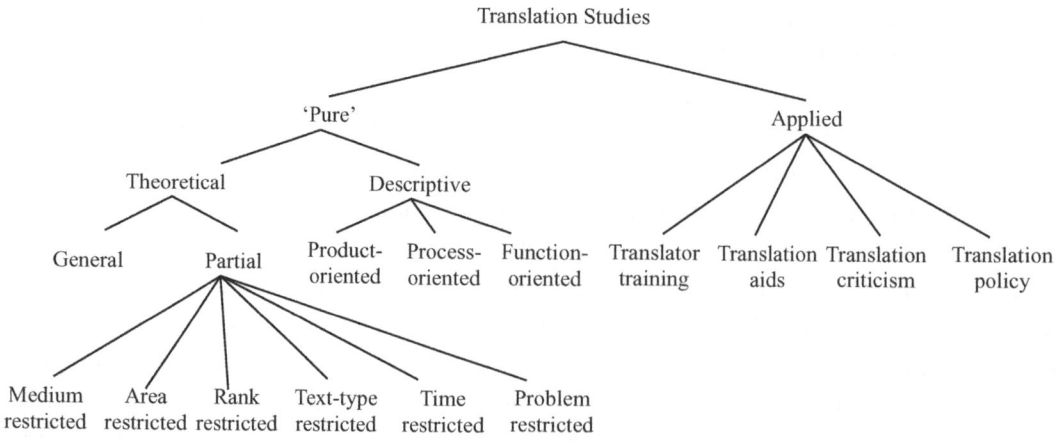

Figure 1.1 Holmes's map of translation studies (adapted from Toury 1995: 10)

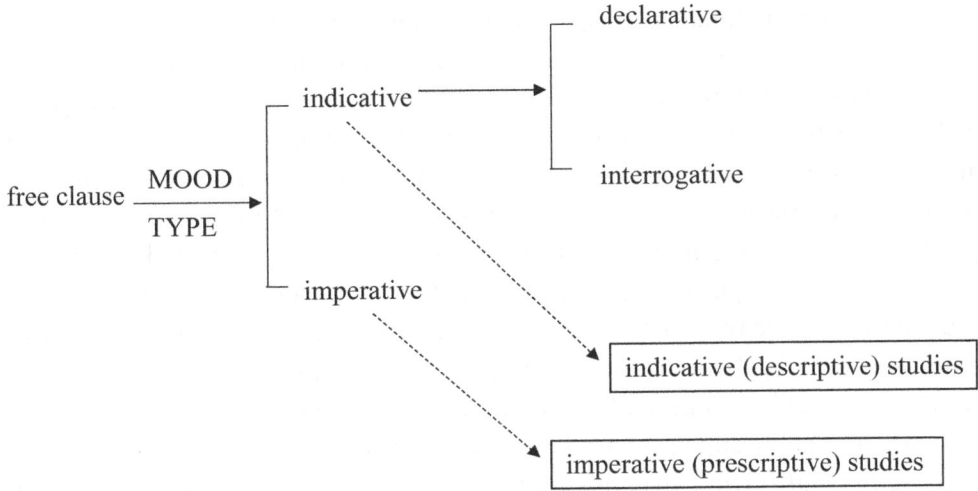

Figure 1.2 Halliday's (2001) categorization of imperative and indicative translation theories

Halliday (2001: 13) provides another way of categorizing translation theories, in relating translation theories to linguistics, by distinguishing **two kinds of translation theories** – the linguist's theory and the translator's theory:

> For a linguist, translation theory is the study of how things are: what is the nature of the translation process and the relation between texts in translation. For a translator, translation theory is the study of how things ought to be: what constitutes good or effective translation and what can help to achieve a better or more effective product.

Halliday (2001) further expresses this distinction in grammatical terms, and associates translation theories with the system of MOOD in SFL. As shown in Figure 1.2, translation theories are divided into the following two categories: (i) the linguist's indicative (descriptive) theories, and (ii) the translator's imperative (prescriptive) theories.

Based on this categorization, a linguist's translation theory, generally, is descriptive – this concerns the nature of the translation process and the relationship between the source text and the target text. In particular, translation studies from the SFL perspective are indicative rather than imperative.

1.2 Mapping Systemic Functional Translation Studies

Systemic functional translation studies (SFTS) is used in this book to refer to studies in translation that are informed by systemic functional linguistics (SFL) (cf. Matthiessen 2009a; Matthiessen, Wang, & Ma 2017b). Unlike other linguistic theories, application is central to SFL, and its application to translation dates as far back as the 1950s when SFL theory was still in its early days (see Halliday 1985b; Halliday & Matthiessen 2014; Matthiessen & Halliday 2009 for introductions to SFL).

SFTS, though 'functional' as suggested in its name, differs from the other functionalist approaches to translation such as **German functionalism** (Bühler 1933, 1934), whose history can be traced back to the work by scholars of the Prague School, such as Jakobson (1959) and Procházka (1964), who offer multifunctional approaches to translation. **Karl Bühler**'s (1934) famous model distinguishes three functions of language: (i) informative function (*Darstellungsfunktion*), (ii) expressive function (*Ausdrucksfunktion*), and (iii) appellative function (*Appellfunktion*). These three functions are, in fact, derived from the person systems of language, which include the function-oriented to 'me' (first person), the function-oriented to 'you' (second person), and the function about the reality (third person) (see Halliday & Hasan 1985; Section 4.1). These functions represent the extrinsic functionality of language, and are philosophical and psychological in nature, rather than functions deeply engaged with language (see Martin 1991).

Jakobson (1960) further expands Bühler's three functions into six, i.e. referential, emotive, conative, poetic, phatic, and metalingual, which are in turn determined by the constitutive factors in communication – context, addresser, addressee, message, contact, and code. Instead of delving into the inherent functions of language, Jakobson and Bühler's models categorized the uses of language. If we compare the functions proposed by Jakobson and Bühler with Halliday's (e.g. 1967/1968, 1973, 1979) metafunctions, we can find that both Bühler and Jakobson have not foregrounded the textual metafunction, which is instead found in Mathesius's (1928, 1975) work on theme and Daneš's (1974) functional sentence perspective. However, the Prague School scholars did not combine these functions into a unified theory of the intrinsic functionality of language. One reason behind this may be the limited number of textual-based studies readily available. Therefore, the works by Jakobson and Bühler merely represent a functional model of language, without considerations of grammar per se (Firbas's 1992 opening chapter consists of translations of short literary text, but he does not overtly focus on translation).

The functional tradition in the Prague School was followed by skopos theory put forward by **Katharina Reiss** and **Hans J. Vermeer** in Germany (e.g. Reiss 1971; Reiss & Vermeer 1984). Reiss's (1971) functional studies are based on the concept of equivalence on a higher level of communication rather than on the lexicogrammar. Further

Table 1.1 Bühler's functions and Halliday's metafunctions (cf. Halliday & Hasan 1985: 17; see also Section 2.3)

Bühler (1934)	representational [3rd person]	conative [2nd person]	expressive [1st person]	–
Halliday (e.g. 1973)	ideational	interpersonal		textual
Language use	informative uses (orientation to content)	interactive uses (orientation to effect)		–

developing Bühler's (1934) functions, Reiss (1971) characterizes text types as informative, expressive, and operative, relating the functions of text to text types or communicative situations, with purposes of helping translation assessment. The term 'skopos', which means 'purpose' in Greek, is used to refer to the purpose of translation and the action of translating (e.g. Vermeer 2012). These approaches have highlighted the target context of translation, but they have not differentiated translation from other forms of multilingual text production. Other influential functional theories include Nord's works (e.g. 1991, 1995, 1997) on pre-translational text analysis. Her linguistic model for text description includes the mainstream linguistic tools, which offer more insights than the traditional models of language that lack theoretical depth, and are helpful in translation practice.

Other functional schools of grammar, such as Kay's (e.g. 1979) Functional Unification Grammar (FUG), Fawcett's (e.g. 2008) Cardiff Grammar, Bresnan and Kaplan's (e.g. Bresnan et al. 2016) Lexical Functional Grammar (LFG), and Dik's (e.g. 1997a, 1997b) functional grammar (see Matthiessen 2015a: 150 for the origin and development of the different schools of functional grammar), have not yet been applied to translation studies due to their restricted interest in how clause internal mechanisms can be diversified in terms of their functions. Moreover, these theories have never made such attempts as to relate texts to the context of situation.

Informed by SFL, an appliable linguistics, SFTS provides answers to the two questions Firth (1968a: 83; cf. 1968b) raised when discussing the need of a linguistic theory in translation – 'Do we know how we translate?' and 'Do we even know what we translate?'. If we try to map SFTS with the tree structure representation of translation studies in Figure 1.1, we will find that SFTS can shade into the branches and sub-branches in the map. SFTS incorporates the 'partial' sub-branches sketched in Figure 1.1, and is not restricted to one or several such topics, such as translation medium (e.g. spoken and written, human and machine translation), area (linguistics, cultural studies), rank, and text type (e.g. literary text, advertisement, legal documents; see Chapter 4 for a detailed discussion on register and SFTS). In addition, the text analysis informed by SFL can be applied to the various sub-fields in the 'applied' branch of the map.

Compared to translation studies, SFL has a wider coverage in terms of the scientific engagement with language. As early as the 1970s, Halliday (1978) mapped out the domain of a general theory of linguistics, such as SFL. As shown in Figure 1.3, the fields of research within the broken line are all considered as branches of linguistics. The triangle in the centre of the figure identifies the central areas of linguistics. There are projections of the triangle, which are the specific sub-disciplines in the central area, such as linguistic change, history of linguistics (historical linguistics), phonetics, and language varieties: dialect/register. Also, outside the triangle, there are areas that represent how linguistics impinges on other disciplines, such as language as art, language as knowledge, and language as behaviour. For instance, language as art is associated with literary studies located outside the broken line. Although the domains of language studies envisaged by Halliday (1978) were proposed forty years ago, it still enlightens us on the interaction between linguistics and many other disciplines today. The two maps shown in Figures 1.1 and 1.3 are similar in that both linguistics and translation studies have various interface areas with other disciplines. However, compared to Holmes's map, the domain of language in Figure 1.3 is more insightful in that concrete connections are made between linguistics and various disciplines, upon which translation studies can dwell. Hence, we suggest that, despite gaining its autonomy and having its own territories, translation studies should not move too far away from linguistics.

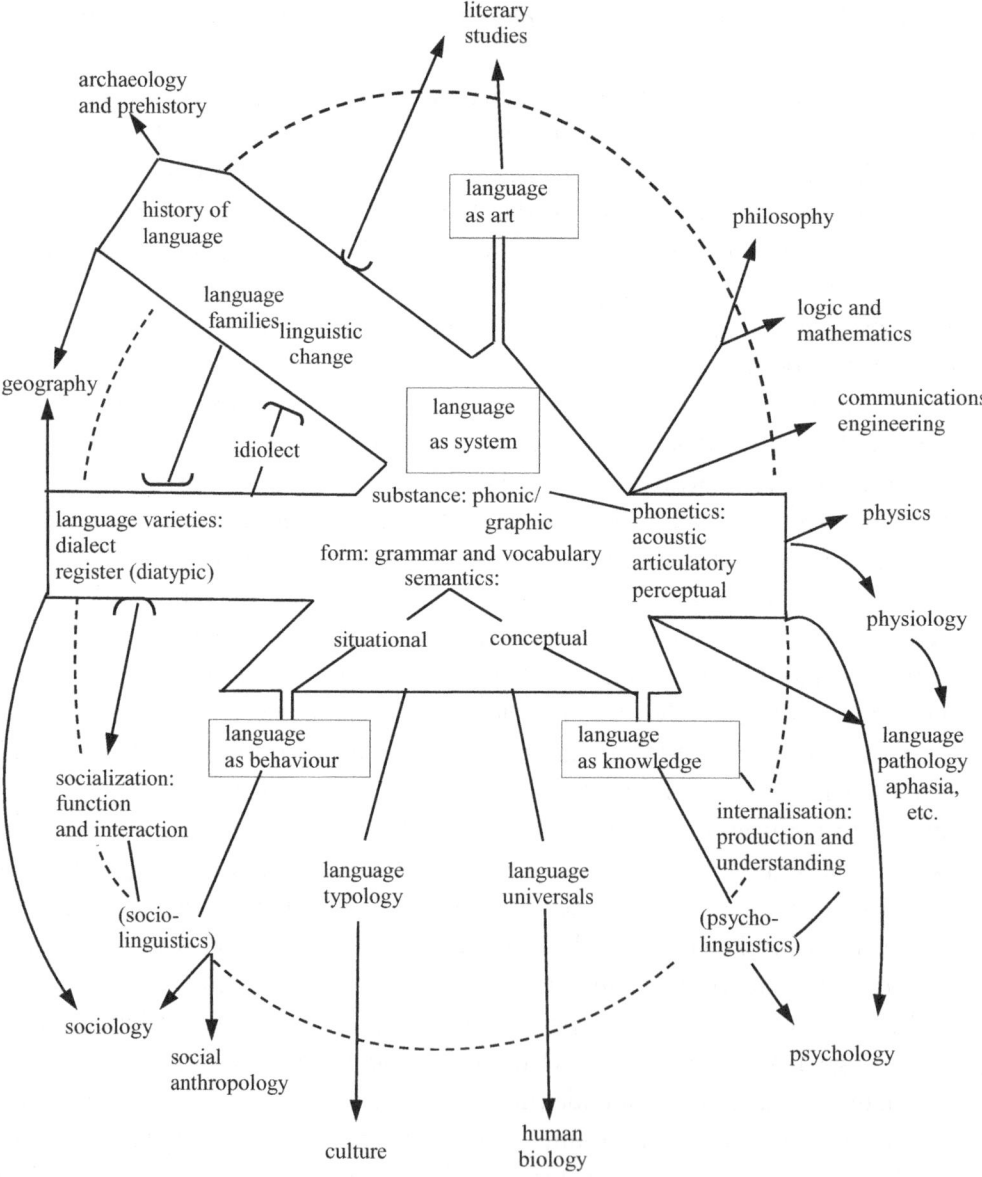

Figure 1.3 The domain of language studies (adapted from Halliday 1978: 11)

One way of bridging the gap between translation studies and linguistics is through language typology or **multilingual studies** (Matthiessen, Teruya, & Wu 2008), which connects different strands of research engaging with the multilingual phenomena. Areas such as translation studies, language description, and language typology are all interconnected with one another, and can be located either at the instance end, at the system end, or somewhere in the middle of the cline of instantiation (see Sections 2.3 and 6.2.1). On the one hand, rather than being institutionalized separately and insulated from each other, engagements with translation can be informed by a rich and powerful theory that offers a comprehensive description of the languages involved. On the other hand, by offering rich bilingual examples under various contexts, translation studies can inform works on language description, comparison, and typology. Otherwise, translation studies may risk ignoring the fact that translation (like literature), is made of language, if language is not given enough attention.

1.3 A Brief History of Systemic Functional Translation Studies

The earliest history of SFTS can be traced to **Bronisław Malinowski**'s (e.g. 1923, 1935) anthropological work on the almost completely unknown languages, cultures, and contexts on the Trobriand Islands in Papua New Guinea. In Steiner's (2005, 2015b, 2019) writings, he regards Malinowski's influence on J.R. Firth, Michael Halliday, and SFL as 'early British contextualism', which highlights Malinowski and Firth's contributions to context. For Malinowski (1935), translation plays an important role in his understandings of language, and is crucial in explaining the differences between the meanings in some other cultures and the anthropologist's English-speaking readership. Different from the missionary linguists' Eurocentric view of translation according to which the foreign culture should be assimilated into the target culture, Malinowski (1935) acknowledges the differences between the source culture and the target culture.

Also, Malinowski (1935) considers translation as a process of iterative contextualization of linguistic structures. For instance, words are contexualized in groups/phrases, groups/phrases in clauses, clauses in sentences/clause complexes, sentences in contexts of situation, and contexts of situation ultimately in contexts of culture. In this way, meaning is interpreted through a sequence of linguistic and cultural levels, until the complete meaning of the linguistic activity is understood by the readers. Reflecting on his way of translating, Malinowski (1935: 17, original emphasis) has the following observation:

> We see then that it is impossible to define a word by mere equation. Translation in the sense of *exact and exhaustive definition of meaning* cannot be done by affixing an English label … Translation in the sense of *defining a term by ethnographic analysis,* that is, by placing it within its context of culture, by putting it within the sets of kindred and cognate expressions, by contrasting it with its opposites, by grammatical analysis and above all

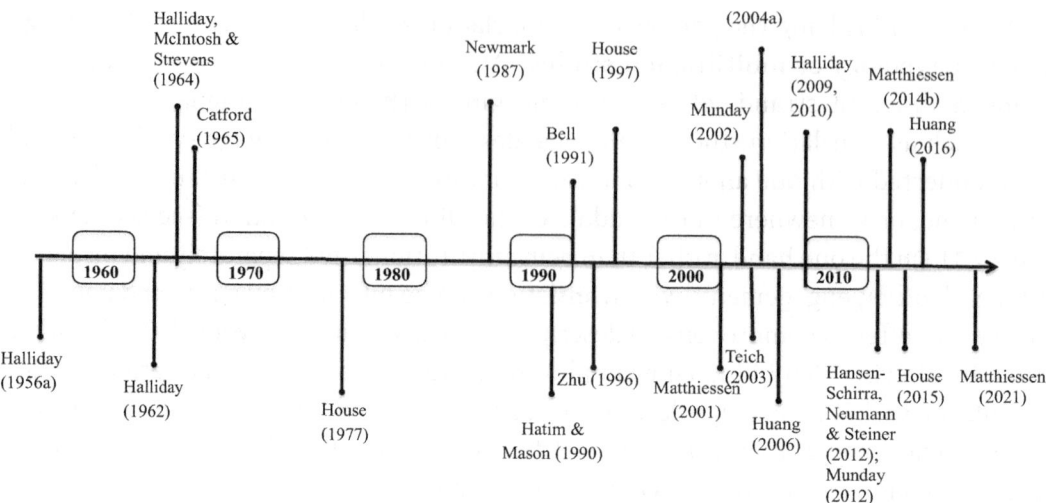

Figure 1.4 A timeline of the chronological development of SFTS

by a number of well-chosen examples – such translation is feasible and is the only correct way of defining the linguistic and cultural character of a word.

Influenced by Malinowski, **J.R. Firth** takes over the notion of context, passes it down to Michael Halliday, and eventually influences SFL and SFTS. Even though Firth (1968a, 1968b) does not contribute much to translation, various notions proposed by him have the potential to be applied to translation, such as register as 'restricted languages' (Firth 1968c; see Chapter 4), his work on person and personality (Firth 1950, 1968c), his concern with collocation (Firth 1968d), and his suggestion of treating each language in its own right (Firth 1968e), which is against the universalist's conception of language (cf. Greenberg 1966).

In Figure 1.4, we provide a timeline to reflect the chronological development of SFTS and to highlight some significant studies. Most studies included are widely known for their application of SFL to the theorizing and modelling of translation.

1.3.1 Systemic Functional Translation Studies in the 1950s and the 1960s

Translation has been on the agenda from the very beginning of SFL. As early as the 1950s, **Michael Halliday** (e.g. 1956a, 1962) began to research **machine translation** by emphasizing the significance of choice in translation as well as highlighting the value of thesaurus as a lexical resource (see Section 5.1 for discussions on machine translation and SFL). From the early work, we note that the value of a theory lies in its application, and SFL is essentially a consumer-oriented theory (cf. Halliday 1964). In Halliday (2009: 17), when expressing the need to apply SFL to translation, he comments on the relationship between linguistics and translation:

[T]ranslation can be seen as a fairly specialized domain, in the sense that relatively few linguists working in either functional or formal linguistics have paid explicit attention to translation; but it has been recognized as a kind of testing ground, since if your theory cannot account for the phenomenon of translation it is clearly shown up as inadequate.

Halliday, McIntosh, and Strevens (1964), in their co-authored *The Linguistic Sciences and Language Teaching*, include a chapter on 'Comparison and Translation', in which they contextualize translation in language teaching methodology by pointing out the relationship between language comparison, translation, and language teaching. While discussing how description and comparison between languages should be carried out, they suggest three steps of language comparison: (i) the separate description of related features of each language, (ii) the establishment of comparability, and (iii) the comparison itself. They also explore linguistic description in comparison and translation, comparison between different strata and ranks, and the future of machine translation.

The overall application of SFL in SFTS began with **J.C. Catford**'s (1965) monograph – *A Linguistic Theory of Translation*, in which scale and category grammar, an early version of Halliday's (1961) systemic functional grammar, was applied to the description and analysis of translation. By implementing the Hallidayan concept of rank and stratification (level), Catford (1965) formulates a general theory of translation and theorizes translation as a relationship between units in structures. The levels of language analysed include context (including features of situation where language operates), form (grammar and lexis), and substance (graphology and phonology). In this way, equivalence and shift, two central notions in translation studies, are modelled from a linguistic approach on the basis of stratification and units in structures. Catford (1965) considers finding translation equivalents in the target language as the central problem of translation practice, and the nature and conditions of translation equivalence as the central task of translation theory. He further distinguishes between translation equivalence and formal correspondence:

> A textual equivalent is any TL [target language] text or portion of text which is observed on a particular occasion ... to be the equivalent of a given SL [source language] text or portion of text. A formal correspondent, on the other hand, is any TL category (unit, class, structure, element of structure, etc.) which can be said to occupy, as nearly as possible, the 'same' place in the 'economy' of the TL as the given SL category occupies in the SL.
> (Catford 1965: 27)

Translation equivalence then occurs 'when an SL and a TL text or item are relatable to (at least some of) the same features of substance'. 'For total translation it is situation-substance, for phonological translation it is phonic-substance, for graphological translation it is graphic-substance' (Catford 1965: 50).

1.3.2 Systemic Functional Translation Studies from the 1970s to the Millennium

After Catford (1965) and before the end of the millennium, unlike the limited contribution on translation by SFL scholars, scholars in translation studies have made significant strides, including House (1977), Hatim and Mason (1990), Bell (1991), and Baker (1992). Although these scholars may not be described as 'systemicists' in a very strict sense, their works have very strong connections with the core elements of SFL, and are influential both in SFL and translation studies.

In the 1970s, **Juliane House** proposed the model of translation quality assessment based on her PhD thesis (House 1976). Her model, which she terms as linguistic, functional, and pragmatic, remains one of the most influential approaches to translation criticism, and is firmly based on the equivalence between the source text and the target text. The target text is thus doubly constrained, both by the source text and the communicative conditions. House (e.g. 2018) maintains that equivalence is the primary criterion of translation quality; and that one of the fundamental purposes of such a model is to specify and operationalize the equivalent relations.

House (1977) first puts forward her model by defining three dimensions for the author – his/her temporal, geographical, and social provenance, as well as five dimensions of language use – the topic of the text, the interaction of and relationship between author and recipient's social relationship or social attitude, the degree of participant involvement, and the writtenness or spokenness of the text. As to the operation of the model, the original text is firstly analysed according to the five linguistic dimensions or dimensions of language use. The linguistic correlates are the means by which textual function is realized, and the textual function is the result of linguistic-pragmatic analysis along the dimensions of language use, with each dimension contributing to the ideational and interpersonal metafunction. The text analysis on the above dimensions will yield a textual profile, which is characterized by the textual, ideational, and interpersonal metafunctions, and is seen as the individual textual norm, against which the translated texts will be measured. The extent to which the textual profile and function of the original match those of the translation is the extent to which translation equivalence is maintained by the translation.

In her revised models (e.g. House 1997, 2015, 2018), some of the components in her earlier model are integrated into the Hallidayan register analysis of field, tenor, and mode (see Figure 1.5; see also Section 5.2). Notwithstanding the complex taxonomies of the model, it can be simplified as register analysis of both the source text and the target text in terms of their realization through lexical, syntactic, and textual means.

House's model has provided theoretical motivations and consistent explanations for the concept of **overt and covert translation**. In an overt translation, addressees of the text are not 'overtly' addressed, and an overt translation must be a translation rather than a 'second original'. A text that requires an overt translation may be one that enjoys

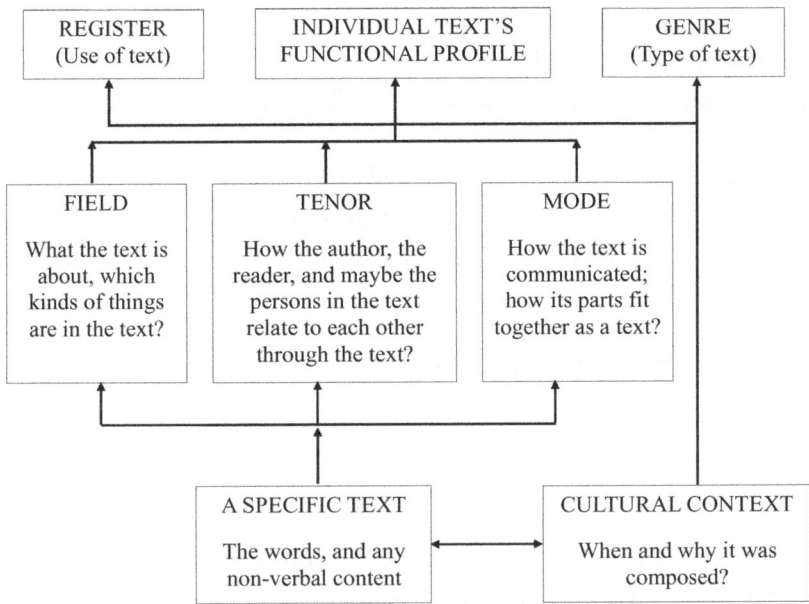

Figure 1.5 House's model of translation quality assessment (adapted from House 2018: 88)

established worth in the source language culture, or it may be a historical text for a specific occasion and for specific audience, or even a timeless work of art. In contrast, a covert translation may enjoy the status of an original text in the target culture; it is not marked as a translation, and has been created in its own right as an independent text. Rather than targeted to the source language addressees, texts of covert translation are of comparable interests to both the source language and the target language addressees. In this case, 'a cultural filter' can be used to account for the differences between an overt and covert translation.

The concept of **cultural filter** serves as 'a means to capturing socio-cultural differences in expectation norms and stylistic conventions between the source and target lingua-cultural communities' (House 2016: 77). The concept emphasizes an empirical basis for 'manipulation' made by the translator. The existence or non-existence of such empirical basis is required in the translation quality assessment. To achieve the aim of functional equivalence between the original and the translation, manipulation of the original should not be made before the careful examination of such cultural differences.

In the 1980s, **Peter Newmark** (1987) was one of the first scholars in translation studies to acknowledge the appliability of SFL and to regard Hallidayan linguistics as an effective tool of text analysis in translation. He agrees with Halliday's (1966a) notion that translation theory is an important aspect of general linguistics, and suggests three stages of translation: (i) item for item equivalence, (ii) reconsideration in the light of the linguistic environment and a consideration of the context of situation, and (iii) reconsideration in the light of the lexicogrammatical features of the target language. By adding 'cohesion' to the translation stages (cf. Halliday & Hasan 1976), Newmark (1988, 1991) renames these stages as 'levels' for translators to consider while translating, including levels of (i) textual, (ii) referential, (iii) cohesive, and (iv) naturalness. He also compares SFL with the German functionalist theories, and highlights the social and the cultural uses of language.

By approaching translation as a linguist and orienting towards translation practice, **Roger Bell** (1991: 13) demonstrates the significance of a linguistic theory to translation. He draws a distinction between translating, a translation, and translation in the following way:

(i) translating: the process (to translate; the activity rather than the tangible object);

(ii) a translation: the product of the process of translating (i.e. the translated text);

(iii) translation: the abstract concept which encompasses both the process of translating and the product of that process.

He maintains that a comprehensive theory of translation must describe and explain both the process and the product part of translation. His model of translation not only involves psycholinguistics and artificial intelligence on real-time language processing, but also absorbs various ideas from SFL. For instance, he regards a clause as the basic unit of analysis, and adopts both bottom-up and top-down approaches – two approaches from the trinocular perspectives in SFL (e.g. Halliday 1978, 1996), namely from below and from above. The analyses in various linguistic systems are included in the model in its syntactic, semantic, and pragmatic processes.

In this way, Bell (1991: 44, original emphasis) assumes that the process of translation:

(1) is a special case of the more general phenomenon of human information processing;

(2) should be modelled in a way which reflects its position within the psychological domain of information processing;

(3) takes place in both short-term and long-term memory through devices for decoding text in the source language (SL) and encoding text into the target language (TL), via a non-language-specific semantic representation;

(4) operates at the linguistic level of **clause**, irrespective of whether the process is one of the analysis of incoming signals or the synthesis of outgoing ones (monolingual, reading and/or writing, or bilingual, i.e. translation);

(5) proceeds in both a **bottom-up** and a **top-down** manner in processing text and integrates both approaches by means of a style of operation which is

both cascaded and interactive, i.e. analysis or synthesis at one stage need not be completed before the next stage is activated and revision is expected and permitted;

(6) requires there to be, for both languages
   (i) a visual word-recognition system and a writing system
   (ii) a **syntactic processor** which handles the options of the MOOD system and contains a
   (iii) frequent lexis store (FLS), a lexical search mechanism (LSM), a frequent structure store (FSS) and a parser, through which information passes to (or from) a
   (iv) **semantic processor** which handles the options available in the TRANSITIVITY system and exchanges information with a
   (v) **pragmatic processor** which handles the options available in the THEME system, and there is also an
   (vi) **idea organizer** which follows and organizes the progression of the speech acts in the text (and, if the text type is not known, makes inferences on the basis of the information available) as part of the strategy for carrying out plans for attaining goals, devised and stored in the
   (vii) **planner** which is concerned with creating plans for reaching goals of all kinds. Some of these plans may involve uses of language such as text-processing. This might include translating a text and this decision might well have been made even before its first clause had been processed.

There is another strand of works that considers translation at the stratum of semantics by considering concepts in SFL such as register, genre, and cohesion (e.g. Hatim & Mason 1990, 1997; Taylor 1998). **Hatim and Mason** (1990), for example, highlight the significance of context and register. They take a fairly eclectic approach to the investigation of discourse and translation by drawing on various linguistic concepts such as context, register, dialect, pragmatic theories such as cooperative principle and speech act, semiotics, intertextuality, text type, text structure, and thematic development.

Chunshen Zhu (1993, 1996, 2008) also adopts a linguistic approach to translation. He constructs his Structure of Meaning (SOM) model by integrating SFL with Austin's (1962) speech act theory. The model covers three linguistic areas, namely: (i) linguistic composition, with a focus on lexicogrammar, phonology, and graphology, (ii) interactional dynamic that highlights the exchange of connotative meaning and the illocutionary forces, and (iii) aesthetic impact that manipulates information through textual means. His reason for not choosing the well-developed account of speech function in SFL and instead opting for speech act theory is that the latter adds an aesthetic dimension to linguistics and also provides a linguistic background to literary criticism. As suggested by Zhu (1996: 342), 'speech act theory brings under focus our concern with reference/meaning conventions, and their consequence in language use'. However, it can be argued that speech act theory, as formulated by philosophers in the 1960s, does not pay much attention to (the instantiation of) context of culture, nor does it draw on authentic instances of language use.

We also note that it was in this period during the 1970s that SFL was introduced to Chinese academia with the publication of a paper titled 'On the Three Systems in Modern English Grammar and Communicative Grammar' by Fang Li, Hu Zhuanglin, and Xu Kerong (1977). The theoretical engagement of SFL with translation in China was then traced back to the co-authored textbook – *A Survey of Systemic-functional Grammar* by Hu Zhuanglin, Zhu Yongsheng and Zhang Delu (1989) (see Hu et al. 2008 for an updated edition of the book), in which suggestions of applying SFL to the Chinese context were proposed. In the section on human translation and machine translation, the authors briefly model translation according to rank, metafunction, and stratification, explaining translation equivalence with literal and free translation strategies as well as highlighting the specificity of machine translation.

1.3.3 Systemic Functional Translation Studies after the Millennium

Since the millennium, there was a renewed interest in applying SFL to translation, along with the publication of *Exploring Translation and Multilingual Text Production: Beyond Content*, edited by **Erich Steiner and Colin Yallop** (2001). As the title of the book suggests, one of the motivations for Steiner and Yallop (2001) to edit the volume is to model texts in translation and multilingual text production as configurations of multidimensional meanings, to challenge the folk notion of translation which considers translation as transfer of content from the source language to the target language, and to move beyond the notion of content in conceptualizing language and translation. All chapters in the book are informed by SFL notions to a certain degree. Some chapters theorize translation (Gregory 2001; Halliday 2001; Matthiessen 2001), while some apply the authors' own models to translation practice (House 2001; Steiner 2001a; Teich 2001; Yallop 2001). Some studies approach translation from the technological perspective, searching for technological solutions to problems in multilingual text production (Hartley & Paris 2001; Taylor & Baldry 2001; Teich 2001), while some are explicitly concerned with translation pedagogy (Shore 2001; Taylor & Baldry 2001). Steiner and Yallop's (2001) book widely covers a number of topics in SFTS, and succeeds in illustrating the appliability of SFL as well as introducing the theoretical aspects of SFTS.

In Steiner and Yallop (2001), **Christian Matthiessen** (2001) contextualizes translation and locates it within a typology of systems, which he names as 'the environments of translation', i.e. what translators have access to that informs their choices in translation. Following this approach, translation has been examined within an overall architecture of language in context. His approach is praised as 'the most comprehensive statement of an SFL-based view' (Steiner 2015b: 420).

The motivation of working on Matthiessen (2001) is to update Catford's (1965) work based on scale and category grammar, which does not include later theoretical updates such as metafunction, instantiation, stratification of language in context, and axis. Inspired by Halliday's (1966a) example of translation between languages at different ranks (see Figure 2.8), Matthiessen (2001) holds that the notion of the environment of rank scale can also be applied to other orders of environments. Thus, the amount of information available to translators depends on the environment they have access to. In literal translation, translators have access to a fairly narrow grammatical environment of the text in this context of situation; whereas in free translation, translators have access to a wide environment. Thus, the general principle is that 'the wider the environment of translation, the higher the degree of translation equivalence' (pp. 74–75). This can also be seen as the principle of contextualization: 'the "widest" environment is that in which the text is "maximally contextualized" – and therefore, by the same token, is likely to be "maximally effective"' (Halliday 2010: 16). Matthiessen (2001) summarizes six dimensions which together define the environments of translation, including stratification, instantiation, rank, metafunction, delicacy, and axis (see Chapter 2 for a detailed account of the dimensions). Along these dimensions, we can configure equivalence and shift between the source text and the target text.

As a continuation of the environments of translation, Matthiessen (2014b) proposes the notion of **'choice in translation'**, which focuses on **metafunction** – one of the six dimensions. He considers translation equivalence and translation shift as 'two opposite poles on a cline of difference between languages' (Matthiessen 2001: 78), and examines texts in terms of the metafunctional modes of meaning. Figure 1.6 shows the degree of congruence (distance) between the choices made in the source text and the target text. Choice in one metafunction may be closer to the equivalence pole of the cline, while choice in another metafunction may be closer to the shift pole of the cline. Thus, translation involves **trade-offs** in choices made in different metafunctional modes of meaning.

According to Matthiessen (2014b), translation is understood as the recreation of meaning in context through choice, or 'an ongoing process of choosing options within the systems of the source language and of the target language' (2014b: 272). Both in the interpretation of the original text and in the generation of the translated text, translators make choices in the meaning potential. Specifically, under consideration of the metafunctional organization of language, translators will be faced with choices located in the experiential, logical, interpersonal, and textual systems (see Chapter 3 for discussions on metafunction).

Based on the automated and manual analysis of multilingual corpora, Matthiessen (2014b: 283) summarizes different types of metafunctional translation shifts in the following matrix (see Figure 1.7 and Section 2.4), which 'provides a simple way of

20 • *Systemic Functional Translation Studies*

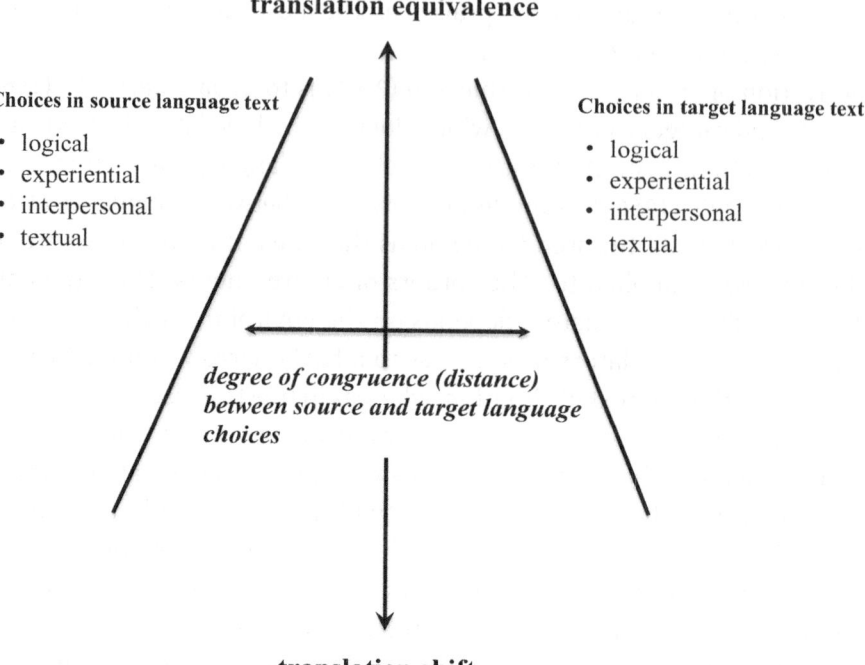

Figure 1.6 The cline from 'translation equivalence' to 'translation shift' as degree of congruence between source and target texts in terms of all four metafunctional modes of meaning (adapted from Matthiessen 2014b: 280)

TRANSLATION SHIFTS

From [source text]:

		textual	ideational: logical	ideational: experiential	interpersonal
To [target text]:	textual	textual > textual: e.g. theme shift	logical > textual: e.g. complex to cohesive sequence		
	ideational: logical	textual > logical: e.g. cohesive sequence to complex	logical > logical: e.g. tactic shift		interpersonal > logical: e.g. mood or modality represented by verbal or mental clause in clause complex of projection
	ideational: experiential		logical > experiential: e.g. clause > phrase	experiential > experiential: e.g. process type shift	
	interpersonal				interpersonal > interpersonal: e.g. mood type shift

Figure 1.7 Matrix of metafunctional translation shifts (adapted from Matthiessen 2014b: 284)

probing translation shifts, sorting them into very general classes of choice according to metafunction'. It can be noted that some boxes in the matrix are empty since these shifts are less likely to be found. With the analysis and comparison of more texts of different languages in the long term, some boxes may be filled, while some may remain empty (cf. Matthiessen, Wang, & Ma 2017a, 2018).

Also based on the dimensions in SFL, **Elke Teich** (2001, 2003) puts forward a model of contrastive-linguistic descriptions for investigating cross-linguistic commonalities and differences (see Figure 1.8).

Teich (2003: 50 original emphasis) has made the following observations of the six dimensions:

1. As a tendency, different languages show more similarities on the more abstract *strata* of linguistic organization than on the less abstract ones, i.e. they tend to express similar meanings, but cast them in different lexical-grammatical terms.

2. Different languages may distribute functional responsibilities differently across *metafunctions*.

3. At the level of grammar, there may be different preferences in different languages concerning the grammatical *rank* (clause, nominal group, prepositional phrase etc.) at which a particular meaning is expressed.

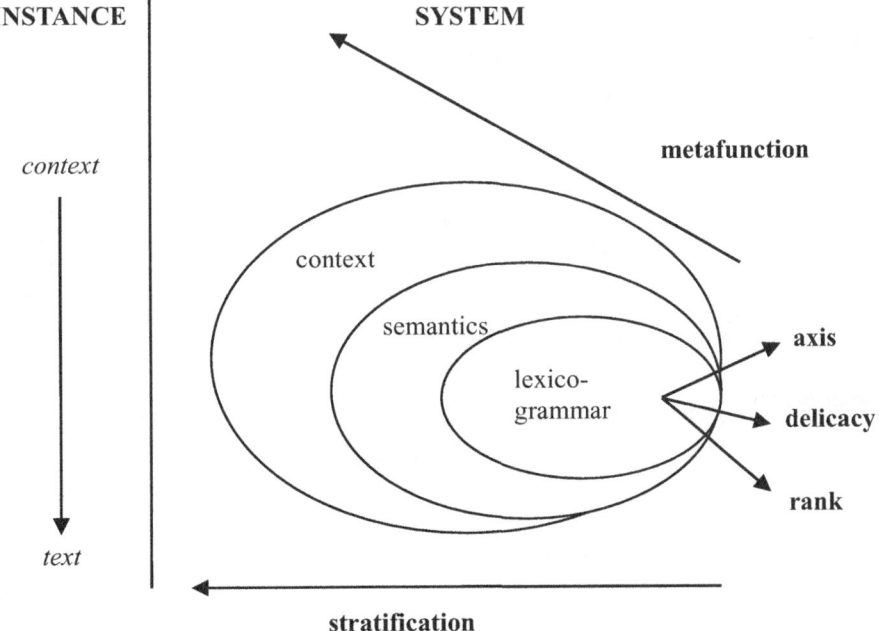

Figure 1.8 Dimensions relevant for contrastive-linguistic descriptions of translations (adapted from Teich 2001: 199; 2003: 60)

4. At the level of grammar, languages tend to be similar in terms of functional paradigms and different in terms of syntagmatic, surface-syntactic realization, i.e., there is cross-linguistic variation according to *axis*.

5. At the level of grammar, systems of low *delicacy* (more general grammatical types) tend to be similar across languages, and systems of higher delicacy (more specific grammatical types) tend to be dissimilar.

6. If there is a basic commonality in a particular grammatical system between two languages, in texts, i.e., in *instantiations* of the grammatical system, the two languages may still have different choice preferences according to situational context (i.e. register).[1]

In addition, Teich (2001) locates some key concepts of translation theory, including translation type, translation strategy, equivalence, and translation procedure in her model. As shown in Figure 1.9, translation type is located in the stratum of lexicogrammar and in the column of register/text type along the cline of instantiation, because

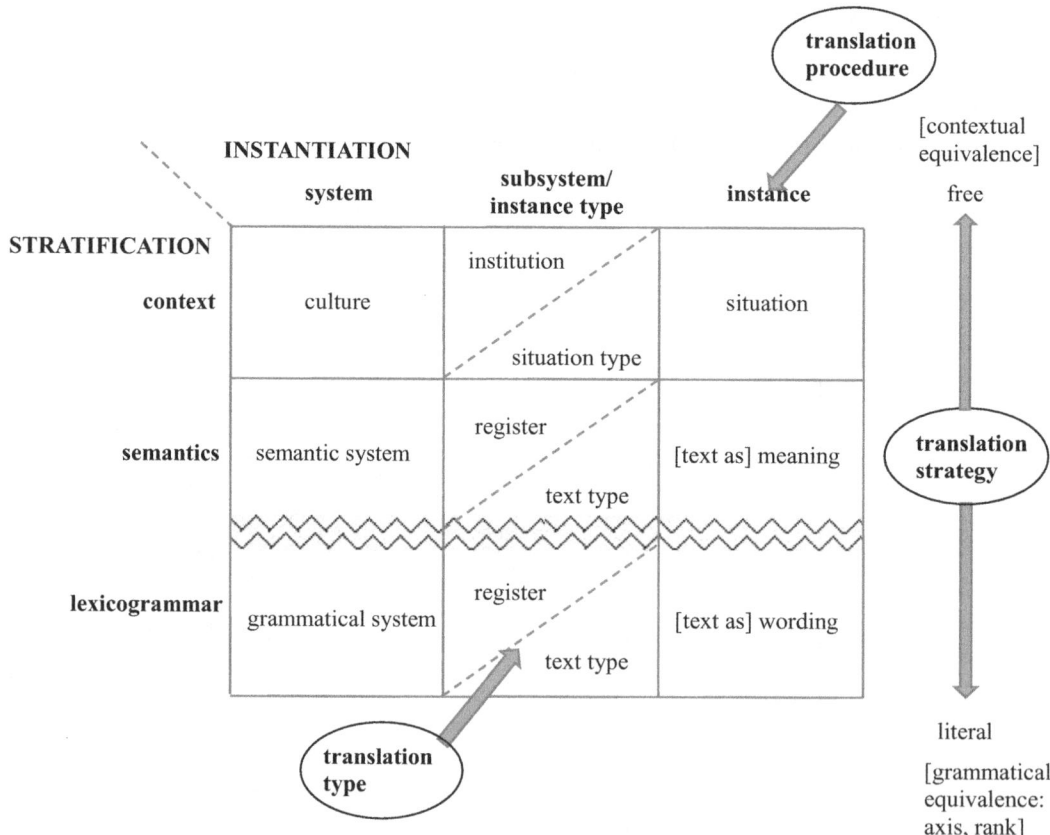

Figure 1.9 Locating translation methods in the matrix of stratification and instantiation (adapted from Teich 2001: 213)

the choice of a translation type has to be determined in accordance with text type or register in the target language.

Translation strategy is located in stratification. Seen from this perspective, translation correspondence at the stratum of context implies strategies such as free translation, dynamic equivalence, communicative translation, or covert translation. At the stratum of lexicogrammar, translation correspondence implies strategies such as literal translation, formal equivalence, semantic translation, or overt translation. In terms of axis, formal equivalence is located at the syntagmatic axis or at the realization level, while functional equivalence is located at the paradigmatic axis or at the systemic level. In terms of rank, when the choices in the target text are consistent with those in the source text, the translation is more literal. On the contrary, when the choices in the target text are inconsistent with those in the source text, the translation is less literal, with translation strategies such as transposition and modulation being used (see Teich 2001).

Translation procedures are located at the instance end along the cline of instantiation, as instance is related to the system end via subsystem, register, text type, or instance type. The cline of instantiation is crucial for translators in making their decisions on the translation procedure. To find a suitable procedure, a translator not only needs to know the similarities and differences between the language systems typologically, they also need to have enough understanding about the register of the target text.

In **Cross-Linguistic Variation in System and Text**, Teich (2003) elaborates on her model, exploring the comparable registers of English and German texts as well as the relationship between translated texts and texts originally produced in English and German. Various parameters of cross-linguistic variation are taken into consideration, including variation in system and text, variation in function and form, as well as variation in and across the different strata of language. Through corpus methodology, the analysis reveals how the source language shines through in the target texts, i.e. the target texts may be oriented more towards the source language (cf. Baker 1993, 1995, 1996) and how the target texts try to be even more normalized or typical of the target language compared to original texts in the same language.

Erich Steiner, one of the key scholars in SFTS (see Steiner et al. 2018a), is not only important institutionally in training scholars such as Elke Teich, Stella Neumann, Kerstin Kunz, and Silvia Hansen-Schirrra, but is also a significant person as far as writing about the development of SFTS (e.g. Steiner 2005, 2015b, 2019) and tracing the history of SFL's application in translation to Malinowski (e.g. 1923, 1925). Coming from a background in English and German philology, he started to work on translation since **EUROTRA**, a former EU machine translation project (e.g. Steiner 1986, 1992; Steiner et al. 1988; see Section 5.1). Many of his later studies are related to register and translation, e.g. **Translated Texts: Properties, Variants, Evaluations** (Steiner 2004a), which is a collection of his works. These papers approach register as a resource for translators to analyse the source text before translation, to evaluate the target text after translation, to control multidimensional variation in texts, and to relate such variation to lexicogrammar. His studies (e.g. Steiner 1997, 1998a, 2004a) on advertisements of Rolex watches investigate the translators' choices by identifying the variations between the source text and target text in terms of register (especially tenor relations) and lexicogrammatical realizations. We will return to these studies in Chapter 4 and categorize the advertising texts as recommending texts (see Section 4.3.3).

In addition, Steiner and his research team in Saarbrücken contributed to the development of corpus methodology in SFTS (see Section 5.2.1). From 2009 onwards, they started to build their first family of corpora – **CroCo (Crosslinguistic Corpora for Translation)**. CroCo has been used in various studies on contrastive linguistics and translation studies (Hansen-Schirra, Neumann, & Steiner 2012). Based on CroCo, the team continued to build the second family of corpora called **GECCo (German–English Contrasts in Cohesion)**. These corpora provide resources for a number of studies on various topics, such as explicitation as a possible property of translated texts (Steiner 2008, 2012a), translation of grammatical metaphor (Steiner 2002a, 2002b, 2004b), and comparison of cohesion between German and English (Steiner 2017).

Apart from Steiner and his team's works, there are also other studies that highlight the application of corpus in SFTS, especially those by **Jeremy Munday** (e.g. 1997, 2002), who builds his model on SFL, corpus linguistics, descriptive translation studies, and the sociocultural framework (see Section 5.2.3).

In the Chinese context, a number of papers on the translation of Chinese classical poems based on SFL have been written by **Huang Guowen** since 2002. A wide range of theoretical perspectives have been covered, including interpersonal meaning (Huang 2002a), logical meaning (2002b), reported speech (2002c), overall analysis (2002d), tense (2003a), dynamic and static realization (2003b), and formal equivalence (2003c). A collection of these papers was published in book form in Huang (2006). The analysis is not only carried out at the clause rank, but also at the rank of group/phrase. Huang (2006) suggests six steps for SFTS, which include (i) observation, (ii) interpretation, (iii) description, (iv) analysis, (v) explanation, and (vi) evaluation. He also situates the six steps on a cline from subjective to objective, with observation being located at the objective end and evaluation at the subjective end. Further, he notes that the analysis is helpful in answering the two possible goals in text analysis suggested by Halliday (2001: 13; cf. Halliday 1994):

> When we analyse a text linguistically, we usually have one of two possible goals. One is to explain why the text means what it does: why it is understood the way it is – by the analyst, or by anyone else. That is the lower of the two goals, the one that is easier to attain. The higher goal is to explain why the text is valued as it is – again, by anyone who may be evaluating it: this might be, in the case of a literary or religious text, by a general consensus within the culture. This second goal is more difficult to attain, if only because it includes the first one: to be able to explain why a text is more, or perhaps less, effective in its context one must first be able to explain why it means what it is understood to mean.

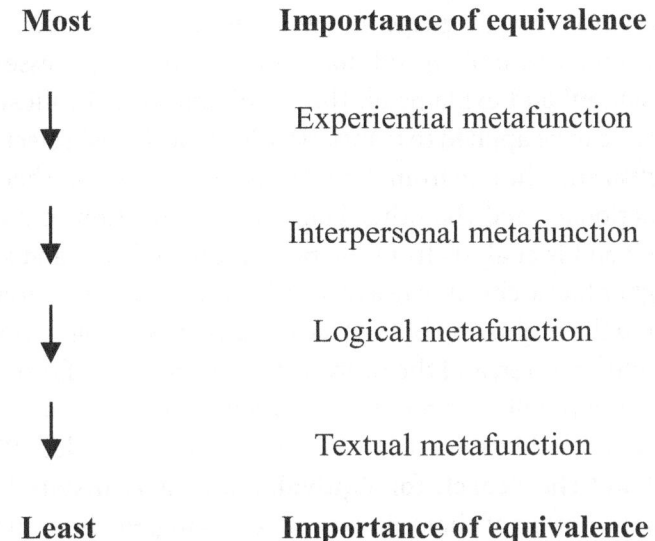

Figure 1.10 Order of importance of metafunctional equivalence (adapted from Huang 2016: 301)

In Huang (2016), he demonstrates Matthiessen's (2001: 78) claim that 'translation equivalence and translation shift are two opposite poles on a cline of difference between languages ... from maximal congruence to maximal incongruence'. Examples are selected from his analysis of Confucius's *The Analects* and its translations (see also Huang 2014), based on which the priority of equivalence in terms of the different modes of meaning are ordered by importance, with the experiential metafunction ranked as the most important and the textual as the least important (see Figure 1.10).

Zhang Meifang is another important figure of SFTS in China. Her monograph, *Functional Approaches to Translation Studies* (Zhang 2005, 2015), introduces various functional theories and illustrates their applications to translation. She categorizes functional theories into two types. The first is micro functional theories, including the works by Catford (1965), House (e.g. 1977), Halliday (1985b), Hatim and Mason (1990), Bell (1991), and Baker (1992), which are informed by SFL. The second is macro functional theories, i.e. German functionalist works by Reiss (1971), Holz-Mänttäri (1984), Nord (1997), and Vermeer (2012), which originate from Prague School works and Bühler's functions of language (see Section 4.1). In addition to a wide coverage of the functional approaches to translation (cf. Zhang 2001; Zhang & Huang 2002), the book collects Zhang Meifang's previously published papers on the application of functional theories, with examples being selected from texts of different registers.

After the millennium, **Michael Halliday** also had publications on SFL and translation, further placing translation studies on the agenda of SFL theory. There were two insightful papers that introduce major ideas in SFTS, and illustrate how SFL can be applied to translation studies. In '**The Gloosy Ganoderm: Systemic Functional Linguistics and Translation**', Halliday (2009: 17) defines translation as 'a relation between languages', 'a process of moving from one language into another', and 'an extraordinarily complex achievement of the human brain'. In addition, he highlights Matthiessen's (2001) 'environments of translation' and explains all the six dimensions. To illustrate how these dimensions from SFL can be applied to translation, Halliday (2009) selects two translated texts between English and Chinese from two different registers – one being introductory remarks from a dictionary and the other being an introduction to an exhibit from a tourist guide. Based on his analysis from the perspectives of rank and stratification, he shows how the higher hierarchical scales of stratification and rank carry higher values. Then he moves on to the evaluation of the translations by relating to House's (e.g. 1997, 2001) model, the cultural filter, and the overt/covert distinction of translation strategy.

As a continuation to the discussion on translation equivalence and translation shift in Catford (1965) and Matthiessen (2001), in another study entitled '**Pinpointing the Choice: Meaning and the Search for Equivalents in a Translated Text**', Halliday (2010) emphasizes the notion of choice in meaning-making. He differentiates shift from errors in translation, though a translation error will always involve a shift, and makes the following observation:

> Indeed there will almost always be shift on some dimension or other, because there is seldom total equivalence between choices in two languages; the translator shifts here to gain equivalence there, according to the value inhering in equivalence of different kinds in the nature of the task in hand.
>
> (Halliday 2010: 17)

Halliday (2010: 18–19) further explains the notion of 'pinpointing the choice', which means 'locating, within the systems of the two languages concerned, the moments of equivalence and shift that come to our attention …'. While making choices, the translator will give priority to these forms of equivalence, and accept the resulting shift elsewhere. Translation work is always 'the exercise of choice, conscious or unconscious'.

Another strand of influence on SFTS comes from the **Sydney School** of SFL represented by **James R. Martin**. Though Martin himself has few works on translation, some of his theories, especially appraisal (Martin & White 2005), instantiation and individuation (e.g. Martin 2009), have been applied to translation,

APPRAISAL, together with NEGOTIATION and INVOLVEMENT, are considered as semantic systems. Appraisal concerns with the resources for appraising and evaluation: 'the kinds of attitudes that are negotiated in a text, the strength of the feelings involved and the ways in which values are sourced and readers aligned' (Martin & Rose 2003: 22). In the system of APPRAISAL, there are sub-systems of ENGAGEMENT, ATTITUDE, and GRADUATION. When applied to translation, researchers mainly analyse and compare the lexical choices in the source text and the target text, looking for the interpersonal meanings that have been added or omitted, and then giving interpretations to these translation shifts. **Zhang Meifang** (e.g. 2002, 2013) and **Jeremy Munday** (e.g. 2012, 2018) have several studies in this area (see Section 3.2).

For the application of **re-instantiation** in translation, **Ladjane de Souza** (2010, 2013) proposes a model of conceiving translation as interlingual re-instantiation, which involves a three-dimensional perspective of realization, instantiation, and individuation in SFL. Drawing on Martin's (e.g. 2009) hierarchies of instantiation and individuation, this model defines translation as the sourcing of target text on source text, applies the conceptual toolkit of instantiation to text analysis, which includes re-instantiation, coupling, and commitment, and highlights the individual users involved in translation. From the perspective of individual users, 'the instantiation/re-instantiation of texts becomes a matter of projecting reading, managing intertextual relations, and negotiating meaning with different communities of users based on specific repertoires' (de Souza 2013: 592). In a recent study, Chang (2018) further explores how translation can be modelled as a process of re-instantiation by focusing especially on the different degrees of commitment. His analysis reveals the differences between the various target texts both ideationally and interpersonally, and is related to the translators' different purposes, thus confirming the potential of applying the hierarchy of instantiation to study translation.

To sum up, Section 1.3 has provided a brief introduction to the history of SFTS and has highlighted a number of major studies and frameworks as well as the time period of these works. Our discussions on topics such as metafunctional modes of meaning, register, machine translation, and corpus are rather brief because we will return to these topics in later chapters, and provide further details.

Chapter 2

The Environments of Translation

This chapter elaborates on Matthiessen's (2001) **environments of translation**. Following our discussion in Section 1.3, we know that by employing the environments of translation, translation can be examined within an overall SFL-architecture of language in context, involving six dimensions, i.e. stratification, instantiation, metafunction, rank, delicacy, and axis (see Figure 2.1). Outlined by these dimensions, the environments of translation that the translators have access to will determine the amount of information available to them when making choices in translation. As a result, in literal translation, translators will have access to narrow grammatical environments of the text in the context of situation; whereas, in free translation, translators will in principle have access to wider grammatical environments.

The six dimensions, as commented on by Halliday (2009: 17), 'give language its inexhaustible power of making meaning, opening up all the different vectors – of abstraction, of combination, of depth in detail, of functional specialization and so on'. In addition, they are 'critical to any comparison of two or more different languages; and hence to

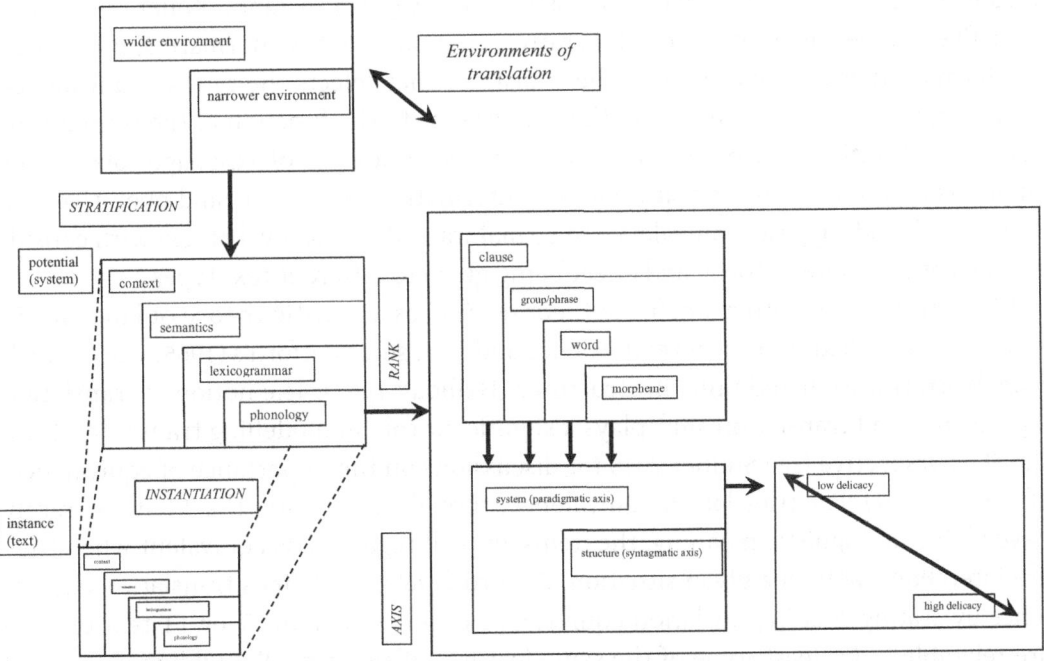

Figure 2.1 The environments of translation (adapted from Matthiessen 2001: 77)

the process of translation, because they are the parameters that define equivalence (and therefore also non-equivalence, or shift)' (p. 19). In the following sections, we will first discuss the significance of measuring translation equivalence and shift and then introduce the six dimensions in detail.

2.1 Measuring Translation Equivalence and Shift along the Dimensions

Since we conceive translation as recreation of meaning, choices in the recreation then become the central issue. Translators then have to make choices not only when they interpret the source text, but they also make choices when they generate the target text. These choices are all made along the various dimensions in the architecture of language outlined by SFL. As researchers, we can investigate these choices and point out the equivalences and the shifts made by translators. In certain cases, a shift may provide one way for translators to maintain equivalence elsewhere, and equivalence is always relative to the multilingual meaning potential that translators have mastered (see Matthiessen 2018).

For the non-SFL approaches to translation equivalence, Halverson (1997) has conducted a review on this topic. Comparison is essential because '[i]n studying translation and equivalence, we are studying the means by which all things can be compared' (p. 227). In addition, Pym (2014) considers equivalence as a relation of equal value, which can be established on any linguistic level, ranging from form to function. Different kinds of equivalence or solutions can be evaluated in this way. For instance, Koller (1979) suggests five degrees of equivalence: denotative, connotative, text-normative, pragmatic, and formal. He maintains that it is the translator that selects the type of equivalence according to the appropriateness of the equivalence to the function of the source text. Reiss (1971), influenced by Bühler's (1934) three functions of language, places her emphasis on the three basic text types, i.e. informative, expressive, and operative (see Section 4.1), and suggests equivalence to be maintained on the level of text with considerations of the content, form, and effect being given to different text types.

Different from the other linguistic theories, SFL, as a holistic theory of language in context, has studied translation equivalence and shift since Catford's (1965) work, which models stratification and units in structures (Halliday 1961). The notion of translation equivalence and translation shift plays a significant role in modelling translation from the SFL perspective (see Steiner 2019 for discussions on the importance of equivalence; cf. Yallop 2001). For translation equivalence, though the ST and the TT items rarely have identical linguistic meaning, the items are still regarded as equivalent when they are interchangeable in a given situation. Catford (1965: 50) defines translation equivalence by stating that '[t]ranslation equivalence occurs when an ST or TT text or item are relatable to (at least some of the same features of substance)'. Building on Catford (1965)'s work, Matthiessen (2001) characterizes equivalence by referring it to the widest environment of stratification, rank, and axis, and describes it as a matter of degree. In terms of stratification, the highest degree of equivalence is to be found in the widest environment – the context (see Section 2.2). By the same token, for rank scale, the widest environment in the stratum of lexicogrammar is clause (see Section 2.5); while for axis, the widest environment is system (see Section 2.7). In these wide environments, translators tend to adopt free strategies of translation rather than literal strategies to maintain translation equivalence (see Figure 2.2).

Translation shift, which refers to the departure from formal correspondence in the process of the ST to the TT, includes level shift and category shift (Catford 1965). Level shift means an item on one linguistic level in the source language has an equivalence at a different level in the target language. Category shifts can mean changes of rank (when equivalence is established between sentences, clauses, groups, words, or even morphemes), changes of class, changes of term, etc. As summarized by Fang and Wu (2009), translation shifts occur when equivalence is achieved at a higher rank when it cannot be realized at the current rank.

Matthiessen's (2001) environments of translation make it possible to systemically examine translation equivalence and translation shift in terms of the dimensions based on the linguistic analysis of the ST and the TT. In addition, instead of separating translation equivalence and translation shift, Matthiessen (2001: 78) places them as 'two opposite poles on a cline of difference between languages'. Equivalence and shift can then be configured within all the dimensions in the environments of translation. Since equivalence between the ST and the TT cannot always be achieved on all dimensions, translation shift thus has to take place, because translators have to shift in one dimension

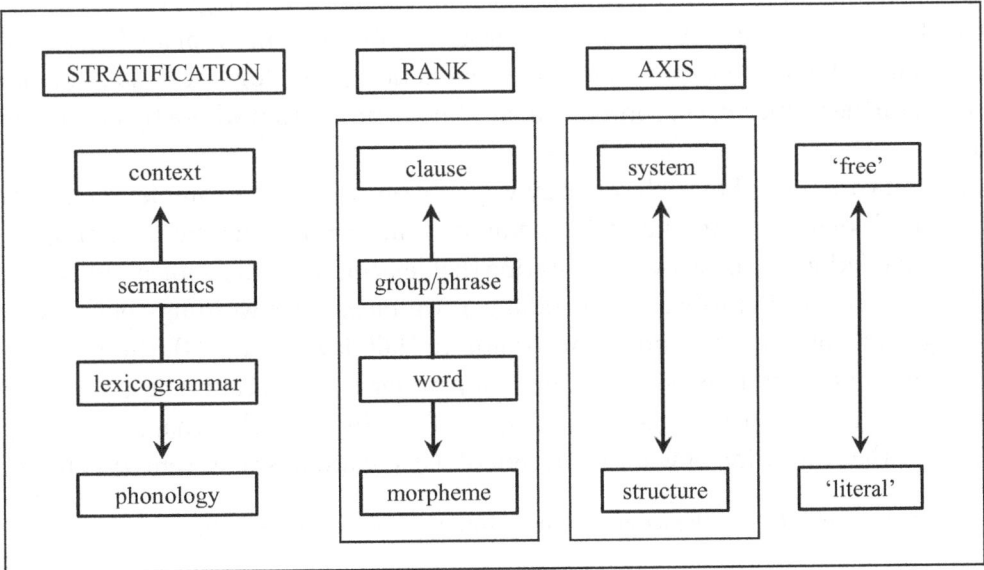

Figure 2.2 The environments and nature of translation (adapted from Matthiessen 2001: 81)

or another to gain equivalence elsewhere, especially to maintain semantic equivalence (Halliday 2009, 2010). It must also be noted that translation shifts are not equal to errors in translation. Although some shifts may be errors, many of them are not.

Teich (2001, 2003) relates the works by non-SFL scholars and re-interprets them in relation to the environments of translation. She identifies various translation types, translation strategies, and translation procedures in accordance with the dimensions (see Figure 1.8). Venuti's (2008) advocacy of 'foreignization' can be located as an orientation towards the context stratum in stratification, and similar strategies are also found in Malinowski's (1935) anthropological works, where emphasis is given to the differences between the foreign culture and the target culture. In addition, translation strategies can be interpreted in accordance with stratification. Thus, strategies like free translation, dynamic equivalence, communicative translation, and covert translation orient towards the stratum of context, suggesting wide environments the translators have access to; on the contrary, literal translation, formal equivalence, semantic translation, or overt translation orient towards lexicogrammar – a narrow environment (see e.g. Nida 1964; Newmark 1988; House 2001, 2015; cf. Wang & Ma 2016).

2.2 Stratification

Stratification is a global dimension that organizes language in context into a hierarchy of strata or levels (Matthiessen 2007; Halliday & Matthiessen 2014). Along the hierarchy of stratification, there are different orders of symbolic abstraction. Such strata within the organization of language include semantics, lexicogrammar, phonology (or graphology), and phonetics (or graphetics) (see Figure 2.3). Phonetics and phonology are the expression strata in oral language, while graphetics and graphology are the strata in written language. These four strata can be grouped into the content plane (lexicogrammar, semantics) and the expression plane (phonetics, phonology). Outside language, there is a further stratum, i.e. context – a non-linguistic stratum where texts come into being.

The strata are related to each other by way of realization. For example, semantics is realized by lexicogrammar, and lexicogrammar is in turn realized by phonology. The realization relationship is two-way. By stating that lexicogrammatical formations (wordings) realize semantic formations (meanings), we mean that wordings both express meanings and construct meanings. According to Halliday (1992a: 24), the realization relationship in the strata is one of redundancy rather than causality: 'it is not that (i) meaning is realized by wording and wording is realized by sound, but that (ii) meaning is realized by the realization of wording in sound'. This relation is represented as follows:

context ↘ (semantics ↘ (lexicogrammar ↘ (phonology ↘ phonetics)))

According to Matthiessen (2001), in the dimension of stratification, context is the widest environment, while phonetics is the narrowest environment. As a result, in wider

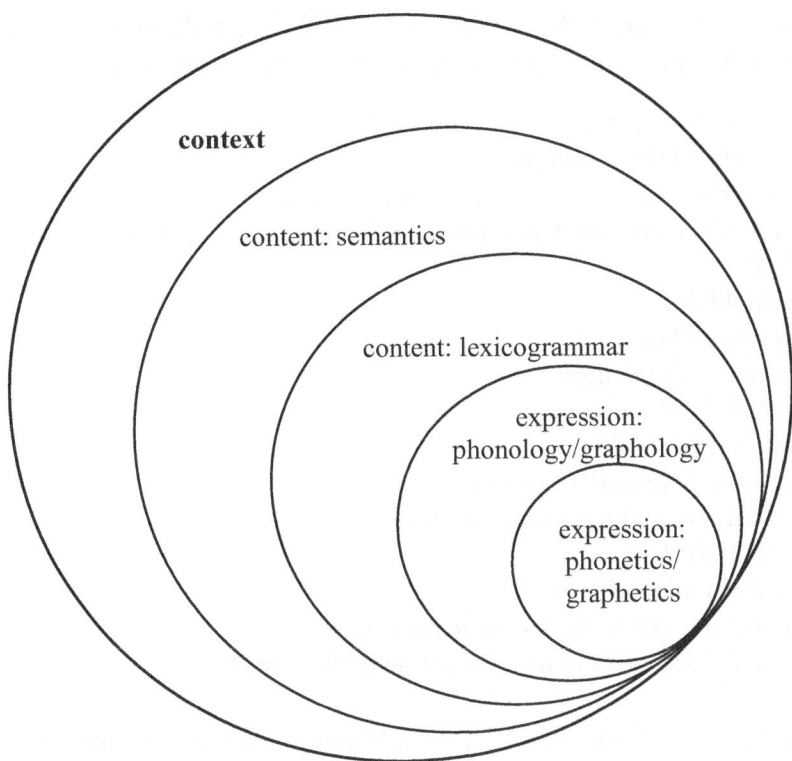

Figure 2.3 Stratification (adapted from Halliday & Matthiessen 2014: 26)

environments along stratification, such as semantics, the degrees of translation equivalence tend to be higher; while in narrower environments, such as phonetics and phonology, there tends to be higher degrees of translation shift, and translation equivalence is more difficult to achieve. Also, it must be noted that stratification and instantiation are two global dimensions that have to be maintained in translation. Therefore, along these dimensions, translation shifts will not be measured. In other words, the process of translation will not move from one stratum in the ST to another stratum in the TT. Instead, shifts can be found in terms of rank and delicacy, which are the two major sources of variation in the environments of translation.

Example 2.1 shows how phonological meaning[1] in the ST has to be abandoned in translation. The example is a story written in classical Chinese by Yuen Ren Chao (1980). The Chinese characters are all of the 'shi' sound but with different tones. When one reads the text aloud, even native Chinese speakers who are acquainted with classical Chinese cannot understand what the text means. However, when one reads the written text, it becomes comprehensible. If the text is translated into another language, such as English, as suggested in the back translation, the phonological meanings of the repetitive 'shi' sound will be lost, and will give way to the semantic meanings in a higher environment, where equivalence is maintained. A translator may need to add notes to inform readers about the phonological features of the text.

Example 2.1: *A History of How Mr. Shi Eats Lions* (施氏食狮史) in classical Chinese and its back translation into English (adapted from Chao 1980: 149)

石室诗士施氏，嗜狮，
PY: shí shì shī shì shī shì, shì shī,
IG: stone room poet Shi surname, be addicted to lion
BT: A poet called Shi from the stone room is addicted to eating lions.
誓食十狮。
PY: shì shí shí shī.
IG: vow eat ten lion
BT: He vows to eat ten lions.
氏时时适市视狮。
PY: shì shí shí shì shì shì shī.
IG: man often go to market see lion
BT: He often goes to the market to see lions.
十时，适十狮适市。
PY: shí shí, shì shí shī shì shì.
IG: ten clock, happen to ten lion go to market
BT: At ten o' clock, ten lions happened to go to the market.

In Example 2.2, we see how choices at the lexicogrammatical stratum have to be abandoned to maintain equivalence at the semantic stratum or elsewhere. In this example, the four German cases are found in the poem by Christian Morgenstern, i.e. the nominative case (subject of the sentence), the genitive case (possessive), the dative case (the indirect object), and the accusative case (the direct object). Different definite articles for masculine are used for the four cases, i.e. 'der', 'des', 'dem', and 'den'. When translating this poem into English (which does not have these four cases), a translator faces the difficulty of translating the case forms of 'wer' (IG: who), which are humorously treated as a pronominal part of 'Werwolf'. The English translation of 'Werwolf' as 'Whowolf' will not convey the humour expressed by the German cases. Consequently, the translator will have to abandon the equivalent lexicogrammatical choices and instead choose other lexicogrammatical resources to maintain the semantic equivalence, such as changing the definite articles to 'the', 'of the', 'to the', and 'a', or find English analogues such as 'werewolf', 'whenwolf', 'whywolf', and 'howwolf'.

Example 2.2: *Der Werwolf* [2]

'Der Werwolf' – sprach der gute Mann,
IG: the (NOM) Whowolf (NOM) spoke the (NOM) good man,
BT: 'The Werwolf', spoke the good man,
'des Weswolfs, Genitiv sodann,
IG: the (GEN) Whowolf (GEN), genitive then,
BT: 'The Weswolfs, genitive then,

dem Wemwolf, Dativ, wie man's nennt,
IG: the (DAT) Whowolf (DAT), dative, how man it called,
BT: the Wemwolf is the dative name how man called it
den Wenwolf, – damit hat's ein End.'
IG: the (ACC) Whowolf (ACC), therefore have it an (ACC) end.
BT: the Wenwolf therefore has an end.

When translating poems, songs or verses that are rhymed, translators have to choose whether to maintain the phonological meaning or not. Example 2.3 is selected from the dramatic monologue of a Chinese play titled *Teahouse* and its two English translations. This monologue is delivered by a beggar who earns a living by chanting rhythmic storytelling. In the example, the Chinese ST rhymes with the same character '儿' (er) at the end of each line to make the doggerel suitable for chanting. In the two TTs, both translators choose to recreate the phonological meaning by finding rhymed patterns, i.e. 'play' and 'pay' in TT1, as well as 'game' and 'claim' in TT2. The recreation of the phonological meaning results in some translation shifts in lexicogrammar in the TTs, such as the alteration of the mental process realized by '爱' (PY: ài; IG: love) with a relational process in TT1, the omission of this mental process in TT2, and the choice of 'Tasty meat balls' as marked topical Theme in TT2 (see also Wang 2017; Wang & Ma 2018, 2020).

Example 2.3 (adapted from Lao 1994: 230–231, 2004: 188–189)

Chinese ST: 爱下棋，（您）来两盘儿，
赌一卖（碟）干炸丸子外洒胡椒盐儿。
PY: ài xià qí, (nín) lái liǎng pán er,
dǔ yí mài (dié) gān zhá wán zi wài sǎ hú jiāo yán er.
IG: love play chess, you (HON) come two MEAS,
bet one MEAS (plate) dry fried meatball outside sprinkle pepper salt
BT: If you love playing chess, come and play,
and bet for a plate of meatballs sprinkled with pepper salt.
English TT1: If you're a chess fan, come in and **play**
For a plate of meatballs – losers **pay**.
English TT2: Here chess players meet for their favourite **game**,
Tasty meat balls, the winners **claim**.

Context, the upper stratum in the hierarchy of realization, can play a significant role in determining the translator's choices. As a higher-order semiotic system above the linguistic systems, context can be characterized in terms of the three parameters, i.e. **field** (what is going on), **tenor** (who is taking part in the activities), and **mode** (what role language is playing). Also, context can be theorized along the cline of instantiation, with the context of culture at the system pole and context of situation at the instance pole. Context of culture, according to Halliday (1978: 55), 'defines the potential, or range of possibilities available in language as a system', while context of situation 'plays a significant role in determining the actual choices among these possibilities' (ibid.).

Example 2.4 is selected from D.H. Lawrence's *Lady Chatterley's Lover* and its two Chinese translations. Chinese TT1, translated by Zhao Susu and published in 2004, involves various deletions of the sexual descriptions. These omissions are shaped by the context, and stem from the censorial practices in China. In various countries, there are rules and regulations, which have become powerful social norms for authors, translators, and editors to follow (see Wong 2018 for an introduction to censorship and translation in the Chinese context). Violating such norms can lead to the withdrawal of the published books, the shutting down of the publishing house, etc. Therefore, it is likely that the editor of the book has deleted the later part of the sentence, with suspension points being used to mark out the omissions. In TT2 translated by Hei Ma and published in 2014, however, no omission is found.

Example 2.4 (adapted from Lawrence 1959: 269, 2004: 262, 2014: 238)

English ST: He was ashamed to turn to her, **because of his aroused nakedness**.
Chinese TT1: 他 不好意思地 调转 身 去 ……
PY: tā bù hǎo yì si de diào zhuǎn shēn qù
IG: he ashamedly turn around body PV
BT: He turned around ashamedly.
Chinese TT2: 他 不好意思 转身，**因为 他的 裸体 正 兴奋 着**。
PY: tā bù hǎo yì si zhuǎn shēn, yīn wéi tā de luǒ tǐ zhèng xīng fèn zhe.
IG: he ashamedly turn around, because his naked body VADV excited VPART
BT: He turned around ashamedly, because his naked body was excited.

Example 2.5, selected from a collection of ghost stories titled *Strange Tales from a Chinese Studio* (聊斋志异), reveals how tenor can be related to the changes made in the translation. Herbert Giles, the translator of TT1, dedicates his translation to his grandchildren. His aims for translating this book include: to glorify virtue, to censure vice, to introduce the knowledge of the folklore of China, and to provide a guide to the manners, customs, and social life of the Empire. Therefore, he purposefully adapts the sexual descriptions in the story. As seen in the example, descriptions of how the man and the lady make love have been changed to the Chinese ritual of getting married by way of worshipping heaven and earth. In TT2, which is translated by John Minford, with aims of introducing the cultural connotation of the tales in his translation, we note that '狎好' (PY: xiá hǎo; IG: make love) has been translated into English in equivalent terms.

Example 2.5 (adapted from Pu 1988: 4, 2006: 23–24, 2010: 31)

Chinese ST: 女回首，举手中花，遥遥作招状，乃趋之。舍内寂无人，遽拥之亦不甚拒，**遂 与 狎好**。

PY: nǚ huí shǒu, jǔ shǒu zhōng huā, yáo yáo zuò zhāo zhuàng, nǎi qū zhī. shě nèi jì wú rén, jù yōng zhī yì bú shèn jù, suí yǔ xiá hǎo.

IG: maiden look back, raise hand in flower, distant do beckon look, so follow her. house in quiet NEG people, quickly embrace her and NEG much refuse, so with make love.

BT: The maiden looked back, raised the flowers in her hand, beckoning him from some distance, so he followed her. The room was quiet and had no person, quickly he embraced her, and she did not refuse, **so he made love with her.**

English TT1: But the young lady, looking back, waved the flowers she had in her hand as though beckoning him to come. He accordingly entered and found nobody else within. **Then they fell on their knees and worshipped heaven and earth together, and rose up as man and wife...**

English TT2: The maiden looked back and beckoned him on with the flower that she still held in her hand. So he followed her into the pavilion, where they found themselves alone, and where with no delay he embraced her and, finding her to be far from unreceptive, **proceeded to make love to her.**

2.3 Instantiation

Instantiation is the scale that links the instance – the text and the usual object of the translation process, with the system of language (see Figure 2.4). A text is meaningful because it is an instance of the entire system. It can be understood by its readers because they are in control of the meaning-making resources. Halliday (e.g. 1992a) makes an analogy by comparing instance and system to weather and climate: the climate is nothing but instances of weather, instances of weather accumulate to form patterns that will be recognized as weather patterns, and, if being further generalized, they will be recognized as the climate. For translators, their job is to move up and down the scale, looking for instances that meet the requirement of a text to be translated.

In translation, the ST and the TT are at the instance pole of the cline, where we can observe language unfolding as texts in their contexts of situation. At the potential pole of the cline, translators make generalizations about the language based on the instances they have observed. Between the two poles, there are intermediate patterns, which are characterized either as instance types from the instance pole (text types operating in situation types) or as sub-potentials from the potential pole (registers operation in institutional domains). We note that in machine translation, emphasis is also given to registers or the sub-potentials of language, which are characterized as '**sublanguages**' (e.g. Kittredge & Lehrberger 1982).

Matthiessen (2021) highlights the importance of register and the cline of instantiation in the engagement with translation and the study of translation from the following two perspectives:

Firstly, when translators do their jobs, they proceed from texts, which are located at the instance pole of the cline of instantiation. Then, the patterns of meaning in the source text are recreated as patterns of meaning in the target text. Such a **process of**

38 • *Systemic Functional Translation Studies*

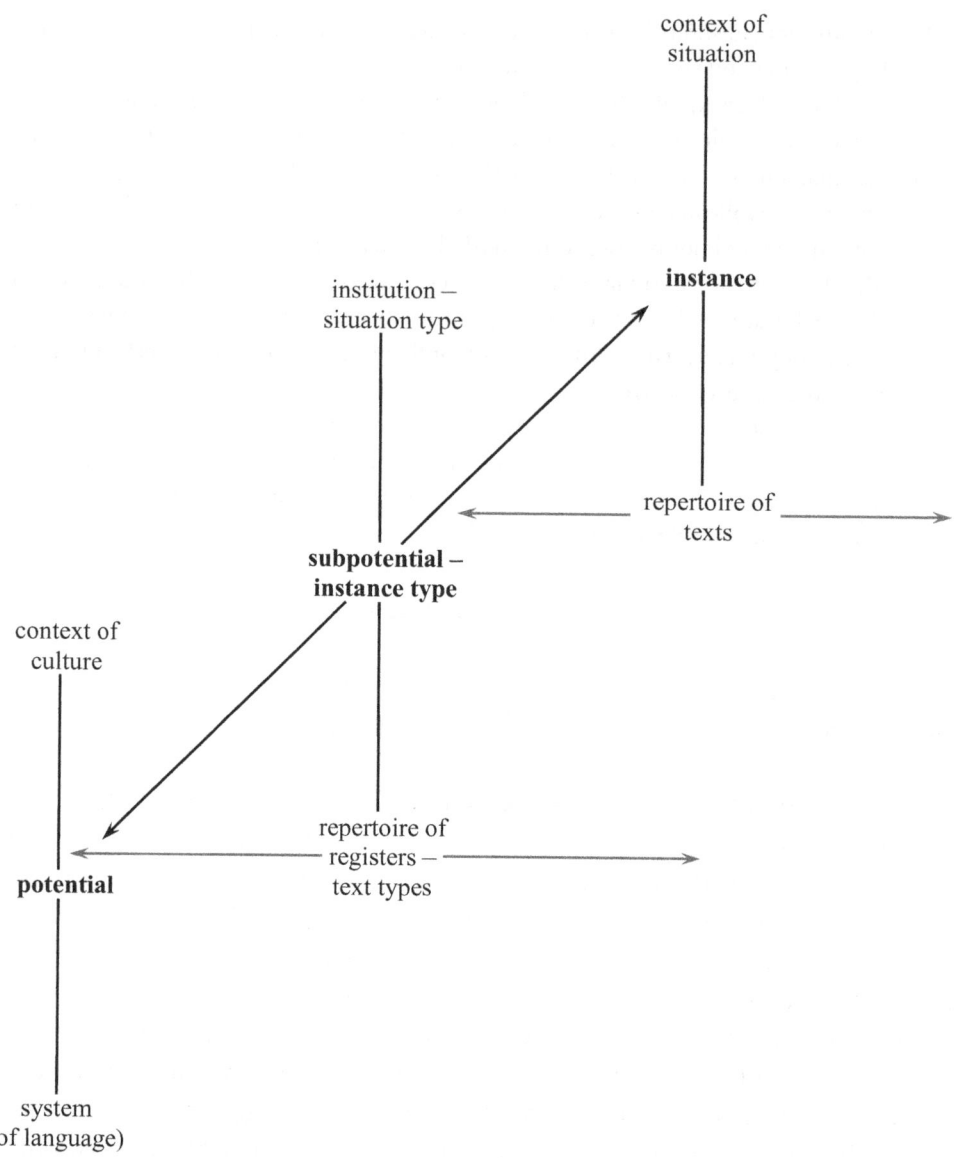

Figure 2.4 The cline of instantiation (adapted from Halliday & Matthiessen 2014: 28)

recreation is also a **process of re-instantiation**, which involves moving up and down the cline of instantiation. Different phases are involved in this process: translators begin to translate, translators keep on translating, translators keep on revising, and translators stop translating; and it is possible for us to investigate the various phases. The traditional focus has been on the first and the final phases by studying the source text and the target text as products. However, the development of technology has equipped us with tools to study the process of translating, enabling us to examine translation as process from below in terms of the ordered typology of systems (see Sections 1.1 and 5.3) (e.g. Alves 2003; Jakobsen 2011, 2014, 2017).

Secondly, when translators translate, they not only have to refer to the meaning potential of the source language (the system pole of the cline), which is instantiated by the source text, but they also have to engage with the meaning potential of the target language, which is instantiated as they recreate the target text. In this way, they are moving from the instantial pole of the cline towards the potential pole and then from the potential pole to the instantial pole. The distance of moving up the cline towards the potential pole will depend on the extent to which they master the registers (sub-potentials) of the source and target language. When translating texts that instantiate conventional registers, translators may already have the knowledge about the registers and do not have to move to the meaning potential end of the cline. It has already been proved in studies on machine translation in the 1970s that when translating particular registers (sub-languages), the automatic translation would be more effective (see Kittredge & Lehrberger 1982). Therefore, the notion of register is suitable to be applied to translation practice and translator training. By setting up a register-based and context-based curriculum, translators can have a clearer sense of the meanings at risk in the source language and target language when they translate texts in different registers (see Section 4.3).

By intersecting stratification and instantiation, we can see that register is located in the mid-region along the cline of instantiation and stratally in semantics (see Figure 2.5). Thus we can approach register stratally from context (from above), from semantics by probing into the semantic strategies that constitute a register (from roundabout),

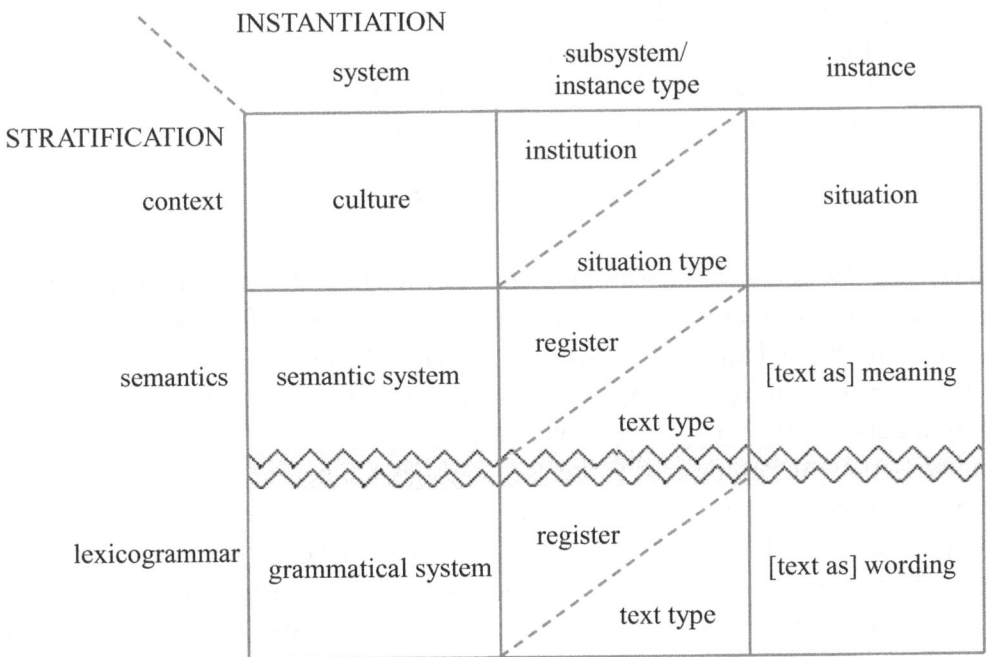

Figure 2.5 Halliday's stratification-instantiation matrix (adapted from Halliday 2002: 14)

and from lexicogrammar by studying the patterns of wording that realize semantics (from below) (see Matthiessen 2019, 2020).

In addition, differences in terms of register between the ST and the TT can lead to various translation shifts in lexicogrammar. Example 2.6 is the English original and the Chinese translation of a poem from *Stray Birds* by Rabindranath Tagore. According to Matthiessen's (e.g. 2014c) context-based registerial typology (see Section 4.2), the register of the ST is enabling, as the poem is characterized by an imperative mood, requesting the addressee – 'my heart' – to undertake certain actions. In the Chinese TT, the register is changed to exploring, which expresses the narrator's opinion, and reveals the narrator's deep love to the addressee of the poem. Besides the change of register, various translation shifts in lexicogrammar are found, such as (i) the addition of three clauses to describe the narrator's mental state in the TT, which leads to an increase in topical Themes, mood types, and process types in the TT, despite the fact that there is only one clause in the ST, and (ii) the omission of the Vocative 'my heart', as the TT is no longer addressed to a certain addressee.

Example 2.6 (adapted from Ma 2018: 257; see also Tagore 1921)

English ST: Listen, my heart, to the whispers of the world with which it makes love to you.
Chinese TT: 静听复静听，静中呼我心。
PY: jìng tīng fù jìng tīng, jìng zhōng hū wǒ xīn.
IG: silence listen again silence listen, silence in call my heart
BT: Listen silently and listen silently, in silence you call my heart.
世间私语处，爱尔意堪寻。
PY: shì jiān sī yǔ chù, ài ěr yì kān xún.
IG: world in private talk place, love you meaning can find
BT: At the place for private talk in the world, I love you, and I will seek the meaning of love.

2.4 Metafunction

Halliday (e.g. 1973) conceptualizes language as a resource for making meaning – the major and primary resource for making meaning in human life. Then, as a resource for making meaning, language is organized systemically as a huge network of interrelated choices of meaning. Halliday observes that these choices in lexicogrammar would sometimes cluster; then, to give an explanation of the clusters, he develops his theory of metafunction. According to this theory, language is inherently organized along the functional lines, and the different clusters are manifestations of different metafunctions, including ideational, interpersonal, and textual. The different metafunctions are in fact different modes of meaning. Therefore, language is a resource for making different modes of meaning simultaneously. When making meaning, we mean ideationally, interpersonally, and textually at the same time.

The ideational meaning provides resources for construing our experience of the world both around us and inside us as meaning. There are two different modes of construing experience, either modelling it configurationally (the experiential mode) or serially (the logical mode). The interpersonal metafunction provides resources for interacting with other people and introducing our own judgements, desires, and perspectives on the situation. The textual metafunction provides resources for organizing ideational and interpersonal meanings as a flow of information in the context.

As the basic unit in SFL analysis, a clause is the combination of the different strands of meaning in accordance with the metafunctions, which include clause as a representation, i.e. a construal of some process in ongoing human experience (ideational metafunction), clause as an exchange, i.e. a transaction between speaker and listener (interpersonal metafunction), and clause as a message, i.e. a quantum of information (textual metafunction). For these different modes of meaning, different systems will be involved (see Table 2.1, see also Chapter 3 for SFTS and the different modes of meaning). In this section, we will briefly introduce Matthiessen's (2014b) categories of metafunctional translation shifts (see Figure 1.7), illustrating how choices between the ST and the TT will differ in terms of the metafunctional modes of meaning. Some shifts are fairly common, such as shifts between the experiential and the logical modes of construing experience as well as shifts between the logical and the textual ways of indicative rhetorical relations. Some shifts, such as those between the interpersonal and the other metafunctions, are less likely to be found, but they do occur. In terms of grammatical metaphor of the interpersonal kind, the ideational metafunction and the interpersonal metafunction may be 'co-selected' in one language, but such a choice may not be selected in another language (see Halliday & Matthiessen 2014: chapter 10; Matthiessen 2021).

Translation shifts can remain **within the textual metafunction (from textual to textual)**. In Example 2.7 (see Figure 2.6), a **theme shift** takes place when the Theme in the ST – '我们的 舞台 上' (PY: wǒ men de wǔ tái shàng; IG: our stage on) – is changed to 'the stove' in TT1 and 'though for the stage' in TT2. In our studies (e.g. Wang & Ma 2020;

Table 2.1 Three lines of meaning in the clause (Halliday & Matthiessen 2014: 83)

Metafunction	Clause as...	System	Structure
textual	message	THEME	Theme ^ Rheme
interpersonal	exchange	MOOD	Mood [Subject + Finite] + Residue [Predicator (+ Complement) (+ Adjunct)]
experiential	representation	TRANSITIVITY	process + participant(s) (+ circumstances), e.g. Process + Actor + Goal

ST	我们的 舞台 上	可以 不 要	炉灶
PY	wǒ men de wǔ tái shàng	kě yǐ bú yào	lú zào
IG	our stage on	can NEG want	stove
TT1		can be dispensed with	the stove
TT2	though	for the stage	we can do away with	the stove
	Theme	Rheme		

Figure 2.6 Example 2.7 (adapted from Lao 1999: 4–5, 2004: 12–13)

Ma & Wang 2021), we have categorized the delicate kinds of theme shift, pointing out the delicate categories such as theme addition, theme omission, and theme substitution. According to the example, '炉灶' (PY: lú zào; IG: stove), which is in the culminative position in the ST, has been put at the beginning of the clause in TT1, thematizing part of the Rheme in the ST. In TT2, a conjunction, i.e. 'though', is added as the textual Theme, and the Theme in the ST is substituted by a circumstance – 'for the stage', which functions as the marked topical Theme.

Translation shifts can take place from **textual to logical**. Example 2.8 (see Table 2.2) is selected from the dramatic monologue of *Teahouse*. It is observed that no textual Theme is found in the ST, whereas several of them are identified in the TTs, including 'But' in TT1, 'But', 'For', and 'nor' in TT2. On the one hand, all textual transitions in the ST are left implicit for readers or the audience to make their own inferences. On the other hand, both translators have made the transitions explicit by adding cohesive conjunctions, leading to a translation shift from textual to logical. The reason is that the Chinese ST is written in the form of doggerel, and the textual connectors are seldom used. Conjunctions in Chinese, such as '然后' (PY: rán hòu; IG: and), '可是' (PY: kě shì; IG: but), and '因为' (PY: yīn wéi; IG: because) will not only be redundant, but will also destroy the rhythmic pattern in Chinese.

Conversely, there can also be translation shifts **from logical to textual**, where the textual transitions are changed from explicit in the ST to implicit in the TT. In Example 2.9 (see Table 2.3), the translator breaks the logical relations between the clauses in the ST by translating the tactically related clauses as structurally unrelated clauses that form a cohesive sequence. In this way, the TT is made less explicit than the ST.

Translation shifts **from logical to logical** can be found within the logical mode of the ideational metafunction. As revealed in Example 2.10 (see Table 2.4), which is selected from Munday's (2001) *Introducing Translation Studies* and its Chinese translation, different logical choices are made in the ST and the TT. Shifts of taxis and logico-semantic type are thus found. The hypotactic relation in the ST is changed to a paratactic one in

Table 2.2 Example 2.8 (adapted from Lao 1999: 234–235, 2004: 192–193)

Tactic structure	Chinese ST	Tactic structure	English TT1	Tactic structure	English TT2
1α	[ø: 他] 动脑筋， PY: tā dòng nǎo jīn, IG: he use brain BT: He uses his brain,	1	**But** all his effort is in vain;	α	**But** all his efforts, alas, are looking pretty thin,
1=β	[ø: 他] 白费力， PY: tā bái fèi lì, IG: he NEG waste strength BT: he wastes strength,	=2	There are certain things you can't attain.	×β α	**For** with heads he lost,
×2	胳膊拧不过大腿去。 PY: gē bo nǐng bú guò dà tuǐ qù. IG: arm wring NEG CV leg PV BT: An arm will not succeed in wringing a leg.			×β+β	**nor** with tails did win.

Table 2.3 Example 2.9 (adapted from Lao 1999: 232–233, 2004: 190–191)

Tactic structure	Chinese ST	Tactic structure	English TT
1	这些事，别多说， PY: zhè xiē shì, bié duō shuō, IG: these matters, NEG much say BT: Do not say much about these matters,		So the less you say about reform.
×2×β	说着 PY: shuō zhe IG: say VPART BT: while you are saying		The longer you'll keep your head from harm.
×2=γ	说着 PY: shuō zhe IG: say VPART BT: while you are saying		
×2α	就许掉脑壳。 PY: jiù xǔ diào nǎo ké. IG: VADV may drop head BT: you may drop your head.		

Table 2.4 Example 2.10 (adapted from Munday 2001: 16, 2007: 25)

Tactic structure	English ST	Tactic structure	Chinese TT
×β	Linked closely to the previous chapter,	1	第六章 和 第五章 紧密 相连， PY: dì liù zhāng hé dì wǔ zhāng jǐn mì xiāng lián, IG: chapter 6 and chapter 5 closely link BT: Chapter 6 is closely linked to Chapter 5
α	Chapter 6 moves on to consider House's register analysis model and the development of discourse-oriented approaches in the 1990s by Baker and Hatim and Mason,	×2	探讨 豪斯（House）的 语域 分析 模式 和 话语 导向 方法 的 发展。 PY: tàn tǎo háo sī de yǔ yù fēn xī mó shì hé huà yǔ dǎo xiàng fāng fǎ de fā zhǎn. IG: discuss House SUB register analysis model and discourse orient approach SUB development BT: discuss House's register analysis model and the development of discourse-oriented approaches.
=γ α	who make use of Hallidayan linguistics	1	话语 导向 方法 是 20世纪90年代 由 贝克、哈蒂姆 和 梅森 所创立的， PY: huà yǔ dǎo xiàng fāng fǎ shì èr shí shì jì jiǔ shí nián dài yóu bèi kè hā dì mǔ hé méi sēn suǒ chuàng lì de, IG: discourse orient approach be 20 century 90 decade PASS Baker Hatim and Mason APART set up SUB BT:
=γ ×β	to examine translation as communication within a sociocultural context.	=2 1	他们 吸收 PY: tā men xī shōu IG: they absorb BT: They absorb
		=2 +2	利用 了 韩礼德 的 语言学， PY: lì yòng le hán lǐ dé de yǔ yán xué, IG: apply ASP Halliday SUB linguistics BT: absorb Hallidayan linguistics
		=2 +3	把 翻译 作为 一个 社会 文化 背景 之下 的 交际 行为 来 进行 研究。 PY: bǎ fān yì zuò wéi yí gè shè huì wén huà bèi jǐng zhī xià de jiāo jì xíng wéi lái jìn xíng yán jiū. IG: DISP translation as one MEAS social cultural background under SUB communicative behaviour CV carry out examination BT: to carry out the examination of translation as a communicative behaviour under sociocultural background

the TT. Also, an enhancing logico-semantic relation (×) in the ST is omitted in the TT, while additional logico-semantic relations are added, such as those of extension (+).

The logical mode and the experiential mode complement each other, both providing resources for the construal of the experiences of the world as meaning. Translation shifts **from experiential to experiential** can be found within the experiential mode of meaning, such as shifts found in the transitivity configuration of process + participants + circumstances. Example 2.11, which is selected from Rabindranath Tagore's *Stray Birds* and Feng Tang's Chinese translation, illustrates how the process type in the ST is changed in the TT. In the example, the substitution of process type takes place when the material process realized by 'fall' in the ST is replaced by the relational: attributive process realized by '无' (PY: wú; IG: NEG have) – the negative lexical choice of '有' (PY: yǒu; IG: have) – in the TT. With the help of the shift, the translator of the TT has deliberately contrasted this line of the poem with a line in the previous stanza – '[ø: 夏日 的 飞 鸟] 翩跹' (PY: xià rì de fēi niǎo piān xiān; IG: summer SUB flying bird flutter).

Example 2.11 (adapted from Ma 2018: 164–168)

English ST: and [ø: yellow leaves of autumn] **fall** there with a sigh. (process type: material)
Chinese TT: [ø: 秋天 的 黄 叶] **无** 翩跹 (process type: relational)
PY: qiū tiān de huáng yè **wú** piān xiān
IG: autumn SUB yellow leaf **have NEG** fluttering
BT: yellow leaves of autumn have no fluttering

Translation shifts **from experiential to logical** take place when the configuration augmented experientially by a circumstance is translated as clauses linked logically through choices made in systems of TAXIS and LOGICO-SEMANTIC TYPE. In Example 2.12 (see Table 2.5), which is taken from the *Universal Declaration of Human Rights* and its Chinese translation,³ the English ST contains a circumstance of Purpose, i.e. 'for the purpose of securing due recognition and respect for the rights and freedom of other'. In the Chinese TT, this circumstance realized by a prepositional phrase in the ST is re-construed as a paratactically related clause linked by the logico-semantic relation of enhancement (×).

Conversely, translation shifts **from logical to experiential** are also possible when translators downgrade a logically related clause in a clause nexus to a circumstance. As shown in Example 2.13 (see Table 2.6), the two clauses in the English ST – 'to install Palm Desktop software' and 'insert the CD into your computer's CD drive' are hypotactically related by the logico-semantic relation of enhancement (×). In the German TT, however, the translator has 'compressed' the first dependent clause in the ST as a circumstance realized by a prepositional phrase in the TT – 'zum Installieren der Palm Desktop-Software'. In this way, the verbal group in the English ST 'to install' is translated as 'Installieren' (IG: installation) – the nominalized equivalent in German, with a grammatical metaphor being used in the German TT.

Translation shifts remaining **within the interpersonal metafunction (from interpersonal to interpersonal)** take place when the translator's interpersonal choices made in systems such as MOOD TYPE, MODALITY, and POLARITY are different from those in the ST. In general, despite the shifts in the system of MOOD, the higher-level choices in the semantic system of SPEECH FUNCTION tend to be retained. As shown in Example 2.14,

Table 2.5 Example 2.12

English ST	Tactic structure of the TT	Chinese TT
In the exercise of his rights and freedoms, everyone shall be subject only to such limitations as are determined by law solely **for the purpose of securing due recognition and respect for the rights and freedom of other…**	1	人人 在 行使 他的 权利 和 自由 时，只 受 法律 所确定 的 限制， PY: rén rén zài xíng shǐ tā de quán lì hé zì yóu shí, zhǐ shòu fǎ lǜ suǒ què dìng de xiàn zhì, IG: everyone CV exercise his right and freedom time, solely subject to law determined limitation BT: When exercising his rights and freedoms, everyone is only subjected to the limitations determined by law,
	×2	确定 此 种 限制 的 唯一 目的 在于 保证 对 旁人 的 权利 和 自由 给予 应有的 承认 和 尊重…… PY: què dìng cǐ zhǒng xiàn zhì de wéi yī mù dì zài yú bǎo zhèng duì páng rén de quán lì hé zì yóu gěi yǔ yīng yǒu de chéng rèn hé zūn zhòng IG: determine this kind limitation SUB only purpose lie in guarantee for other's right and freedom give due recognition and respect BT: the only purpose of determining this kind of limitation lies in the due recognition and respect given to other's rights and freedom

Table 2.6 Example 2.13 (adapted from Matthiessen 2014b: 305)

Tactic structure of the ST	English ST	German TT
×β	to install Palm Desktop software…	Zum Installieren der Palm Desktop-Software,… legen Sie die CD in das CD-ROM-Laufwerk des Computers ein. IG: for the (DAT) installation the (GEN) Palm desktop software,… insert you (HON) the (ACC) CD in the (ACC) CD-ROM drive the (GEN) computer BT: For the installation of the Palm desktop software,… insert the CD into the computer's CD-ROM drive.
α	insert the CD into your computer's CD drive	

the speech function in the ST and the two TTs remains unchanged, while the shifts of mood type are found in the TTs. In the ST, the command is realized by the jussive imperative, by which the addressee – Master Song, is asked to keep the watch. Both translators choose to render the imperative as declaratives, marked by the syntagmatic order of Subjective ∧ Finite, as seen in 'you'd better hang onto' in TT1 and 'you really ought to' in TT2. If translated as imperative mood, the TTs will be expressed as 'hang onto that watch' and 'keep this watch', which will not be as polite as the declaratives used by the speaker, Pock-Mark Liu, to advertise his product to the potential buyer. Moreover, there are additions of modality in both TTs, which result in modality shifts. Though modality is not found in the ST, the modalities of obligation, i.e. 'you'd better' and 'ought to', reveal Pock-Mark Liu's insistence in asking Master Song to keep the tiny watch.

Example 2.14 (adapted from Lao 1999: 26–27, 2004: 28–29)

Chinese ST: 松二爷，留下这个表吧，(mood type: imperative: jussive, speech function: command)
PY: sōng èr yé, liú xià zhèi ge biǎo ba,
IG: Master Song, keep this watch MOD
BT: Master Song, keep this watch!
English TT1: Second Elder Song, **you'd better** hang onto that watch. (mood type: declarative, speech function: command)
English TT2: Master Song, you really **ought to** keep this watch. (mood type: declarative, speech function: command)

In certain cases, the change in mood type results in semantic differences in the system of SPEECH FUNCTION. In Example 2.15, it is found that both the choices of mood type and speech function are changed in the TT. When the imperative mood is changed to declarative, the speech function is also changed from command to statement. However, despite the changes, the clause still serves as the speaker's declining of the compliments from the addressee.

Example 2.15 (adapted from Lao 2004: 32–33)

Chinese ST: 可是，用不着奉承我。(mood type: imperative: jussive, speech function: command)
PY: kě shì, yòng bù zháo fèng chéng wǒ.
IG: but NEG need flatter me
BT: But don't flatter me.
English TT: But you'll get nothing by playing up to me. (mood type: declarative, speech function: statement)

Translation shift may also take place in choices made in the system of POLARITY. In Example 2.16, 'positive' is chosen in the ST between the two choices of 'positive' and 'negative' in the system of POLARITY. In the TT, however, the translator chooses 'negative' in the second clause of the poem, thus leading to a shift of polarity.

Example 2.16 (adapted from Tagore 2015: 10)

English ST: Sorrow is hushed into peace in my heart like the evening among the silent trees.
Chinese TT: 痛 在 我 心 里 渐渐 平和
PY: tòng zài wǒ xīn lǐ jiàn jiàn píng hé
IG: sorrow CV my heart in gradually gentle
BT: Sorrow gradually becomes gentle in my heart.
夜 在 树林 里 一 字 不 说
PY: yè zài shù lín lǐ yí zì bù shuō
IG: night CV wood in one word NEG say
BT: Night does not say a word in the wood.

2.5 Rank

Rank is a hierarchy of units based on composition. It is clearly defined at the inner strata of lexicogrammar and phonology. In English, for instance, the rank scale within lexicogrammar is clause—group/phrase—word—morpheme; within phonology, the rank scale is tone group—foot—syllable—phoneme (see Figure 2.7). The relationship between the units in the rank scale is realization, with one rank being composed of and realized by units of the rank immediately below it. Thus, clause is realized by groups/phrases, whose functions are in turn realized by words. There can be complex extensions of the ranks, such as clause complex, group complex, and phrase complex. Rank is also described in the strata of semantics and context. In semantics, text is the highest rank, while figure/move/message is the lowest rank, which is realized by clause in lexicogrammar.

In addition, rank scale may vary in different languages, but the hierarchy in lexicogrammar is valid for many languages around the world. In Chinese, for instance, since the existence of the rank of morpheme has often been debated (cf. Kennedy 1937), Halliday and McDonald (2004) have regarded word rather than morpheme as the lowest rank in their description.

In lexicogrammar, the widest environment in terms of rank is that of the clause – the most extensive unit of grammar, the narrowest environment is that of the morpheme. As illustrated by Halliday, McIntosh, and Strevens (1966) (see Figure 2.8), when translating from French to English, equivalents can be maintained at different ranks. At the morpheme rank, we only find equivalent choices of 'frott' and 'joue' in English. However, moving up along the rank scale, we find more equivalent choices. At the clause rank, it is appropriate to translate the clause in French into one in English, as clause is the widest grammatical environment where the text is maximally contextualized and where there is a higher degree of grammatically specified translation equivalence.

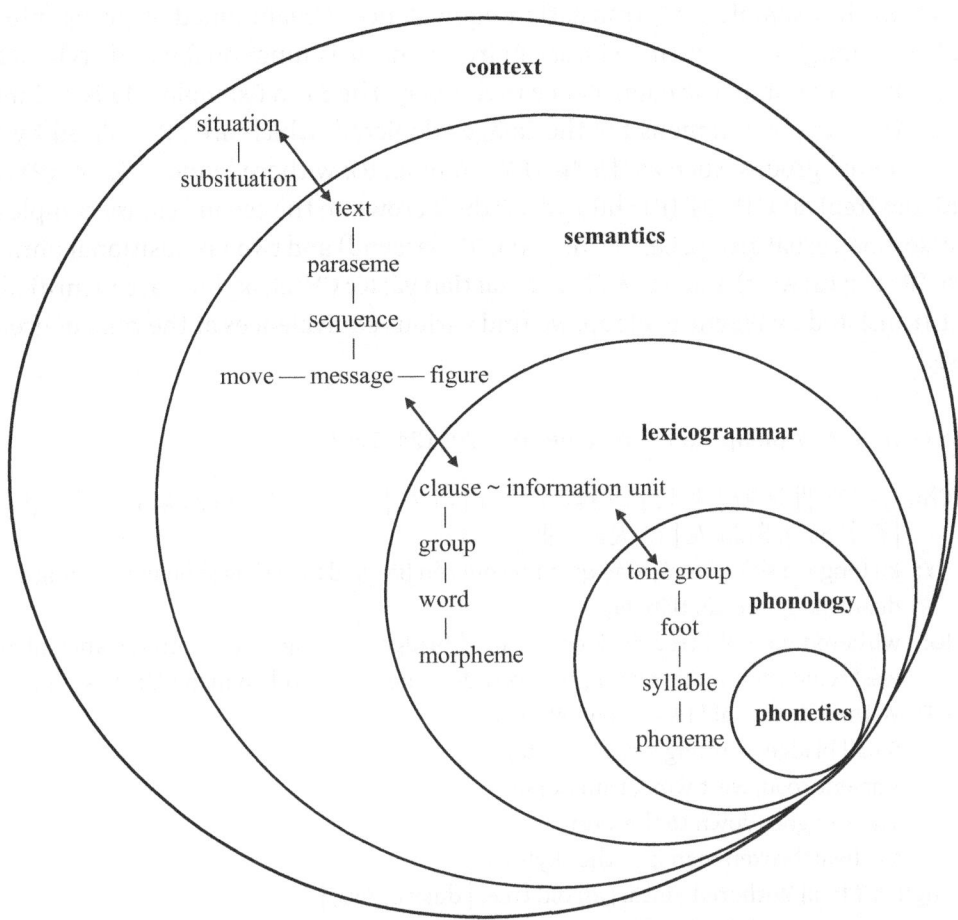

Figure 2.7 The strata of context and language and their internal composition in terms of rank (adapted from Matthiessen, Teruya, & Lam 2010: 207)

Translation at rank of:	||| elle	se	frott+a+				les +	joue +s		
morpheme	X	X	rub	X	X	X	X	cheek	X
word	she/her	X	rubbed				the	cheeks	
group	she		rubbed			herself	his/her	cheeks	
clause	she		rubbed				her	cheeks	

Figure 2.8 Multilingual correspondence and rank (adapted from Halliday, McIntosh, & Strevens 1964: 127)

As shown in Example 2.17, translation equivalence is maintained at group/phrase rank. Even though it is not the widest environment, it is functionally and stylistically appropriate to maintain the equivalence in this way. The ST in Example 2.17 is a Chinese verse in Yuan Dynasty famous for the images depicted, which are all realized by the eleven nominal groups, such as '枯 藤' (PY: kū téng; IG: withered vine), '老 树' (PY: lǎo shù; IG: old tree) and '昏 鸦' (PY: hūn yā; IG: dusk crow). In the second clause complex of the verse, one verbal group, i.e. '下' (PY: xià; IG: descend) and two prepositional phrases, i.e. '西' (PY: xī; IG: west) and '在 天涯' (PY: zài tiān yá; IG: CV: at skyline) are identified. In the TT translated by Wayne Schlepp, we find various equivalences at the rank of group/phrase.

Example 2.17 (adapted from Schlepp 1970: 124–125)

Chinese ST: ||| 枯 藤 | 老 树 | 昏 鸦，| 小 桥 | 流 水 | 人 家，| 古 道 | 西 风 | 瘦 马。||| 夕 阳 | 西 | 下，|| 断 肠 人 | 在 天 涯。|||

PY: kū téng lǎo shù hūn yā, xiǎo qiáo liú shuǐ rén jiā, gǔ dào xī fēng shòu mǎ. xī yáng xī xià, duàn cháng rén zài tiān yá.

IG: withered vine old tree dusk crow, small bridge running water cottage, ancient road west wind thin horse. setting sun west descend, heartbroken man CV: at skyline

BT: Withered vine, old tree, crows at dusk,
Small bridge, running stream, cottages,
Ancient road, west wind, thin horse.
The sun goes down to the west,
the heartbroken man is at the skyline.

English TT: ||| Withered vines, | an old tree, | dusk crows; |
A small bridge, | flowing water, | a few houses; |
Ancient road, | the west wind, | a lean horse; |||
||| Late sun | sets | in the west, ||
A heartbroken man | at the ends of the earth. |||

Rank shift takes place when one unit is downranked or embedded. For instance, in the ST of Example 2.18, 'that took place on the day of my friend's arrival here' is a downranked clause, which modifies 'a conversation', playing a role similar to an Epithet in the nominal group. In the TT, the downranked clause is translated equivalently in terms of rank as an Epithet – '我的 朋友 来 这儿 时 和 你 的' (PY: wǒ de péng yǒu lái zhè er shí hé nǐ de; IG: my friend come here time with you SUB) that modifies the Head '一 场 对 话' (PY: yì chǎng duì huà; IG: one MEAS conversation) in the nominal group.

Example 2.18 (adapted from Christie 2013a: 144, 2013b: 124)

English ST: ||| 'Miss Howard, | do | you | remember | a conversation [[that took place on the day of my friend's arrival here]] ?...' |||

Chinese TT: ||| '霍华德 小姐，| 你 | 还 记得 | **我的 朋友 来 这儿 时 和 你 的** 一 场 对话 吗? ......'|||

PY: huò huá dé xiǎo jiě, nǐ hái jì dé wǒ de péng yǒu lái zhè er shí hé nǐ de yì chǎng duì huà ma?

IG: Howard miss, you still remember my friend come here time with you SUB one MEAS conversation MOD

BT: Miss Howard, do you still remember a conversation that my friend had with you when he came here?

A downranked clause in the ST can also be translated as another clause rather than an Epithet of a nominal group. In Example 2.19, the hypotactically dependent clause in the TT – '如果 一 国 的 美味 对 另一国 人 来说 变得 难 以 下咽' (PY: rú guǒ yì guó de měi wèi duì lìng yì guó rén lái shuō biàn dé nán yǐ xià yàn; IG: if one country SUB delicacy for another country people as for become difficult to swallow) – is translated from the downranked clause in the ST, viz. 'that might seem unpalatable to some'. The translator shifts at the dimension of rank, thus increasing the number of clauses in the TT.

Example 2.19 (adapted from Case 2008: 9, 2012: 9)

English ST: ||| For any country, shared heritage means shared food, || and national delicacies [[that might seem unpalatable to some]] are often based on a plentiful supply of a particular animal or vegetable. |||

Chinese TT: ||| 对于 任何 国家 来说，拥有 共同 的 遗产 就 意味着 他们 会 有 共同 的 食物。||| **如果 一 国 的 美味 对 另一国 人 来说 变得 难 以 下咽**，|| 那 通常 也 是 某 种 动物 或 蔬菜 在 作祟。|||

PY: duì yú rèn hé guó jiā lái shuō, yōng yǒu gòng tóng de yí chǎn jiù yì wèi zhe tā men huì yǒu gòng tóng de shí wù. **rú guǒ yì guó de měi wèi duì lìng yì guó rén lái shuō biàn dé nán yǐ xià yàn,** nà tōng cháng yě shì mǒu zhǒng dòng wù huò shū cài zài zuò suì.

IG: for any country as for, own shared heritage VADV mean VPART they will have shared food. **if one country SUB delicacy for another country people as for become difficult to swallow**, that often also be certain kind animal or vegetable CV make trouble

BT: For any country, to own shared heritage means that they will have shared food. If the delicacy in one country becomes difficult for people from another country to swallow, that trouble is often made by some kind of animal or vegetable.

Similarly, translators can maintain equivalence at a higher rank by translating a group/phrase as a clause. As shown in Example 2.20, which is selected from one of John Milton's sonnets and its Chinese translation, the prepositional phrase 'on his wing' in the ST is rendered as a clause '又 飞走 了' (PY: yòu fēi zǒu le; IG: then fly away ASP) in the TT, with a process '飞走' (PY: fēi zǒu; IG: fly away) being added.

Example 2.20 (adapted from Li & Feng 2003: 23)

English ST: ||| How soon hath Time, the subtle thief of youth, Stol'n **on his wing** my three and twentieth year! |||

From [source text]:

To [target text]:	clause complex	clause	phrase	group
clause complex	clause complex > clause complex	clause > clause complex		
clause	*clause complex > clause*	clause > clause	phrase > clause	
phrase		*clause > phrase*	phrase > phrase	
group			*phrase > group*	group > group

Figure 2.9 Matrix of translation shifts characterized in terms of rank (adapted from Matthiessen 2021: 530)

Chinese TT: ||| 时间，这个狡猾的 小偷，盗窃 了 我 二十 又 三 年，|| 又 飞走 了。|||
PY: shí jiān, zhè gè jiǎo huá de xiǎo tōu, dào qiè le wǒ èr shí yòu sān nián, **yòu fēi zǒu le**.
IG: time this subtle thief steal ASP my twenty and three year **then fly away ASP**
BT: Time, this subtle thief, has stolen my twenty and three years, then flew away.

Similar to the matrix of metafunctional translation shift (see Figure 1.7 and Section 2.4), Matthiessen (2021) also characterizes translation shift in accordance with the dimension of rank. As shown in Figure 2.9, Matthiessen (2021) regards clause complex as the most extensive grammatical domain and a higher rank in the matrix. The diagonal from top left to bottom right in the matrix represents choices made on the same rank in the ST and the TT. However, choices are not always equivalent in terms of rank, the domains in the TT could be either 'up-ranked', i.e. be moved to a higher rank, or 'down-ranked', i.e. be translated to a lower rank. Also, we note that the grammatical classes in the matrix can be distinguished, e.g. the group rank can be specified as nominal, verbal, and adverbial (cf. Dorr 1994 for similar focuses in machine translation).

2.6 Delicacy

Delicacy is a cline from general to specific or a scale from the most gross to the most delicate. In a system network, it corresponds to the ordering of systems from left to right, and is the basic concept behind the system network. As shown in Figure 2.10, which is a simplified system network of MOOD in English, the degree of delicacy increases from left to right. Thus, choices to the left of the network have low delicacy, and those towards the right have relatively higher delicacy. Comparatively, closed systems have low delicacy, open sets have high delicacy, and the semi-closed systems have intermediate delicacy.

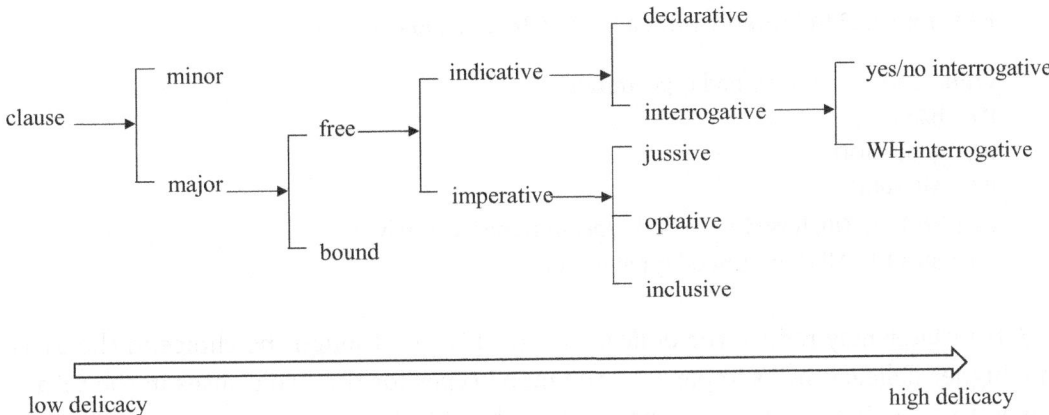

Figure 2.10 Delicacy in the interpersonal system of MOOD (adapted from Halliday & Matthiessen 2014: 24)

In the process of translation, one problem often faced by translators is to locate the degree of delicacy within the ST, and then to maintain equivalence in this respect. According to Halliday (2009), delicacy has relatively received little attention in translation studies, whereas in machine translation it is studied under the heading of 'granularity'. Example 2.21 to Example 2.24 illustrate translation equivalence and shift in terms of delicacy. In Example 2.21, the equivalence in terms of delicacy in the system of MOOD is maintained in the choice of mood type. In both the ST and the TT, declarative mood is selected; thus, the mood choice in the TT is as delicate as that in the ST.

Example 2.21 (adapted from Matthiessen & Halliday 2009: 93, 153)

English ST: In a system network, delicacy corresponds to the ordering of systems from left to right by means of entry conditions. (mood type: declarative)
Chinese TT: 在系统网络中，精密阶对应于以入列条件从左到右的系统的顺序。(mood type: declarative)
PY: zài xì tǒng wǎng luò zhōng, jīng mì jiē duì yìng yú yǐ rù liè tiáo jiàn cóng zuǒ dào yòu de xì tǒng de shùn xù.
IG: CV system network in, delicacy correspond to through entry condition from left to right SUB system SUB ordering
BT: In a system network, delicacy corresponds to the ordering of systems from left to right through entry conditions.

Example 2.22 shows how choice of low delicacy in the system of MOOD is translated as a choice of higher delicacy. In the ST, the mood type is minor, which is low in delicacy. In TT2, the delicacy is maintained equivalently; whereas in TT1, the jussive sub-type of imperative, which is a more delicate choice of mood, is selected by the translator.

Example 2.22 (adapted from Lao 1999: 38–39, 2004: 37–39)

Chinese ST: 好 啦，(mood type: minor)
PY: hǎo la
IG: good MOD
BT: All right,
English TT1: Oh, forget it. (mood type: imperative: jussive)
English TT2: All right, (mood type: minor)

A translator may reduce the delicacy in the TT even though the choice in the ST is of a higher delicacy. In Example 2.23, the mood types for the two clauses in the ST are imperative: jussive and bound respectively. In the TT, the translator chooses the minor mood type, thereby resulting in a translation shift from a wide environment to a narrow environment in terms of delicacy in the system of MOOD.

Example 2.23 (adapted from Lao 2004: 37–39)

Chinese ST: 甭 说 (mood type: imperative: jussive)
PY: béng shuō
IG: NEG say
BT: Don't say
打 洋人 不 打。(mood type: bound)
PY: dǎ yáng rén bù dǎ.
IG: beat foreigners NEG beat
BT: I beat the foreigners or not.
TT: To hell with the foreigners, (mood type: minor)

Similarly, in Example 2.24 (see Figure 2.11), the delicacy of the choice in the English TT is reduced compared to that in the Chinese ST, but the choice is made in terms of experiential meaning in the system of PROCESS TYPE. In the Chinese ST, the process type is material, which is realized by the verbal group '打' (PY: dǎ; IG: fight). For material process, there are further options in the system in terms of type of doing and impact. Therefore, 'transformative' and 'intransitive' are selected here. In the English TT, a process type shift takes place when the process type is changed to experiential, which has no further option in the system network and is thus less delicate as the choice of 'material' made in the ST.

2.7 Axis

The hierarchy of axis is used to distinguish between the paradigmatic organization and the syntagmatic organization. Figure 2.12 illustrates how the systemic (paradigmatic) axis is realized by the structural (syntagmatic) axis. For instance, a major clause in English is realized by the presence of Residue and Predicator; indicative mood is realized

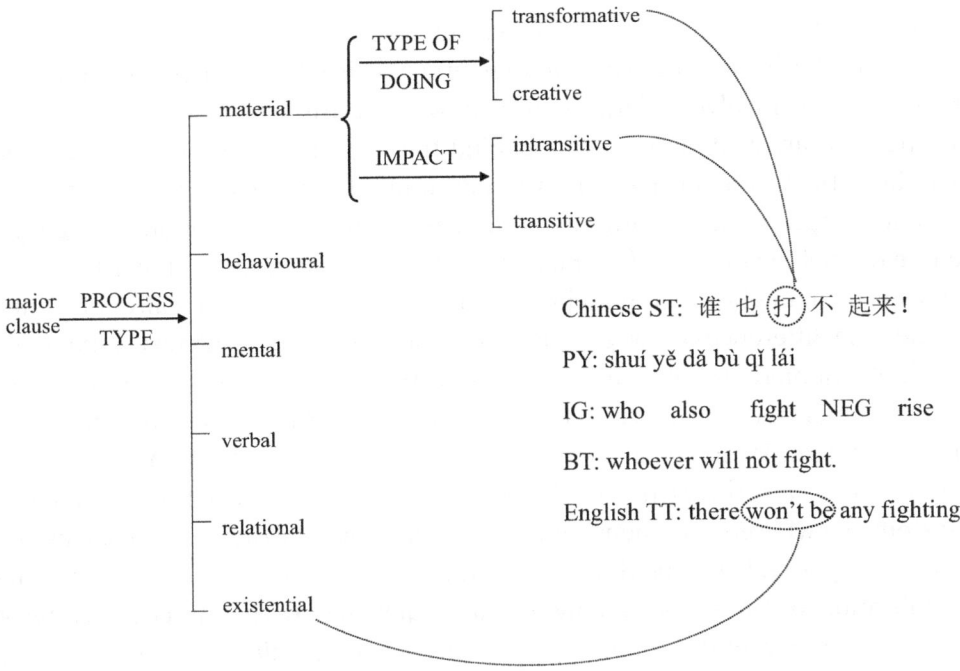

Figure 2.11 Example 2.24 (adapted from Lao 2004: 28–29)

by the occurrence of Mood, which is composed of Subject and Finite; and declarative mood is realized by the syntagmatic order of Subject before Finite (Subject ^ Finite).

The significance of the two axes lies in that they define the space in which the text unfolds, including the structures and grammatical classes, the collocations and the

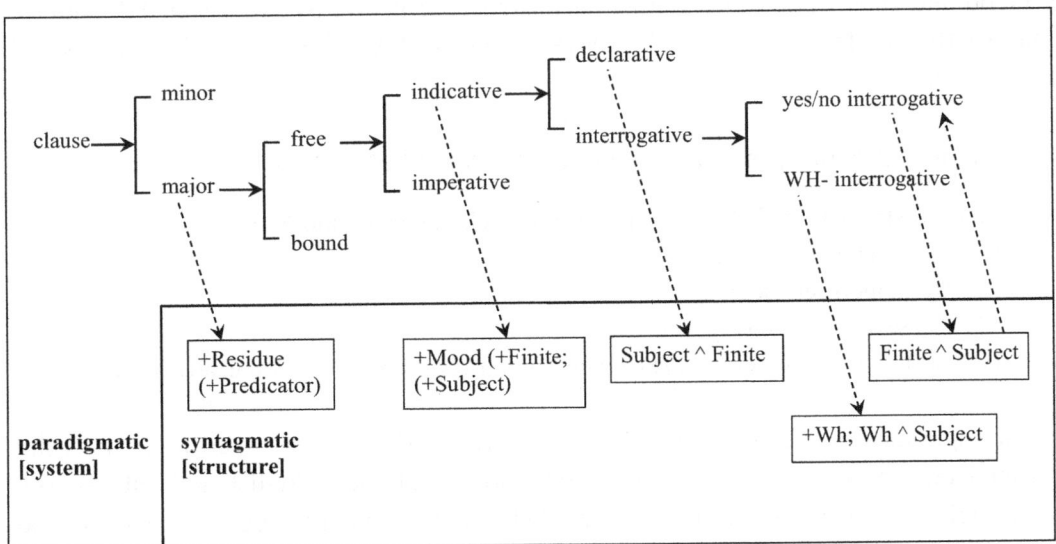

Figure 2.12 The systemic (paradigmatic) axis realized by the structural (syntagmatic) axis (adapted from Matthiessen 2015a: 152)

lexical sets. As noted by Halliday (2009: 19), the meaning of any element is produced by relations on both axes, 'but the paradigmatic axis is what defines the "translation potential", since it involves relations with things that are not present in the particular instance, but are as it were lurking behind the text'. In SFL, scholars have treated the paradigmatic axis as primary. This foregrounds Halliday's conception of making choices among options in meaning and is based on Halliday's conception of language as a resource for making meaning (see Matthiessen 2015b; Matthiessen et al. 2018).

As a result of highlighting the paradigmatic axis, we can paradigmatically point out the similarities and differences between languages. The translated target text is the product and result of innumerbal choices made during the translation process. Therefore, choice is of crucial importance in translation (see Halliday 2010; Matthiessen 2014b), while the syntagmatic marker is merely an automatic realization (see Matthiessen 2021).

In accordance with the principle of the environments of translation, paradigmatic axis (system) is a wide environment, while syntagmatic axis (structure) is a narrow environment. A target text may be different syntagmatically, i.e. shift in terms of syntagmatic realization, but it may be paradigmatically equivalent to the source text. However, it is also possible for shifts to appear paradigmatically. Studies like Teich (1999) and Lavid (2000) have proved the registerial differences in the system of MOOD, even though the systems appear to be similar.

Example 2.25 illustrates a difference in clause structure between Chinese and English. In both the source language and the target language, there is the choice of relational: attributive in the system of PROCESS TYPE. However, in terms of structure, we find no process 'be' in the Chinese ST, with the Attribute being realized by an adjectival verbal group, which is a specific feature in the grammar of Chinese (see Chao 1948; Halliday & McDonald 2004). Thus, the syntagmatic structure in the ST is Carrier ^ Attribute, whereas the one found in the TT is Carrier ^ Process ^ Attribute, with the process 'be' being used.

Example 2.25 (adapted from Halliday & McDonald 2004: 359)

Chinese ST: 这 柠檬 非常 酸。(process type: relational: attributive)
PY: zhè níng méng fēi cháng suān
IG: this lemon very sour
BT: These lemons are very sour.
English TT: These lemons are extremely sour. (process type: relational: attributive)

Paradigmatically, it is possible to find similarities in the system, regardless of how the systemic choices are realized. As shown in Figure 2.13, in both English and Chinese, the basic choices in the system of THEME include textual Theme, interpersonal Theme, and topical Theme. Among these three choices, those of textual Theme and interpersonal Theme in a major clause are optional, whereas the choice of topical Theme is compulsory, which can be further selected as marked or unmarked. Syntagmatically, Theme

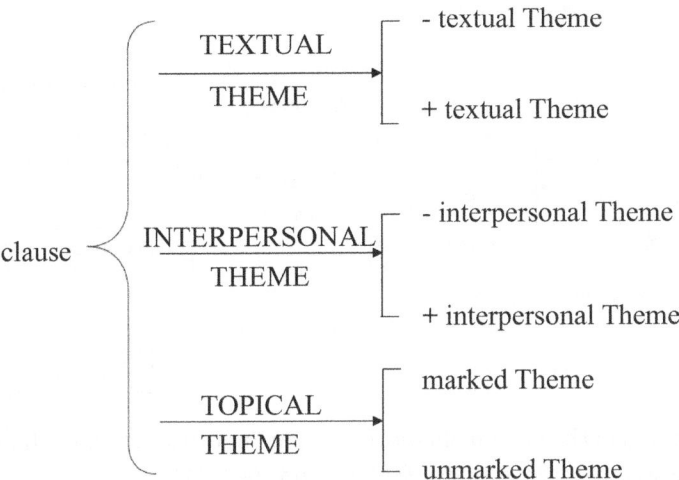

Figure 2.13 Basic choices in the system of THEME (adapted from Halliday & Matthiessen 2014: 106)

choices are realized in both languages based on the order of textual Theme ^ interpersonal Theme ^ topical Theme (see Halliday & McDonald 2004; Li 2007; Halliday & Matthiessen 2014). In Example 2.26 (see Table 2.7), the equivalent realizations of such Theme choices in the ST and the TT can be observed. The textual Themes include 'Hey' in the ST and '嘿' (PY: hèi; IG: hey) in the TT, both being realized by continuatives. The interpersonal Themes include 'bro' in the ST and '哥们儿' (PY: gē men er; IG: bro) in the TT, which are both Vocatives. The topical Themes – 'you' and '你' (PY: nǐ; IG: you) are both unmarked choices.

Table 2.7 Example 2.26 (adapted from Climo 2014: 61, 2015: 54)

	Textual Theme	Interpersonal Theme	Topical Theme	Rheme
ST	Hey	bro	you	've got some toilet paper stuck to your foot.
TT	嘿，	哥们儿，	你	脚上粘着卫生纸啦。
PY	hèi	gē men er	nǐ	jiǎo shàng zhān zhe wèi shēng zhǐ la
IG	hey	bro	you	foot on stuck toilet paper MOD
BT	Hey,	bro	you	have toilet paper stuck to your foot.

However, there can also be differences between languages paradigmatically if we explore the more delicate choices in a system. Figure 2.14 points out a systemic difference between English and Chinese. In Chinese, polar interrogatives can be distinguished as the biassed and the unbiassed sub-types, which are choices not found in English. As shown in Example 2.27, an unbiassed sub-type of polar interrogative is found in the ST in Chinese. When translating this clause into English, there is no systemic equivalent choice of mood in English, the translator thus has to either select yes/no interrogative or other

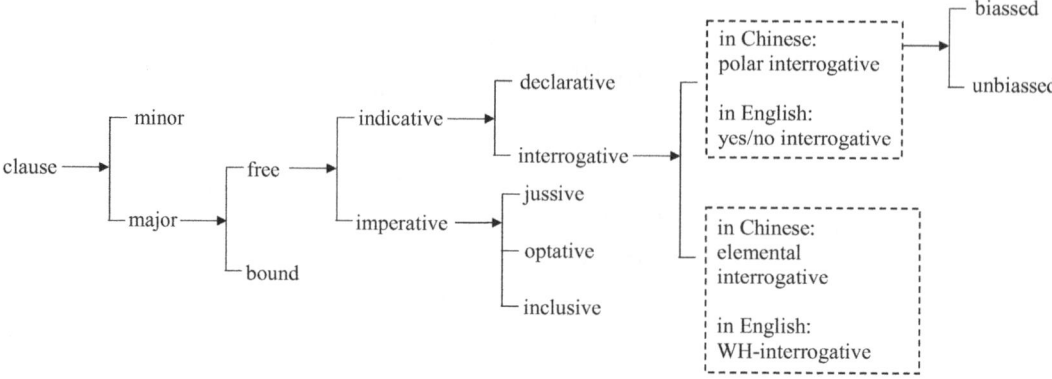

Figure 2.14 Differences in the system of MOOD between English and Chinese (adapted from Halliday & Matthiessen 2014: 24; Halliday & McDonald 2004: 343)

mood types. Therefore, in the TT, one yes/no interrogative and two bound clauses are used. In practice, the awareness of such systemic differences between languages is helpful and has implications for translator training. This requires translators to be equipped with descriptions of the languages in their contexts of cultures that are in focus. Then translators can compare the choices they make in terms of both interpreting the ST and recreating the TT, and be aware of the choices they make in translation.

Example 2.27 (adapted from Lao 2004: 32–33)

Chinese ST: 小王，这儿的房租是不是得往上提那么一提呢？(mood type: polar interrogative: unbiassed)
PY: xiǎo wáng, zhè er de fáng zū shì bú shì děi wǎng shàng tí nà me yì tí ne?
IG: Little Wang, here SUB house rent be NEG be should up raise then a bit raise MOD
BT: Little Wang, should we raise the house rent a bit?
English TT: Little Wang, don't you agree (mood type: yes/no interrogative)
it's time (mood type: bound)
that that the rent on this place was increased? (mood type: bound)

In the next chapter, we focus on metafunction – one of the six dimensions, and discuss how translation is recreated in accordance with the four different modes of meaning.

Chapter 3

Systemic Functional Translation Studies and the Metafunctional Modes of Meaning

This chapter focuses on metafunction, which is one of the six dimensions previously discussed in Chapter 2. We will explore the role that metafunction has played in SFTS and discuss how translators make their choices in this respect. We begin our investigation of metafunction with the clause (whether spoken or written in terms of mode), which is the basic unit in SFL analysis and the combination of the different strands of meaning in accordance with the metafunctions, including clause as a message, i.e. a quantum of information (textual metafunction), clause as an exchange, i.e. a transaction between speaker and listener (interpersonal metafunction), and clause as a figure/representation, i.e. a construal of some process in ongoing human experience (ideational metafunction) (e.g. Halliday & Matthiessen 1999, 2006). These different kinds of meaning are simultaneously made in the lexicogrammar. Following Halliday (e.g. 1978), meaning is compared to beams of white light made up of different colours. The metafunctional analysis, which works like a prism, is capable of revealing the different strands of meanings. In translation, the four modes of meaning are equally implicated.[1] Thus, translation involves the recreation of ideational meanings of the logical kind, ideational meanings of the experiential kind, interpersonal meanings, and textual meanings (see Figure 3.1):

> In terms of **logical** meaning, translators choose how to interpret logico-semantic relations used in forming 'coherent' source texts, and they choose among the options in the target language to **reconstrue** them in the translation they are producing.
>
> In terms of **experiential** meaning, translators choose how to interpret events as configurations of elements (processes, participants, and circumstances) and larger 'chunks' of experience made up of events such as episodes and procedures, and they choose among the options in the target language to **reconstrue** the experiential meanings in the translation they are producing.
>
> In terms of **interpersonal** meaning, translators choose how to interpret propositions, proposals, and the assessments associated with them in the exchange of meaning embodied in the source text, and they choose among the options in the target language to **re-enact** the interpersonal meanings in the translation they are producing.
>
> In terms of **textual** meaning, translators choose how to interpret messages and the sequences of messages that create the flow of information in the source text, and they choose among the options in the target language to **re-present** the textual meanings in the translation they are producing. (Matthiessen 2014b: 277, original emphasis)

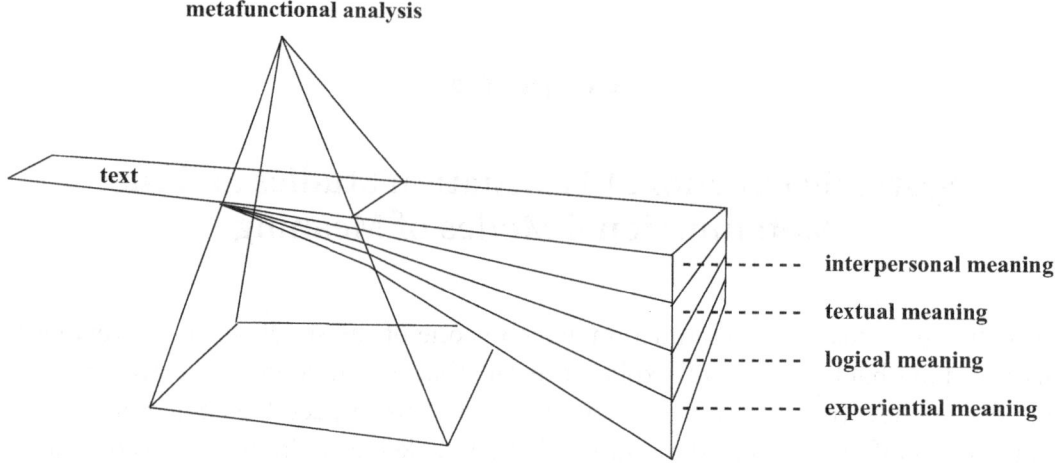

Figure 3.1 Modes of meaning in text revealed by the metafunctional part of discourse analysis (adapted from Matthiessen 2014b: 277)

This chapter explores the relationship between SFTS and the different modes of meaning. Even though the four modes of meaning are equally implicated and are of equal importance to translators, the meanings have not received equal attention in translation studies and practice.[2] There is a tendency for translators and researchers to focus on ideational meaning (also examined under different headings such as denotative meaning, cognitive meaning, and representational meaning), and arguably more on interpersonal meaning. The textual meaning has, to some extent, not been emphasized in practice (cf. Kim & Matthiessen 2015). Matthiessen (2021) holds that translators may prioritize ideational equivalence over interpersonal and textual equivalence; thus we are likely to find more textual and interpersonal translation shifts than ideational ones (see Section 2.4). In the following sections, we will treat each metafunction in its own right, present the choices in terms of the meanings, and discuss how the meanings are investigated in literature.

3.1 Re-presenting Textual Meaning in Translation

Among the four modes of meaning, we will first examine the studies from the textual perspective. These studies focus on choices made in systems such as THEME – a system that provides resources for writers or speakers to guide their readers or listeners as texts unfold in contexts. Halliday (1978) regards the textual metafunction as an enabling one, suggesting that it enables readers and listeners to interpret a text (cf. Matthiessen 1992, 1995a).

Defined as the departure of the message, Theme functions in locating and orienting a clause by making one part of the clause prominent. Theme can be differentiated as textual, interpersonal, and topical. According to the descriptions of English grammar (e.g.

Matthiessen 1995b; Halliday & Matthiessen 2014), choice of textual Theme and interpersonal Theme in a major clause is optional, and choice of topical Theme is compulsory (see Figure 2.12). Moreover, a topical Theme can further be distinguished as marked or unmarked. In Example 3.1 (see Table 3.1), 'However' is the textual Theme, realized by a conjunction; 'frankly' and 'my dear' function as the interpersonal Themes, realized by a modal/comment Adjunct and a Vocative respectively; 'I', realized by a participant, is the topical Theme of the unmarked type, as it is the Subject in the declarative mood. Besides, the unmarked information structure of the clause is Given ^ New, which means that the Theme normally falls within the Given, and the New falls within the Rheme (see O'Grady 2017 for discussions on the prosody of marked Theme).

Table 3.1   Example 3.1

However	frankly my dear,	I	don't give a damn.
textual Theme	interpersonal Theme	unmarked topical Theme	Rheme
Given			New

Textual choices are associated with the flow of information in text. They not only provide translators with the resources to guide their readers to interpret texts, but also help with the composition of the translated texts (see Matthiessen 2014b). Matthiessen (2014b) summarizes the guidance of textual choices to textuality in two domains, i.e. **textual transitions** and **textual statuses** (cf. Matthiessen 1992). In terms of textual transition, the system of CONJUNCTION, one of the systems in the overall network of COHESION (see Halliday & Hasan 1976), is involved. In terms of textual status, other systems of COHESION are related, including REFERENCE and SUBSTITUTION/ELLIPSIS, as well as systems that are capable of generating textual structures in the clause, viz. THEME and INFORMATION, which complement each other in the development of textuality.

Kim and Matthiessen (2015) and Wang (2014) have conducted comprehensive reviews of studies on textual metafunction and translation. The review papers suggest that studies in this area focus on two issues: (i) the recreation of textual choices, i.e. the extent to which the choices in the target text are similar or different to those in the ST; and (ii) the appliability of SFL to translation studies. Wang (2014) also categorizes the studies into those that focus on similar or different thematic structures based on their findings.

In Ghadessy and Gao's (2000) quantitative analysis of thematic development in political commentaries translated from English to Chinese, both similarities and differences are found. (The Themes of the clauses from Example 3.2 to Example 3.4 are underlined.) Firstly, the majority of the additional Themes in Chinese are simple Themes. The amount of multiple Themes does not differ significantly between the two languages. Secondly, Chinese texts have more clauses, which lead to the increase of marked and unmarked Themes. As seen in Example 3.2, three more Themes are added in the Chinese TT, which is a reinterpretation of the ST. Among the Themes in the TT, 'China' and 'weakness' are thematized, while the rest of the information from the Theme in the ST are all found in the Chinese Rhemes. Thirdly, there are more ellipted (omitted) Themes and time as Theme categories in the Chinese texts. Based on these findings, the authors suggest that there is 'a highly significant correlation between the Themes in English texts and Chinese translations in terms of assigned Themes features and Theme patterns selected' (p. 461). The analysis of the thematic patterns is expected to shed light on the teaching of academic writing.

> Example 3.2 (adapted from Ghadessy & Gao 2000: 475)
>
> English ST: <u>With a curious arrogance, made even stranger by its weakness,</u> China at first continued to refuse to accept the West on equal terms and negotiate with them as such.
> Chinese TT: <u>中国 傲慢 自恃</u>,
> PY: zhōng guó ào màn zì shì,
> IG: China proud arrogant
> BT: China is proud and arrogant,
> <u>更 由于 它的 软弱 无能</u> 而 令 人 感到 奇怪。
> PY: gèng yóu yú tā de ruǎn ruò wú néng ér lìng rén gǎn dào qí guài.
> IG: further because its weakness incapability thus make people feel strange
> BT: further because of its weakness and incapability, people feel strange.
> 它 最初 一直 不 承认 与 西方 国家 的 平等 地位,
> PY: tā zuì chū yì zhí bù chéng rèn yǔ xī fāng guó jiā de píng děng dì wèi,
> IG: it at first always NEG admit with Western nations SUB equal status
> BT: It always does not admit its equal status with Western nations at first.
> [ø:它] 并 拒绝 以 平等 地位 与 西方 国家 进行 谈判。
> PY: tā bìng jù jué yǐ píng děng dì wèi yǔ xī fāng guó jiā jìn xíng tán pàn.
> IG: it and refuse with equal status with Western nations carry out negotiations
> BT: It refuses to carry out negotiations with Western nations in equal status.

Kim and Huang (2012) discuss the professional translators' choices of Theme in three translations of a Chinese short story. They find that changes tend to be made in terms of the marked topical Themes in the TT. According to Example 3.3, unmarked choices, i.e. 'six years' and 'since I', are found in TT1, while a marked topical Theme 'in the twinkling of an eye' is seen in TT2, indicating how quickly the six years have passed. In the ST, however, the marked topical Theme is placed in the second clause to orient readers with the circumstantial information. Also, in order to know the readers' response towards these translations, the authors conduct a survey, which has revealed that different thematic choices are considered to be odd by readers, and are thus not welcomed (cf. Kim 2007). This study reflects the importance of metafunctional thinking. It indicates that textual choices are too subtle for translators to focus on and even professional translators may not have paid enough attention to such choices (see also Kim 2011; Matthiessen 2014b).

Example 3.3 (adapted from Kim & Huang 2012: 89)

Chinese ST: 我 从 乡下 跑 到 京城 里，
PY: wǒ cóng xiāng xià pǎo dào jīng chéng lǐ,
IG: I from countryside run to capital in,
BT: I ran from the countryside to the capital,
一转眼 已经 六 年 了。
PY: yì zhuǎn yǎn yǐ jīng liù nián le.
IG: in a wink already six year ASP
BT: In a wink, it has already been six years.
English TT1: <u>Six years</u> have slipped by
<u>since I</u> came from the country to the capital.
English TT2: <u>In the twinkling of an eye</u>, six years have passed
<u>since I</u> left the countryside
[<u>ø: I</u>] to come to the capital.

In addition, in some studies, different thematic structures are found between the ST and the TT. For example, Ventola (1995) explores the Theme/Rheme structures between German and English academic texts in terms of thematic progression and development in the parallel texts. She further discusses the structures of Theme/Rheme and Given/New information, which are both factors that lead to the differences found. As Halliday (1985b) points out, the information structure normally coincides with the topical Theme/Rheme structure of the clause, so that in the unmarked cases the topical Theme can also be the Given information and the Rheme can be the New information. This study concludes that, in academic registers, 'the Theme/Rheme patterns are important in guiding the reader through the logical paths constructed by the writer' (Ventola 1995: 102). As shown in Example 3.4, we find two different English translations of the clause in German. The translator of TT1 was first asked to do the job. However, the German author was not fully satisfied with the first version, thus the second translator was found to provide another translation based on TT1. In TT1, which is a literal translation of the ST in terms of the thematic structure, the information structure is the same as that of the ST. TT2, which is a revised version of TT1, is characterized with the free strategy adopted in translation, as the translator tries to 'Anglicize' the literal translation by changing the marked topical Theme to an unmarked one.

Example 3.4 (adapted from Ventola 1995: 91–92)

German ST: <u>Kennzeichnend für diese Diskussion</u> ist eine breite thematische und argumentative Auffächerung.
IG: characteristic for this (ACC) discussion is a (NOM) broad thematic and argumentative breakdown
BT: Characteristic for this discussion is a broad and thematic breakdown.

English TT1: <u>Characteristic for this discussion</u> is the broad breakdown of topics and arguments.

English TT2: <u>A wide range of issues and arguments</u> is characteristic for this discussion.

In another study, by examining the thematic and information structure between English and Portuguese translations, Vasconcellos (2008) emphasizes the translators' competence and the variations between the two languages. It is concluded that 'professional translators choose to preserve the original Theme and focus despite the constraints of a different target-language syntax' (p. 63). Meanwhile, it is suggested that the translator should take several aspects into consideration, such as 'gaps in the lexicon, fusion of multiword concepts, differences in register, cultural differences, etc.' (ibid.), as it is impossible for a translator to capture all kinds of meaning.

Among the studies found in the literature, both Halliday's (1985b) SFL model and the Prague School's Functional Sentence Perspective (FSP) model (e.g. Mathesius 1928, 1975; Daneš 1974; Firbas 1992) have the potential to be selected as the theoretical model. Comparatively speaking, the FSP model is primarily adopted to analyse languages such as Spanish, Russian, German, and Finnish in studies such as Contreras (1976), Hickey (1990), and Nord (1991), while Halliday's model is applied in more recent studies that cover a wider range of language pairs (see Kim & Matthiessen 2015).

Baker (1992, 2018) highlights the importance of textual equivalence, and emphasizes the need to raise translators' awareness of marked Theme choices in translation. (Presumably these will have different realizatons in different languages, such as English and Greek.) On the one hand, translators are encouraged to preserve the marked Theme choices in their TTs, even though some thematic choices in the ST have to be abandoned due to the typological differences between languages. On the other hand, the TT will also have its own thematic features. It is not only a coherent text in its own right, but is also a recreation of the ST in terms of the information structure.

3.2 Re-enacting Interpersonal Meanings in Translation

Interpersonally, clauses are considered as exchanges, involving grammatical systems such as MOOD and MODALITY. In the system of MOOD, all major clauses can select one specific mood type. Take the grammar of English for example (see Figure 2.10 for MOOD system of English; see Figure 2.14 for comparison of system between English and Chinese), there is the choice for a major clause to be either indicative or imperative. If it is indicative, it can be either declarative or interrogative. If it is interrogative, it can be further refined into yes/no and wh- sub-types. In addition, the system of MODALITY concerns itself with 'the speaker's judgement, or request of the judgement of the listener, on the status of what is being said' (Halliday & Matthiessen 2014: 172), with four major types of modality being involved: probability, usuality, obligation, and readiness.

Huang (e.g. 2002a, 2006) explores the interpersonal systems in the translation of Chinese classical poems. His analysis focuses on the following perspectives: mood, question and response, vocative, the questioner, the relationship between the characters in the poem, and speaker/listener relationship. In terms of mood choices, it is found that different translators choose different mood types based on their own interpretations of the ST.

Yu and Wu (2016) investigate the choices in systems of MOOD and MODALITY in the four English translations of *The Platform Sutra*, and relate lexicogrammatical choices to the recreation of the image of Chan master Huineng in the Tang Dynasty of China. *The Platform Sutra*, known as one of the most widely read Chan texts, is a collection of Huineng's personal conversations and public sermons. However, variations in mood and modality choices in the different translations have presented different images of Huineng: 'an authoritative and forceful Huineng versus a cautious and polite Huineng' (p. 19). Among the four TTs, though declaratives are often found, imperatives and indicatives with high-valued modalities are especially favoured by the two American translators. As shown in Example 3.5, in which Master Huineng asks his disciple to repeat the teachings of another master, the translators of TT1 and TT2 recreate the second clause equivalently as imperatives. While in TT3 and TT4, the second clause is translated as yes/no interrogative and declarative respectively. Also, modalities that express readiness, i.e. 'will' and 'can', are added by the translators of TT3 and TT4. Thus, TT3 and TT4 soften the tone of Huineng's command and make Huineng's orders less explicit, thereby portraying Huineng as a polite master who tries to put himself on an equal status to his disciples.

Example 3.5 (adapted from Yu & Wu 2016: 13)

Chinese ST: 彼 有 何 言 句 (mood type: elemental interrogative)
PY: bǐ yǒu hé yán jù
IG: he has what say sentence
BT: What did he say?
汝 试 举 看 (mood type: imperative)
PY: rǔ shì jǔ kàn
IG: you try cite see
BT: Try to cite it.
English TT1: What did he have to say? (mood type: wh- interrogative)
Try to quote him. (mood type: imperative)
English TT2: What instruction did he give you? (mood type: wh- interrogative)
Try to repeat it to me. (mood type: imperative)
English TT3: What instruction did he give you? (mood type: wh- interrogative)
Will you please repeat it? (mood type: yes/no interrogative)
English TT4: What did he say? (mood type: wh- interrogative)
You **can** cite for me some of his teachings. (mood type: declarative)

There are also comparative studies that take the semantic system of SPEECH FUNCTION (or speech act in Lavid's study) into consideration. Lavid (2000) examines the speech acts of requests and questions in administrative forms in three languages, namely English, Italian, and German. Quantitatively, significant differences are found in the realizations of the speech acts. For instance, when realizing requests, imperatives are often found in the English forms characterized with the use of simple and direct language. The politeness marker 'please' is frequently seen in the imperatives, appearing at the beginning of the clause and functioning as the interpersonal Themes (see Example 3.6). Contrastively, in Italian and German, declarative mood and passive voice are often used to realize requests, which make the requests impersonal and distant from the readers. Lavid (2000) further relates the lexicogrammatical variations to the context where the forms are produced, suggesting that the speech functions in different languages have different individual unmarked mood choices. She claims that people in the English socio-cultural setting attempt to 'achieve a clear, friendly, and polite tone which will reduce the distance with the citizens and increase their audience acceptance' (p. 83). By contrast, in the Italian/German context, people tend to choose indirect, impersonal expressions in the form that reflects the 'distant and formal attitude of the administration toward its users' (ibid.).

Example 3.6 (adapted from Lavid 2000: 74)

English version: Please tick all the boxes that apply to you. (mood type: imperative)
Italian version: La cartolina deve essere utilizzata anche per la segnalazione alla Sede INPS di inesattezze od omissioni nei periodi assicurative riportati sull'estratto. (mood type: declarative)
IG: the card must be used also for the signalling all office INPS of inaccuracies from omissions no periods insurance reported on extract
BT: The card must also be used to inform the INPF office of any inaccuracy or omission in the insurance periods reported in the extract.
German version: Der Berichtigungsabschnitt muss bei der Landesstelle NISF oder bei einem der Patronate der Provinz abgegeben werden. (mood type: declarative)
IG: the (NOM) claim for correction must at the (DAT) regional NISF or at a (DAT) the (GEN) patrons the (GEN) province sent get
BT: The claim for correction must be sent to the regional NISF office or to one of the Patrons of the province.

APPRAISAL is an interpersonal semantic system that offers resources for assessing meanings. Appraisal is similar to other linguistic attempts towards the assessment of meaning, like stance (e.g. Biber & Finegan 1989) and evaluation (e.g. Hunston & Thompson 2000), and is concerned with the enactment of appreciation, judgement, affect, or graduation. In SFTS, **Jeremy Munday** (e.g. 2010, 2012) and **Meifang Zhang** (e.g. 2002, 2013) have taken a leading role in applying appraisal to translation. Thereafter, a large number of studies have included appraisal in their frameworks, especially studies on translations of news discourse (e.g. Pan 2015) and political speeches (e.g. Munday 2015, 2018).

Munday's (2012) monograph – **Evaluation in Translation: Critical Points of Translator Decision-making** is one of the first books that investigate translators' subjective evaluation of the positions in the ST. The book includes a survey of SFTS in general as well as studies on the translation of attitude. It also features Munday's (2012) own model that largely draws on Martin and White's (2005) appraisal framework. To apply his model to text analysis, he chooses texts of different registers, including political speeches, technical texts, and literary texts.

By analysing President Donald Trump's inaugural address in 2017, Munday (2018) conducts a follow-up study of his previous analysis of the 2009 inaugural speech by President Barack Obama (Munday 2012). The earlier findings are further generalized and the methodology is adjusted. He again uses the appraisal framework and builds an appraisal profile of the ST, which is then compared with six Spanish TTs (including five simultaneous interpretations and one written translation) to reveal the critical points of the interpreters' and translators' intervention. Based on the appraisal profile of the ST, Munday (2018) compares Obama and Trump's speeches, and finds a smaller number of invoked (i.e. implicit, which is used in contrast to inscribed) evaluations in Trump's speech, which are realized through non-core vocabulary, metaphor, and allusion. Though such allusions are not found in Trump's speech, the one in Example 3.7 has caused some problems for the interpreters of TT1 and TT2. In the ST, 'rusted-out factories' here refers to the Rust Belt of the US, which stretches from the Great Lake to the various states in the Midwest, and helps to shape the image of de-industrialization and economic decline. In addition, the use of a simile, viz. 'like tombstones' has reinforced the sense of decay. In both TTs, such evaluative language is not equivalently interpreted and the simile of tombstones is omitted, with 'rusted-out factories' merely being interpreted as 'closed factories'.

> Example 3.7 (adapted from Munday 2018: 185–186)
>
> English ST: rusted-out factories scattered like tombstones across the landscape of our nation.
> Spanish TT1: fábricas cerradas
> IG: closed factories
> BT: closed factories
> Spanish TT2: fábricas cerradas... en todo ... el paisaje de nuestra nación
> IG: closed factories... in all... the landscape of our nation
> BT: closed factories in all landscape of our nation

By following this approach, Munday (2018) examines the translation shifts in terms of attitude (the principle resource of appraisal, and is further divided into the categories of affect [enactment of affect towards the interactants], judgement [enactment of judgement of behaviour], and appreciation [enactment of evaluation of phenomena]), graduation (the resource of grading or scaling), and engagement (the resource of engaging with others in the process of evaluation). He maintains that his appraisal-based model 'provides a very focused and intricate tool for identifying the power behind evaluative words and expressions' (p. 192). He further confirms that the lexical analysis serves important purposes, including (i) understanding the evaluative strategies in the ST, (ii) the possibility of comparing with previous findings, and (iii) providing solutions of retaining the 'non-core lexis and allusion-laden images' in interpreting based on the analysis of the translation shifts in the TTs (ibid.).

In some frameworks, appraisal is used together with critical discourse analysis (CDA), with appraisal serving the micro analytical purposes and CDA functioning as the explanatory toolkit. For instance, Pan (2015) analyses the Chinese translations of English news in *Reference News* – a state-run newspaper in mainland China. She points out the different kinds of deviations in terms of evaluation and positioning, one type of such deviations being the alterations of the news actors in the Chinese translation. Example 3.8 illustrates the possibility of conducting a social analysis, through which evaluative deviation occurs when identifying news actors. The specific information of the Actor in the ST is omitted in the Chinese TT, with the name of the lawyer anonymized and his/her occupation concealed. Furthermore, Pan (2015) interprets the analysis with the help of CDA, specifically Fairclough's (1995a, 1995b) three-dimensional model, by associating the linguistic choices with the ideology and culture of the Chinese society. She argues that the deviation has ideological implications, as 'human rights lawyer' is a job seldom mentioned in the Chinese media. Also, in terms of social and cultural values, the individualism and aggressiveness seen in Western media are not regarded as suitable in the Chinese media, which propagate collectivism and harmony.

> Example 3.8 (adapted from Pan 2015: 222)
>
> English ST: **Pu, a human rights lawyer** in Beijing, said China's human rights performance should be looked at in historical context.
> Chinese TT: 北京 一 名 律师 也 说，中国 在 人权 领域 的 表现 应 被 放入 历史 背景 中 加以 审视。
> PY: běi jīng yì míng lǜ shī yě shuō, zhōng guó zài rén quán lǐng yù de biǎo xiàn yīng bèi fàng rù lì shǐ bèi jǐng zhōng jiā yǐ shěn shì.
> IG: Beijing one MEAS lawyer also say China CV human rights domain SUB performance should DISP put history background in to look at
> BT: A lawyer in Beijing also said that China's performance in the domain of human rights should be looked at in historical background.

3.3 Re-construing Experiential Meanings in Translation

Experiential meaning is mainly manifested through the TRANSITIVITY system. More specifically, experiential meaning construes our experience of a flow of events, which is in turn seen as quanta of change modelled as figures[3] (Halliday & Matthiessen 1999, 2014).

Mason (2012) regards transitivity as one prominent text parameter used to ascertain translators' strategies and attitudes. To re-construe experiential meaning, translators have to model their experience of the world through the resources of transitivity. Hence, the target text is mapped out by transitivity, and is closely linked to the translators' point of view. Mason (2012) admits that typological differences between Spanish and English lead to various obligatory translation shifts. According to Example 3.9, while translating the Spanish agentless process into an English passive structure, we find two different English TTs: TT1 is a more literal translation (adding 'it' as participants of the clauses) while the translator of TT2 adopts a free strategy by identifying the agents of the material processes as 'he'.

Example 3.9 (adapted from Mason 2012: 403)

Spanish ST: De no hacerse así – y no se ha hecho así – el riesgo que se corre...
IG: if no do so – and no oneself has fact so – the risk that it run
BT: if it is not done so – and it has not in fact been done so – the risk that is run...
English TT1: if it is not done in this way – and it has not in fact been done in this way – the risk that is run
English TT2: if he fails to do this – and he has not done it – he runs the risk

Mason (2012) also finds that, in some cases, the TT adheres to the ST as closely as possible in terms of process type. However, there are also translation shifts that change the experiential meanings of the ST, involving re-lexicalization of processes (Example 3.10), participants (Example 3.11), or circumstances (Example 3.12) in the ST to draw the readers' attention and to intensify the effect of the TT. In Example 3.10, 'poser' (IG: ask) – a process in the ST is changed to 'discuss'. In Example 3.11, we find a participant, i.e. 'homicide' (IG: homicide) in the French ST changed to 'murder' in the English TT. Similarly, a circumstance in Example 3.12 – 'de manière tragique' (IG: of manner tragic) is translated as 'criminally'. (It is also interesting to note the registerial and dialectal variation from 'homicide' in the ST to 'murder' in the TT.)

Example 3.10 (adapted from Mason 2012: 407)

French ST: pour que l'on accepte de **poser** la question de...
IG: in order to what we agree to **ask** the question
BT: in order that we agree to **ask** the question
English TT: before we agree to **discuss**

Example 3.11 (adapted from Mason 2012: 406)

French ST: c'est un **homicide**
IG: it is a **homicide**
BT: It is a **homicide**
English TT: It is **murder**

Example 3.12 (adapted from Mason 2012: 407)

French ST: Le groupe TotalFinalElf récidive, de manière tragique
IG: the group TotalFinalElf recommit, of manner tragic
BT: The TotalFinalElf group has recommitted another offence, **in a tragic manner**
English TT: The TotalFinalElf group... has acted **criminally**, once again

Huang (2013) analyses the two translations of James Joyce's 'Two Gallants' from the perspectives of process type, participant roles, and ergative verbs. According to Example 3.13, it is observed that Joyce uses a material process to describe Lenehan – the flattering man who 'wore an amused listening face', rather than using a behavioural process as would normally be the case for 'smile' and 'laugh'. Such an estrangement is understood as a suggestion that Lenehan's amusement is not behavioural, but a fake one. In TT1, it is translated as '做出 一 副 …… 的 样子' (PY: make one MEAS ... SUB look), which turns out to be more explicit than 'wore' in the ST. Comparatively, TT2 ignores the meaning of 'wore', compensating with '看得出' (PY: kàn de chū; IG: seem), which is semantically closer to the ST, but is too explicit to express the flattery of Lenehan. Hence, Huang (2013) suggests his own translation: '挂着张听得饶有兴致的脸' (PY: guà zhe zhāng tīng de ráo yǒu xìng zhì de liǎn; IG: hang VPART MEAS listen VPART plentifully have interest SUB face), in which '挂' (PY: guà; IG: hang) equivalently re-construes the material process in the ST. Also, '挂' (PY: guà; IG: hang) is semantically similar to 'wore', with its collocation with '脸' (PY: liǎn; IG: face) suggesting the artificial amusement.

Example 3.13 (adapted from Huang 2013: 97–98)

English ST: The other, who walked on the verge of the path and was at times obliged to step on to the road, owing to his companion's rudeness, wore an amused listening face.
Chinese TT1: 另 一 位 走 在 小路 边缘，由于 同伴 张 手 动 脚 的，他 有时 不得不 走到 马路 上，却 做出 一 副 听 得 饶 有 兴味 的 样子。
PY: lìng yí wèi zǒu zài xiǎo lù biān yuán, yóu yú tóng bàn zhāng shǒu dòng jiǎo de, tā yǒu shí bù dé bù zǒu dào mǎ lù shàng, què zuò chū yí fù tīng de ráo yǒu xìng wèi de yàng zi.
IG: another one MEAS walk CV small road verge, because companion wave hand move foot SUB, he sometimes have to walk road on, but make one MEAS listen VPART plentifully have interest SUB look
BT: Another one walked at a small road verge, owing to companion's waving-hand and moving-feet, he sometimes had to walk on the road, but made an amused listening manner.

Chinese TT2: 另一个走在路边，因为同伴的粗野，有好几次不得已只好踏上了马路，从他的脸色看得出，他听得很有兴致。

PY: lìng yí gè zǒu zài lù biān, yīn wéi tóng bàn de cū yě, yǒu hǎo jǐ cì bù dé yǐ zhǐ hǎo tà shàng le mǎ lù, cóng tā de liǎn sè kàn de chū, tā tīng de hěn yǒu xìng zhì.

IG: another one MEAS walk CV road side, because companion SUB rudeness, have several times have to have to step ASP road, from his face look VPART PV, he listen VPART very have interest

BT: Another one walked at the road side, because of his companion's rudeness, for many times he had to step on the road; from his face we see that he listened with amusement.

In addition, based on the analysis of participant roles, Huang (2013) finds that 'little jets of wheezing laugher' rather than 'Lenehan' functions as the Actor in the ST (see Example 3.14), through which James Joyce emphasizes Lenehan's powerlessness. In TT1, '他' (PY: tā; IG: he) is translated as the Actor, while the process of 'follow' is changed to '发出笑声' (PY: fā chū xiào shēng; IG: make laughing sound), erasing Joyce's intention to emphasize laughter. Moreover, TT1 decreases the meaning of 'followed one after another' by translating it as '不断' (PY: bú duàn; IG: constantly), and changes 'out of his convulsed body'. By the same token, TT2 puts '他' (PY: tā; IG: he) into the Actor role and makes similar changes in the translation. Huang (2013) also suggests his own translation: '那微微的嗤嗤的笑声哟！一阵接一阵，从他颤动的身子里迸发出来' (PY: nà wēi wēi de chī chī de xiào shēng yo! yí zhèn jiē yí zhèn, cóng tā chàn dòng de shēn zi lǐ bèng fā chū lái; IG: that subtle wheezing laughter MOD! a burst follow a burst, from his shaking body in burst out), which not only renders '笑声' (PY: xiào shēng; IG: laughter) as the Actor, but also emphasizes the laughter by using the modal particle '哟' (PY: yo; IG: MOD) and the exclamation mark.

Example 3.14 (adapted from Huang 2013: 99)

English ST: Little jets of wheezing laugher followed one another out of his convulsed body.
Chinese TT1: 他不断发出嗤嗤的笑声，且笑得身体前仰后合。
PY: tā bú duàn fā chū chī chī de xiào shēng, qiě xiào de shēn tǐ qián yǎng hòu hé.
IG: he constantly make wheezing laughter, and laugh VPART body forward rock backward rock
BT: He constantly made wheezing laugh noises, and laughed to rock his body backward and forward.
Chinese TT2: 他颤动着身子，迸发出一阵接一阵微微的嗤笑。
PY: tā chàn dòng zhe shēn zi, bèng fā chū yí zhèn jiē yí zhèn wēi wēi de chī xiào.
IG: he convulse VPART body, burst one burst follow one burst subtle wheezing laughter
BT: He convulsed his body, and burst one following another little wheezing laughter.

In Cheng and Liang's (2008) study, transitivity analysis is used to point out the lexicogrammatical shifts in translation that function to suit the target language. Various changes made to the process type are identified. As shown in Example 3.15, an additional relational process is found in the TT, and is translated from a nominal group in the ST – 'my disintegrating copy of Edith Hamilton's "Mythology"'. The TT also features with an addition of a logico-semantic type, which is logically linked to the other clause simplexes in the clause complex.

> Example 3.15 (adapted from Cheng & Liang 2008: 44)
>
> English ST: I grabbed my disintegrating copy of Edith Hamilton's 'Mythology' to refresh my memory on the Chimera.
> Chinese TT: 我赶紧拿起我的那本伊迪丝•汉密尔顿的《神话》，虽然那是一个破损的版本，但仍然能唤起我对凯米拉的许多回忆。
> PY: wǒ gǎn jǐn ná qǐ wǒ de nà běn yī dí sī hàn mì ěr dùn de shén huà, suī rán nà shì yí gè pò sǔn de bǎn běn, dàn réng rán néng huàn qǐ wǒ duì kǎi mǐ lā de xǔ duō huí yì.
> IG: I quickly grab my that MEAS Edith Hamilton SUB Mythology, although that be one MEAS outworn edition, but still can evoke I to Chimera SUB many memory
> BT: I quickly grabbed my *Mythology* by Edith Hamilton, although that was an outworn edition, it still can evoke many of my memory on the Chimera.

Apart from the addition of process type to the TT, Cheng and Liang (2008) find omissions of processes. In Example 3.16, the clause complex in the ST is translated as four nominal groups in the TT, with the process of 'run' being omitted. We note that the translator also shifts in the dimension of rank scale, moving from clause rank to group/phrase rank.

> Example 3.16 (adapted from Cheng & Liang 2008: 44)
>
> English ST: Two cars and four men can run upwards of $10,000 a day.
> Chinese TT: 两辆车，四个人，一天，一万美金。
> PY: liǎng liàng chē, sì gè rén, yì tiān, yí wàn měi jīn
> IG: two MEAS car, four MEAS man, one day, ten thousand US dollar
> BT: Two cars, four men, one day, ten thousand US dollar.

3.4 Re-construing Logical Meanings in Translation

Logical meaning provides resources for linking all kinds of complexes, such as clause complexes and group complexes. The logical systems are investigated by analysing systems like TAXIS and LOGICO-SEMANTIC. For instance, Wang and Ma (2018) compare the choices of taxis and logical-semantic type in a Chinese drama titled *Teahouse* and its two English translations. They observe some quantitative differences, and find that the translator of TT2 has used a larger number of hypotaxis out of the consideration of the lyrical form. In Example 3.17 (see Table 3.2), instead of choosing parataxis, the translator of TT2 selects hypotaxis on purpose, by adding a hypotactic clause beginning with 'till'.

Table 3.2 Example 3.17 (adapted from Wang & Ma 2018: 151)

Tactic structure	Chinese ST	Tactic structure	English TT1	Tactic structure	English TT2
1	（我）大傻杨， PY: wǒ dà shǎ yáng, IG: I Silly Yang BT: I am Silly Yang,		I'm Oddball Yang, a balladeer.	1	I'm Silly Yang,
+2	[ø: 我] 打 竹板儿， PY: wǒ dǎ zhú bǎn er, IG: I beat bamboo clapper BT: I beat bamboo clapper,	1	This is Yutai Teahouse;	+2α	and from shop to shop, I make my rounds
+3	[ø: 我] 一来 PY: wǒ yì lái IG: I come BT: I come	+2	I'm always here.	+2×β	till here I stop.
=4	[ø: 我] 来到大茶馆儿。 PY: wǒ lái dào dà chá guǎn er. IG: I come PV big teahouse BT: I come to the big teahouse				

In this way, the clause complex ends with the lexical choice of 'stop', which rhymes with 'shop' in the previous line of the text.

In terms of logico-semantic type, extension (+), the preferred choice in the ST and TT1, turns out to be the least favoured choice in TT2. A detailed analysis reveals eight shifts in logico-semantics type in TT2, due to the 'free' translation strategy adopted by the translator, which allows him to alter the logico-semantic meanings. In Example 3.18 (see Table 3.3), an extra clause – 'Life's hard for a rhymester', is found, with which the logico-semantic type of enhancement (×) is added.

In addition, Wang and Ma (2018) quantify and discuss the metafunctional translation shifts (see Section 2.4), such as those from textual to logical. As shown in Example 3.19 (see Table 3.4), most conjunctions in the ST are omitted, which means translators have to understand these implicit transitions and try to mark them out explicitly in the TTs. The shift takes place when the lexical choices of 'so' are added to reveal the enhancing relation (×) in both TTs, even though there is no equivalent lexical choice of '所以' (PY: suǒ yǐ; IG: so) in the ST.

Logical meaning can be balanced with textual meaning, with the aim of realizing coherence in lexicogrammar. The logical and the textual meanings have exerted a mutual impact on the construction of coherence, which can be examined in terms of clause complexing and cohesion of the text in SFL. Li and Wu (2017) explore this area by investigating clause complexity and cohesive chains in a Chinese novel titled *Hong Lou Meng* (*The Story of the Stone*) and its two English translations. Based on their quantitative analysis, they point out the clause types (whether being clause simplex, hypotactically

Table 3.3 Example 3.18 (adapted from Wang & Ma 2018: 151)

Tactic structure	Chinese ST	Tactic structure	English TT1	Tactic structure	English TT2
1	[ø: 我]打 竹板 PY: wǒ dǎ zhú bǎn IG: I beat bamboo clapper BT: I beat bamboo clapper	1 1	My clapper [ø: is] clacking,	1 α	Beating my clappers,
+2	我又来, PY: wǒ yòu lái, IG: I again come BT: I come again,	1+2	I'm here once more.	1×β	here I am again,
+3	数来宝的还是没发财。 PY: shǔ lái bǎo de hái shì méi fā cái. IG: rhythmic storytelling SUB still NEG get rich BT: The singer of rhythmic storytelling still does not get rich.	+2 1	Tongue a'wagging	+2 1	Life's hard for a rhymester,
		+2+2	[ø: I'm] still dirt-poor.	+2×2	so a beggar I remain.

Table 3.4 Example 3.19 (adapted from Wang & Ma 2018: 156)

Tactic structure	ST	Tactic structure	TT1	Tactic structure	TT2
1×β	为打仗, PY: wèi dǎ zhàng, IG: to fight BT: To fight,	1×β	But in order to fight	1×β	In order to fight,
1α	要枪炮, PY: yào qiāng pào, IG: want gun BT: they want guns,	1α	they've got to have guns,	1α	one must buy guns,
×2	一堆一堆给洋人老爷送钞票。 PY: yì duī yì duī gěi yáng rén lǎo ye sòng chāo piāo. IG: one pile one pile CV foreigner lord send money BT: they send piles of money to foreign lords	×2	**So** they waste our wealth on foreign ones.	×2	**So** to foreign countries went silver by the tons.

Table 3.5 Example 3.20 (adapted from Li & Wu 2017: 11)

Tactic structure	ST	Tactic structure	TT
1	李纨道： PY: lǐ wán dào IG: Li Wan say BT: Li Wan said	"1	"I won't let **you** go!"
"2	"偏不许你去。 PY: piān bù xǔ nǐ qù. IG: EMPH NEG allow you go BT: "I don't allow you go.	2	said Li Wan.
×β	显见得只有凤丫头， PY: xiǎn jiàn dé zhǐ yǒu fèng yā tou, IG: obviously only Feng BT: Obviously you only listen to Feng,	1	"The only person **you** ever take any notice of is that precious Feng of **yours**;"
α	就不听我的话了。" PY: jiù bù tīng wǒ de huà le. IG: VADV NEG listen to my words ASP BT: you do not listen to my words."	+2 α	**you** think
		+2 'β	**you** don't need to obey me;
		+3	but **you** shall."

related or paratactically related clause complex) and the logico-semantic types in the cohesive chains. According to Example 3.20 (see Table 3.5), the projecting clauses are translated explicitly rather than implicitly, which is regarded as one of the styles of the translator. Also, no cohesive chain in terms of personal identity is found in the ST; whereas in the TTs the cohesive chain is made explicit with the help of personal pronouns like 'you' and 'yours', with only one clause being disconnected from the chain, i.e. 'said Li Wan'. Using this approach, Li and Wu (2017) find both similarities and differences between the ST and the two TTs in the distribution of logico-semantic type, and summarize the styles of the translators.

Studies have also focused on the more delicate choices in the overall logical system, such as projection (e.g. Hu & Zeng 2012; Zeng 2016) and reporting clauses (e.g. Huang 2014). For instance, Zeng (2016) proposes a model of analysing and comparing projection in translation, according to which comparisons are made in terms of the realization of projection (the signal of projection, the message being projected, whether the projection is quoting or reporting), the unit being projected (whether it is clause complex, clause complexes, paragraph, or paragraphs), and the tactic relation (hypotaxis or parataxis). According to Example 3.21 (see Table 3.6), it is found that the projected clause, namely '子曰' (PY: zǐ yuē; IG: Confucius say) and 'Confucius once remarked' are not omitted in the ST and the TT, while the difference lies in the syntagmatic realizations

Table 3.6 Example 3.21 (adapted from Zeng 2016: 50)

Tactic structure	Chinese ST	Tactic structure	English TT
1	子曰： PY: zǐ yuē IG: Confucius say BT: Confucius said:	1	Confucius once remarked,
"2	"吾未见刚者。" PY: wú wèi jiàn gāng zhě. IG: I NEG see strong person BT: "I do not see a strong person."	"2	"I do not now see a man of strong character."
1	或对曰： PY: huò duì yuē IG: somebody reply BT: Somebody replied:	"1	"There is So – and – so,"
"2	"申枨。" PY: shēn chéng. IG: Shencheng BT: "Shencheng."	2	said **somebody**.
1	子曰： PY: zǐ yuē IG: Confucius say BT: Confucius said:	"1	"No,"
"2 1	"枨也欲， PY: chéng yě yù, IG: Cheng MOD desire BT: "Cheng has desire,	2	replied Confucius,
"2×2	焉得刚？" PY: yān dé gāng? IG: how can strong BT: How can he be a strong person?"	"3 1	"he is a man of strong passions;
		"3 =2	he is not a man of strong character."

of the projection. In the ST, the projecting clauses are followed by the projected clauses; whereas in the second and the third clause complexes in the TT, the projected clauses are placed before the projecting clauses. Zeng (2016) further notes that the omitted Sayer in the second clause complex is explicitly translated as 'somebody' in the TT.

3.5 Some Implications

3.5.1 Imbalanced Metafunctional Considerations

Based on our brief survey, we find that the frequencies of the studies focusing on different metafunctional modes of meaning are unevenly distributed. A large number of studies have focused on the textual and the interpersonal metafunction, while very limited amount of studies have centred on the ideational (experiential and logical) metafunction. On the one hand, experiential meaning has primarily been the focus of translators; thus, the amount of translation shifts in certain texts may be smaller than those in other modes of meaning. On the other hand, studies on experiential meaning have not yet gained the attention of SFL scholars, and have instead been investigated in translation studies under the headings of denotative meaning, representational meaning, ideology, etc.

We suggest that interesting observations be made based on the ideational analysis of the data, complementing textual and interpersonal analysis. One example is Ma's (2018) study that examines process type in the Chinese translations of Rabindranath Tagore's *Stray Birds* (see also Ma & Wang 2021). Drawing on stratification, Ma's (2018) analytical framework enables her to point out the process type shifts in the data, and to relate the shifts to the choices made graphologically and phonologically as well as the contextual features analysed in terms of field, tenor, and mode, which also function as the principle controlling variables of register, i.e. the variation of language according to use (see Chapter 4).

3.5.2 Variation and Creativity in Analytical Frameworks

We hope the analytical frameworks used in SFTS can be diversified by taking different systems and different environments of translation (Matthiessen 2001) or texts of different registers into consideration. The construction of one's analytical framework can be informed by various factors, such as the nature of the data, the aims of the research, or comments from editors, supervisors, or anonymous reviewers. Also, one needs to determine the comprehensiveness of the analysis: whether the analysis can be highly selective, involving a limited number of systems, or exhaustive, by investigating as many systems as possible. To make one's analysis maximally reliable, one has to make a trade-off, and try to construct comprehensive analytical frameworks rather than an analytical toolkit subject to analytical bias.

After a preliminary review of the literature, we find that there are still perspectives or analytical tools in SFL that have not or have seldom been applied in SFTS. One example is the ergative model of transitivity, which is based on the variable of external cause (the Agent), and has a complementary relation with the transitive model. The transitive model has received considerable attention in SFTS, with various attempts at analysing process types and participant roles (see Section 3.3). However, it would also be interesting to compare the ST and the TT based on an ergative analysis (e.g. Wang 2019). Another theory seldom applied in SFTS is Rhetorical Structure Theory (RST), including both classical RST and Matthiessen's Rhetorical System and Structure Theory (e.g. da Cunha & Iruskieta 2010; Wang 2015, 2020; see Wang & Ma in prep. for a brief introduction to RST). Located on the semantic stratum, RST is capable of sketching out both the local and the global logical relations in a text, and is suitable for application to different domains of text analysis, including translation. Many interesting possibilities in building up analytical frameworks await future explorations by scholars and researchers.

3.5.3 Systemic Functional Theory and Description

Analysis in SFTS is dependent on the development of systemic functional theory and its application to language description. To carry out an analysis that compares the ST and the TT, one needs suitable descriptions of the languages involved. *Halliday's Introduction to Functional Grammar* (Halliday 1985b, 1994; Halliday & Matthiessen 2004, 2014) and *Lexicogrammatical Cartography* (Matthiessen 1995b) have provided detailed descriptions of the grammar of English. However, many languages have still not been described in systemic functional terms, thus leading to difficulties for SFTS. Besides, the existing descriptions of many languages may not be thorough and delicate enough. Therefore, it is hoped that future work in this area will be carried out both in terms of the systemic organization and structural organization, and the descriptions will involve not only systems of low delicacy, but also systems of higher delicacy. Matthiessen (2004), Teruya and Matthiessen (2015), as well as Mwinlaaru and Xuan (2016) have presented summaries of current contributions as well as the ways by which systemic functional language description and typology can be advanced (see also McDonald 2020; McGregor 2021). Hopefully, there will be more developments in this area, as SFTS stands to benefit from this development (see Section 6.2.1).

Chapter 4

Register and Systemic Functional Translation Studies

This chapter examines the relationship between register, text type, and SFTS. Section 4.1 discusses text type and translation, introducing Katharina Reiss's (1971) text typology and its application. The section also links Reiss's (1971) strand of work to Karl Bühler's (1934), and relates these studies to SFL. In Section 4.2, we elaborate on the notion of register in SFL as well as Christian Matthiessen's long-term project of registerial cartography, sketching out the potential of its application to translation studies. In SFL, register is conceptualized as a central property of language and defined as variation in language according to context of use (see e.g. Halliday, McIntosh, & Strevens 1964; Gregory 1967; Hasan 1973; Halliday 1978). It has been essential in SFL application, notably in text analysis and translation. As early as the 1960s, Catford (1965) has related register to translation as part of a general exploration of language varieties in translation. Since then, register has continued to play an important part in SFTS. Section 4.3 reports on a survey of text types in SFTS by building on the context-based register typology introduced in Section 4.2.

4.1 Text Type and Translation

In translation studies, **Katharina Reiss** (1971) represents one of the pioneering scholars who build a text typology aimed at assessing translations. She borrows the three functions of language from the Austrian psychologist **Karl Bühler** (1934), and asserts that the equivalence of such functions is of crucial importance in translation. Inherited from Plato, Bühler's (1934) conceptual framework is, in fact, the distinction of personal pronouns in grammar, i.e. first person, second person, and third person (Halliday & Hasan 1985; see Table 1.1). It is on this basis that Reiss (1971) categorizes the three text types, and puts forward methods for translating texts of different types. In Table 4.1, we tabulate Reiss's (1971, 1976) three text types, their corresponding functions, and the suggested translation methods.

In addition, Reiss (1971: 108–109) characterizes the features of the three text types as follows:

(i) **Informative text type.** 'Plain communication of facts': information, knowledge, opinions, etc. The language dimension used to transmit the

Table 4.1 Text types and their translation methods according to Reiss's text typology (adapted from Reiss 1971, 1976; Nord 2002/2003)

Language function	Informative (representing objects and facts)	Expressive (expressing sender's attitude)	Appellative (making an appeal to text receiver)
Language dimension	Logical	Aesthetic	Dialogic
Text type in Reiss (1971)	Representational (content-dominated)	Expressive (form-dominated)	Appellative (appeal-dominated)
Text type in Reiss (1976)	Informative	Expressive	Operative
Text focus	Correctness of contents, acceptability of form	Correctness of contents, corresponding form	Effect has priority over content and form
Translation method	'Plain prose', explicitation as required	'Identifying' method, adopt perspective of ST author	'Adaptive', equivalent effect

information is logical or referential, the content or 'topic' is the main focus of the communication.

(ii) **Expressive text type.** 'Creative composition': the author uses the aesthetic dimension of language. The author or 'sender' is foregrounded.

(iii) **Operative text type.** 'Inducing behavioural responses': the aim of the appellative function is to appeal to or persuade the reader or 'receiver' of the text to act in a certain way, for example to buy a product (if an advert), or to agree to an argument (if a political speech or a barrister's concluding statement). The form of language is dialogic and the focus is appellative.

Reiss (1971) further provides examples of the text types ('Textsorte'). As shown in Figure 4.1, reference work, poem, and advertisement are the ideal informative, expressive, and operative texts respectively. There are other hybrid text types which are situated somewhere within the triangle shown in the figure. For instance, the tourist brochure straddles informative and expressive text types, and operative instruction lies between informative and operative text types. The limitation of Reiss (1971), as identified by House (2018), lies in that precise indications of text types are not properly given and the assessment of text type equivalence between the ST and the TT are not clearly presented.

From the perspective of SFL, a **text** is a semantic unit. Defined as language functioning in context, it is the highest unit on the rank scale in semantics. In terms of stratification, a text can be viewed trinocularly, i.e. from above (top-down) by looking at the contextual parameters, from roundabout by considering the semantic parameters, and

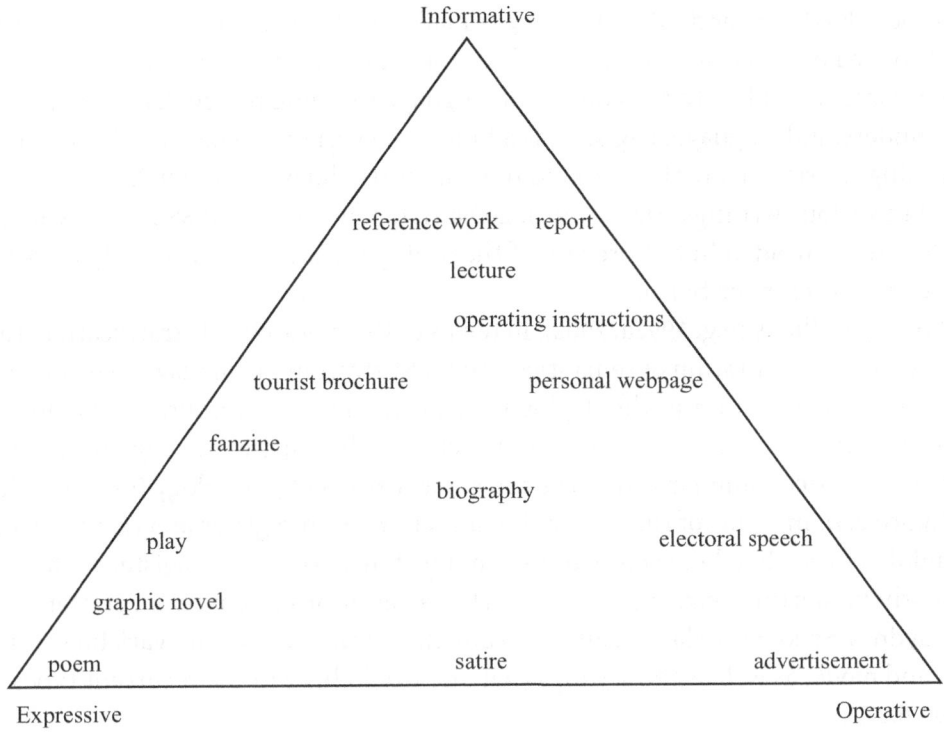

Figure 4.1 Reiss's (1971) text types and text varieties (adapted from Munday 2016: 116)

from below (bottom-up) by investigating the lexicogrammatical parameters. In addition, a text is located at the instance pole of the cline of instantiation, with the recurrent patterns in the unfolding of texts being recognized as **text type**. Both register and text type are in the mid-areas of the cline of instantiation, while text type is viewed from the instance pole (text) as instance type, and register is seen from the potential pole (language system) as sub-potential of language (see Figure 2.4). In the next section, the concept of register in SFL and Christian Matthiessen's (e.g. 1993, 2014c, 2015c, 2015d, 2020) project of registerial cartography will be discussed.

4.2 Register and the Registerial Cartography Project in Systemic Functional Linguistics

Reid (1956) is generally regarded as the first scholar to introduce the concept of register. Besides, **register** has a history in the Firthian tradition in the UK. According to **Firth** (1957a), certain contexts are so constrained that we can be specific about the aspects of the overall resources of language that are to be taught and learned. Such situations are generalized in accordance with the notion that language is inherently variable in context. Complementing dialect, which refers to variation according to language user, register has been introduced as the term and the theory for variation according to language use.

The post-Firthians and SFL scholars gradually established the concept of register. One of the major publications is the book by Halliday, McIntosh, and Stevens (1964), in which register is applied to the context of language teaching to help language teachers better understand language. Register, as a functional variety of language, is interpreted as meanings at risk in a particular kind of context (Halliday 1978, 2002), and is further refined in various writings (Hasan 1973, 2009; Halliday & Hasan 1985). Meanwhile, the term 'genre' is avoided in the process of theorizing register, as it is closely associated with genre in literary criticism.

Following Halliday (e.g. 1992a, 2002), in terms of the hierarchy of stratification, register is located at the stratum of semantics – the first stratum in language to be impacted by context. It is variation in the deployment of the meaning resource of language in accordance with the nature of context. But there are also 'ripples' through from semantics down to lexicogrammar and at least to some aspects of phonology (or graphology) (see Figure 2.5). In terms of the cline of instantiation, both register and text type are in the middle of the cline between potential and instance. However, register is theorized differently in Martin's (e.g. 1992, 1998) works as variations in context. For Martin and other Sydney School scholars, register means the parameters of the variables of field, tenor, and mode, as well as the settings that one would have in the recurrent types (see Section 6.2.3).

Register is central to various applied research goals of SFL. Since the 1960s, register has been fundamental to the various areas of application, including education (although explored under the heading of 'genre') (e.g. Martin & Rose 2007; Rose & Martin 2012), healthcare communication (e.g. Matthiessen 2013), and multimodal analysis (e.g. Bateman 2008; Matthiessen 2009b). Translation and interpreting is certainly one of the areas, and the ealiest attempt was made by Catford (1965) as a general exploration of language varieties in translation. The significance of register is also seen in various works by Steiner (2004a) and the various corpus-based studies by Steiner's team in Saarbrücken (e.g. Hansen-Schirra, Neumann, & Steiner 2012) (see Section 5.2.1).

Registerial cartography is **Christian Matthiessen**'s (e.g. 1993, 2014c, 2015c, 2015d) long-term project of mapping out registers to investigate language as an aggregate of different registers. For him, there are two roots of the registerial cartography project (see Matthiessen, Wang, & Ma 2019a). One is his experience with computational linguistics and artificial intelligence as well as his observation of the tension between general problem-solving (goal-pursuit) and special cases while working at the Information Sciences Institute in the US in the 1980s. The other is the context of SFL, which provides a theory to link the two notions in computational linguistics. The first publication of this project – Matthiessen (1993) – declares that more descriptions are needed in studies on register. In contrast to de Beaugrande (1993), who demands more theories on register, Matthiessen (1993) emphasizes the significance of descriptive work to support further theorization, instead of theorizing without grounds in description.

The **field of activity** provides useful resources in reasoning about registerial cartography from the projection of context based on field, complementing tenor and mode at the same time. Based on Jean Ure's (1989; cf. Ure & Ellis 1977) text anthology, which originally serves as an appendix of a book on discourse analysis, Matthiessen's (e.g. 2014c, 2015c) field of activity characterizes texts contextually from the perspective of the eight **socio-semiotic processes**, including 'expounding', 'reporting', 'recreating', 'sharing', 'doing', 'enabling', 'recommending', and 'exploring' (see Figure 4.2). The eight primary fields of activities can be grouped into three major categories: process of meaning (semiotic processes), process of behaving (social processes), and transition between the two

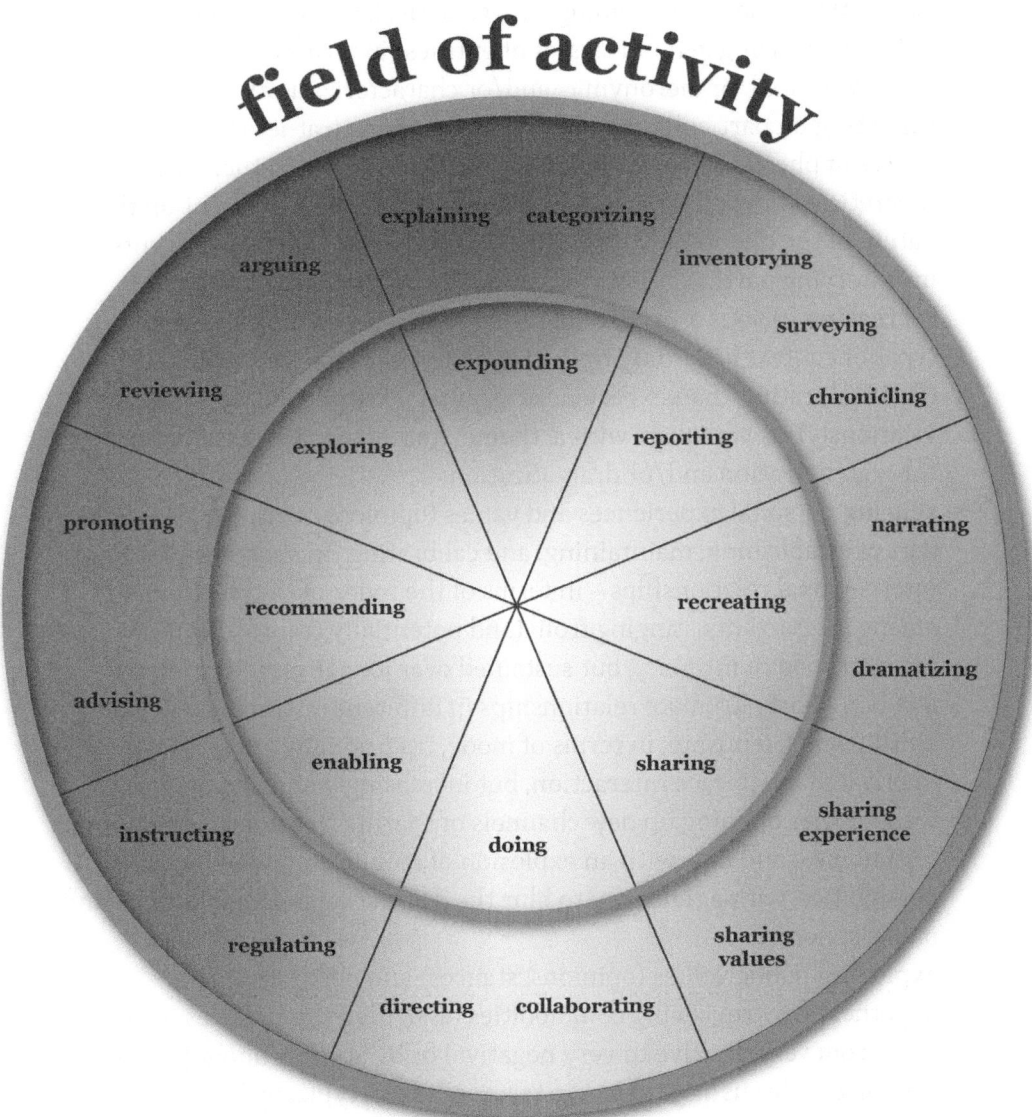

Figure 4.2 The eight primary fields of activity and their sub-types

(semiotic processes potentially leading to social processes). Also, these social-semiotic processes can all be extended with delicacy into sub-types. The definitions of the fields of activity are as follows (Matthiessen & Teruya 2016: 207–209):

- **semiotic processes** (i.e. 'meaning' processes – semiotic processes constitutive of context, constitute as semiotic processes and manifested through social processes):
  - **expounding** knowledge about general classes of phenomena (rather than particular instances of phenomena), theorizing our experience of the world in terms of a commonsense (folk) or uncommonsense (scientific) model by explaining why general classes of events take place or by categorizing general classes of entities (in terms of taxonomies, hyponymic and/or meronymic, and/or characterization);
  - **reporting** on particular instances of phenomena (rather than general classes of phenomena) creating 'episodic' knowledge (rather than theoretical knowledge), the type of reporting being dependent on the nature of the phenomena: chronicling (the flow of) particular events, inventorying particular entities, or surveying particular places;
  - **recreating** various aspects of life – involving any of the eight different types of context according to field of activity, typically imagined (fictional) rather than experienced (factual: experienced personally or vicariously), as verbal art with a 'theme' (in the sense of Hasan 1985), through narration and/or dramatization;
  - **sharing** personal experiences and values (opinions, attitudes, feelings) as part of establishing, maintaining, and calibrating (in short, negotiating) interpersonal relationships – in terms of the tenor of the relationship among interactants, ranging from (and potentially transforming) strangerhood to intimacy, but sustained over longer periods of time involving fairly intimate relationships in different institutions such as kinship and friendship; in terms of mode, traditionally and prototypically in private face-to-face interaction, but increasingly enabled by new technologies opening up new channels of sharing (epistolary, telegraphic, telephonic – and now with an explosion of mobile and internet-based possibilities, with a tendency to blur the distinction between private and public spheres);
  - **exploring** public values (opinions, stances) and positions (ideas, hypotheses) by reviewing commodities (assigning them values on a scale from very positive to very negative) or by arguing about positions, debating or discussing them – in terms of tenor, typically between one person (a professional or a member of the general public) and some segment of the general public, so between strangers; in terms of mode,

typically using media channels, either 'old' media channels (print, radio, TV) or 'new' media channels (mobile and/or internet-based);

- **semiotic processes** potentially leading to social processes (i.e. 'meaning' leading to 'doing'):
  - **recommending** some course of action (typically some kind of social process – exhortation in the strong form), either for the sake of the addressees by advising them to undertake it for their own good or for the sake of the speaker by promoting some type of goods-&-services;
  - **enabling** some course of action (typically some kind of social process), either literally enabling (empowering) them by instructing them in some type of procedure or constraining them by regulating their behaviour;
- **social processes** (i.e. 'doing' processes – social processes constitutive of context, semiotic processes facilitating [i.e. 'meaning' facilitating 'doing']):
  - **doing** – performing some form of social behaviour, on one's own or as part of a team, with semiotic processes ('meaning') coming in to facilitate this social behaviour through direction or collaboration.

Together with scholars like Kazuhiro Teruya and Wu Canzhong (e.g. Matthiessen, Teruya, & Wu 2008; Matthiessen & Teruya 2016), Matthiessen has introduced the field of activity in various contexts such as language description, discourse analysis, and translation studies, exploring the manifestations of these fields in semantics and lexicogrammar, and investigating how the fields put different meanings and wordings at risk. The goal of the registerial cartography project is to collect all descriptions of contextual structures, to fit them into the field of activity, as well as to find and analyse the representative texts comprehensively and critically.

Matthiessen's (e.g. 2014c, 2015c) field of activity is not the only way of describing context in terms of field. There have been various proposals of contextual descriptions in terms of field in David Butt's unpublished manuscript and work by James Martin (1992) and Ruqaiya Hasan (1999, 2009). However, the field of activity certainly represents one way of sorting out texts into different categories. In the next section, we will apply the criteria of field of activity to characterize the texts analysed in SFTS.

4.3 Explorations in the Registers in Systemic Functional Translation Studies

In this section, we conduct a survey in SFTS to point out the registers involved in the existing studies. We attempt to answer the following questions: (i) Which fields of activity are frequently researched in SFTS? (ii) Which fields of activity need more attention in SFTS? (iii) What text types are involved in these studies? (iv) What are the findings of such studies in relation to the fields of activity?

We have compiled a database of 161 publications (100 in English and 61 in Chinese) between 1992 and April 2019 that explicitly focus on translation from the SFL perspective. Three types of publications are involved, i.e. monographs, book chapters, and journal papers (see Table 4.2). PhD theses are excluded, as most of them have been published in other forms already. For instance, Espindola (2016) is based on her PhD thesis – Espindola (2010), both of which share the same motifs and deal with the same data of subtitles from *Star Wars*. Also, given our focus on empirical rather than theoretical issues, all studies in the database involve analysis of texts from one or a limited number of registers. Thus, theoretical discussions such as Matthiessen (2001) and Matthiessen (2014b) are excluded. For journals, we include eight prominent and internationally recognized journals of translation studies and linguistics. For journals published in China, we include ten CSSCI (Chinese Social Sciences Citation Index) journals on language and linguistics. Table 4.2 provides information on the modes of publication and the number of publications involved.

Table 4.2 Mode and number of publication in the database

Mode of publication	Number of publications	
	In English	In Chinese
Book	3	4
Book chapter	19	17
Journal paper	78	40
Total	100	61

Figure 4.3 shows the frequencies of the studies in the database in accordance with the field of activity involved, based on which we can observe the fields frequently examined and those seldom explored. Sixty-nine studies analyse recreating texts, which have the largest frequency compared to the other fields. Reporting texts rank the second in the database, with a frequency of 37 – a much smaller number compared to that of recreating. Texts of some fields have seldom been studied, with occurrences fewer than five. Such fields include enabling and sharing. No study on doing field is found, indicating that doing text is seldom studied in SFTS. Also, 22 studies are characterized as hybrid ones that involve more than one field of activity, with different combinations such as 'enabling, exploring and reporting' and 'expounding and reporting' (see Section 4.3.8).

4.3.1 Recreating Texts in Systemic Functional Translation Studies

Most **recreating** texts are **novels** and **poems**, which respectively account for 49.3% and 48.8% of the total recreating texts. It is not surprising to find that literary texts are frequently selected as data. In the community of translation studies, there has been

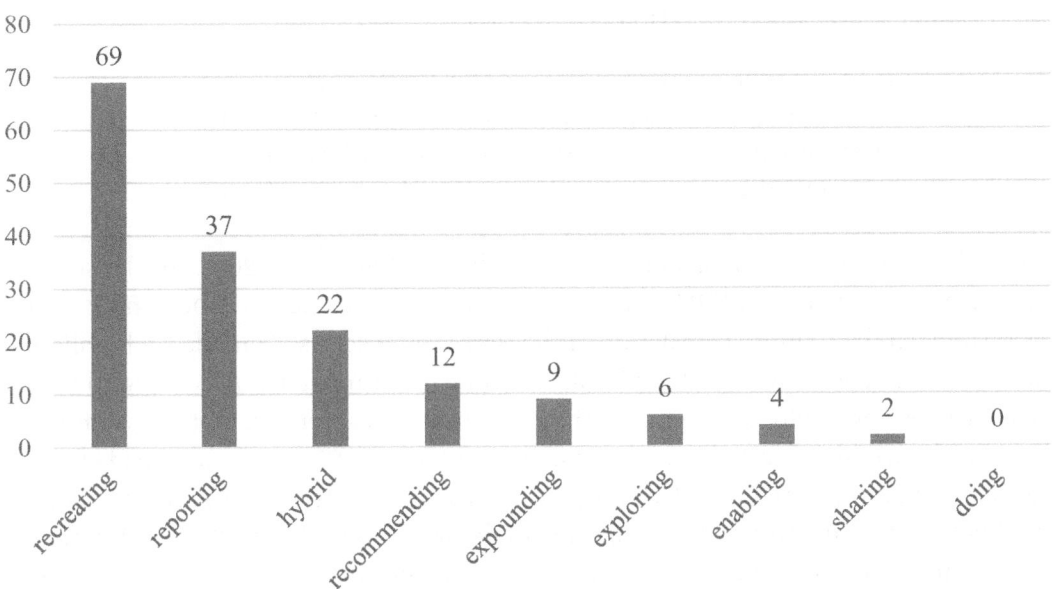

Figure 4.3 Frequency of the studies characterized according to the field of activity involved

a long-standing tradition of scholars' focus on **literary texts**. Tymoczko (2014) claims that literary texts are a good model for translation theory and practice. Similarly, in *The Translator's Invisibility*, Venuti (2008: 34) emphasizes the role that literary translation plays, and holds that humanistic translation, which is literary in the broadest sense, has 'traditionally been the field where innovative theories and practices emerge'.

For some studies in our database, recreating texts are used to demonstrate a certain model or framework. House (2001), for instance, analyses *Peace at Last* – a children's book by Jill Murphy, and its German translation – *Keine Ruh für Vater Bär* as an illustration of her functional-pragmatic model of translation quality assessment. The analysis is carried out from four perspectives, including field, tenor, mode, and genre. Mismatches from different dimensions between the English ST and the German TT are found. For example, lexical mismatches are found in the translation of the leading characters' names – Mr Bear, Mrs Bear and Baby Bear, which are translated as Vater Bär (IG: father bear), Mutter Bär (IG: mother bear), and Baby Bär (IG: baby bear). The TT is not only sentimentalized and infantilized, but also leads to a loss of humour. By naming teddy bears, which play the role of children's toys in daily life, as Mr and Mrs Bear, a clash is created in the English ST, and leads to a humorous effect. In terms of syntactic mismatch, House (2001) finds that the clause structures of the TT are simpler than those in the English ST. As shown in Example 4.1, an additional clause complex is found in the German TT, which converts a longer but coordinated clause complex in the ST to two simple and short clause complexes in the TT. Thus, the German translation is described as a covert one, where a cultural filter has been applied.

Example 4.1 (adapted from House 2001: 151)

English ST: So he got up and went to sleep in Baby Bear's room.
German TT: Er stand auf und ging ins Kinderzimmer. Dort wollte er schlafen.
IG: he stand up and go into the children's room there will he sleep
BT: He stands up and goes into the children's room. He will sleep there.

Novels also function as data for empirical studies. In Wang's (e.g. 2007, 2008) research, tools such as WordSmith and SPSS are applied to investigate choices in MOOD and MODALITY systems in the Chinese translation of the *Harry Potter* series. Example 4.2 highlights the differences between English and Chinese in terms of modality. According to Wang (2008), the use of 'could' and 'have' in the English ST has given rise to the assumption that 'Charlie Weasley is capable of doing it'. In the Chinese TT, the choices made by the translator are interpreted from three aspects: (i) the use of '做不到' (PY: zuò bú dào; IG: could not do) that expresses the inclination of doing, (ii) '呀' (PY: ya; IG: MOD), a modal particle that weakens the degree of the inclination, and (iii) the question mark, which is added in the TT to weaken the degree of '做不到' (PY: zuò bú dào; IG: could not do). Based on a corpus-based automated analysis, frequencies of different types of modality are calculated and further related to the gender and age of the characters.

Example 4.2 (adapted from Wang 2008: 22)

English ST: Charlie Weasley **couldn't** have done it.
Chinese TT: 查理·韦斯莱 也 做不到 这一点 啊？
PY: chá lǐ wéi sī lái yě zuò bú dào zhè yì diǎn a?
IG: Charlie Weasley also could not do this MOD
BT: Even Charlie Weasley couldn't have done this.

As another kind of frequently used recreating text, **poetry** is especially adopted as data in papers written in Chinese in the database, represented by various studies by Huang (e.g. 2002a, 2002b, 2002c). For instance, Huang (2002a) discusses the similarities and differences between the ST – a poem titled '清明' (Qing Ming) in Chinese and its six English translations from the interpersonal perspective. As shown in Example 4.3, the person who asks the question is not explicitly mentioned in the Chinese ST. In the English TTs, however, the participant is either translated as 'I' in TT1 and 'they' in TT2 or omitted in TT3. In terms of mood, we also find differences in translating the clause complex as a bound clause (TT1), a declarative (TT2) or a yes/no interrogative (TT3).

Example 4.3 (adapted from Huang 2002a: 35)

Chinese ST: 借问 酒家 何处 有？
PY: jiè wèn jiǔ jiā hé chù yǒu?
IG: ask tavern where be

BT: May I ask where the tavern is
English TT1: When I ask a shepherd boy where I can find a tavern
English TT2 They ask where wineshops can be found or where to rest
English TT3 'Is there a public house somewhere, cow boy?'

Film subtitles, as another kind of recreating text closely associated with research areas such as audio-visual translation and multimodal analysis, has gradually gained researchers' attention in SFTS. We find an increasing number, 13 studies, that deal with this text in the database, all of which appear after 2003 (e.g. Taylor 2003; Baines 2015). For instance, Espindola (2016) analyses the film subtitles of Master Yoda – a hero from *Star Wars*, and illustrates how Master Yoda is depicted as a wise and powerful character with the help of the thematic choices. In Example 4.4, 'hard to see' and 'Difícil ver' (IG: difficult to see) function as the marked topical Themes in both the ST and the TT. They represent the most relevant points of departure of the message from Yoda's perspective, thus highlighting the need to regard the dark side as an evil energy. Also, the marked topical Themes express Yoda's ideological stance, because the dark side is the most unpleasant place for a member of the Force like Yoda.

Example 4.4 (adapted from Espindola 2016: 29)

English ST: Ah, **hard to see** the dark side is.
Portuguese TT: **Difícil ver** o lado negro é.
IG: difficult to see the side dark is
BT: Difficult to see the dark side it is.

In some researches, the field being recreated is directly pointed out, given the fact that all fields of activity have the potential to be recreated (see also Wang & Ma 2020). In her study of Rabindranath Tagore's *Stray Birds* and its Chinese translations, Ma (2018) finds that the fields being recreated in her data include reporting, sharing, enabling, and exploring (see also Ma & Wang 2021). According to Example 4.5, the ST is addressed to the Vocative – 'troupe of little vagrants of the world', requesting the addressees to perform certain services, i.e. to leave their footprints in the narrator's words. Thus, the field being recreated in the ST is enabling. When translating the ST, the translator can choose to translate the enabling field equivalently, as the translator of TT1 does in retaining the Vocative and the imperative mood. Alternatively, a translator can change the field. In TT2, the field is changed to reporting, which results in a translation providing readers with information about the situation of human beings rather than regulating one's behaviour.

Example 4.5 (adapted from Ma 2018: 242)

English ST: O troupe of little vagrants of the world, leave your footprints in my words.
Chinese TT1: 世界 上 的 一 队 小小的 漂泊者 啊， 请 留下 你们的 足迹 在 我 的 文字 里。
PY: shì jiè shàng de yí duì xiǎo xiǎo de piāo bó zhě a, qǐng liú xià nǐ men de zú jì zài wǒ de wén zì lǐ.
IG: world on SUB one group little vagrant MOD, please leave your footprint CV my word in
BT: One group of little vagrants in the world, please leave your footprints in my words.
Chinese TT2: 生世 等 萍 聚， 漂泊 终 何 依。
PY: shēng shì děng píng jù, piāo bó zhōng hé yī.
IG: life wait buckweed union, wander finally what rely on
BT: Man waits for union in life, he wanders and has nobody to finally rely on.
萍 去 踪 仍 在， 临 流 歌 芳菲。
PY: píng qù zōng réng zài, lín liú gē fāng fēi.
IG: buckweed leave trace still exist, beside stream sing fragrance
BT: The buckweed leaves. Its trace still exists. Beside the stream, man sings about the fragrance.

4.3.2 Reporting Texts in Systemic Functional Translation Studies

Reporting texts in the database include news (18 out of 37 studies, e.g. Károly 2017), political texts such as **governmental reports** (8 studies, e.g. Wang & Feng 2018), **tourist and museum texts** (5 studies, e.g. Jiang 2010), **company introductions** (5 studies) (see Section 5.3 for Alves et al.'s 2010 study, in which translators are required to translate company introductions) and **historical accounts** (1 study, i.e. Li's 2017 analysis of sensitive biographies of political figures in terms of modality choices). Reporting texts provide readers with particular instances of phenomena by way of chronicling, inventorying, or surveying. Among the reporting texts, **news reports** constitute the largest proportion. They are examined to address the potential differences in translation strategy between the languages involved (e.g. Károly 2017), highlight the role that ideology played (e.g. Wu & Zhang 2015), and explore the news translator's subjectivity and the constraints involved in the editing process (e.g. Chen 2011). They are also used to investigate the relationship between genre structure and grammar by analysing student errors, thereby shedding light on translation pedagogy (e.g. Choi 2013).

For instance, Károly (2017) examines Hungarian-English **news** translation from the perspectives of conjunctive cohesive structure and Rhetorical Structure Theory (RST). Based on rigorous quantitative analysis, no statistically significant translation shift is found in terms of the frequency of conjunctions and conjunctive relations. Qualitatively, however, considerable translation shifts have occurred in the global organizations of the rhetorical structure, thus affecting the global meaning of the translations. As revealed in Example 4.6, the conjunction 'Ennek eredményeként' (IG: as a result) is omitted in the TT, leading to differences in terms of cohesion and rhetorical structure. Consequently, the TT is more implicit than the ST, and the evident logical relation has to be inferred by readers of the TT.

> Example 4.6 (adapted from Károly 2017: 282)
>
> Hungarian ST: **Ennek eredményeként** az Alkotmánybíróság megállapította a jogszabály Szász Károlyt és helyetteseit elmozdító rendelkezésének alkotmányellenességét.
> IG: **as a result** the constitutional declared the legislation Szász Károlyt and deputies removal unconstitutional
> BT: As a result, the Constitutional Court declared the clauses regulating the removal of Mr Károly Szász and his deputies unconstitutional.
> English TT: The Constitutional Court declared the clauses regulating the removal of Mr Károly Szász and his deputies unconstitutional.

Wang and Feng (2018) conduct research on **political text** by using a corpus of press conferences interpreting from Chinese to English. They employ Martin and White's (2005) appraisal framework, specifically stance-taking, to investigate how ideology influences the interpreter's lexical choices, and how the attitude of the Chinese government is reflected in interpreting. They find that the stance-taking of the Chinese interpreters is largely attributed to their compliance with the institutional norm of interpreting in mainland China, as interpreters have to adopt the ideology of the Chinese government. In Example 4.7, we find how '问题' (PY: wèn tí; IG: question/issue/problem) in Chinese is interpreted differently in English, revealing the degree of engagement. When associated with international affairs, it is interpreted as 'issue', indicating that the issue is debatable. When related to sensitive issues in China, it is interpreted as 'question', which implies that the topic is beyond discussion and does not allow alternative viewpoints. Guo Jiading (2002), the former director of the Translation and Interpreting Office, China Ministry of Foreign Affairs, has made the following comments on the reason for translating '台湾 问题' (PY: tái wān wèn tí; IG: Taiwan question/issue/problem) as 'Taiwan question' instead of 'Taiwan issue'. Such an explanation provides further proof for the existence of the institutional norm:

> Taiwan is an inseparable part of China's territory, which will be united with the motherland in the end. Besides, settling the Taiwan question is China's internal affair that allows no interference from any outsiders. As the Taiwan question is a question left behind by history, we should use the word 'question', but not 'issue', which means 'a matter that is in dispute between two or more Parties'.
>
> (Wang & Feng 2018: 258)

Further, in Example 4.8, '问题' (PY: wèn tí; IG: question/issue/problem) is interpreted as 'problem' when discussing domestic affairs in China. Such a lexical choice reflects the interpreter's attitude, as 'problem' is used in a positive or neutral manner, which means that the matter can be eventually settled.

Example 4.7 (adapted from Wang & Feng 2018: 257)

Chinese ST: 我 现在 不 想 把 台湾 **问题** 跟 美国 联系起来，更 不 想 把 台湾 **问题** 跟 中美 关系 的 其他 **问题** 联系 起来。

PY: wǒ xiàn zài bù xiǎng bǎ tái wān wèn tí gēn měi guó lián xì qǐ lái, gèng bù xiǎng bǎ tái wān wèn tí gēn zhōng měi guān xì de qí tā wèn tí lián xì qǐ lái.

IG: I now NEG want DISP Taiwan **question** with US relate to, less NEG want DISP Taiwan **question** with China-US relation SUB other **problem** relate to.

BT: Now I do not want to relate Taiwan question to the US, less do I want to relate Taiwan question to other problems of China-US relation.

English TT: For now I do not have any intention to embroil the Taiwan **question** with the United States, and still less do I want to embroil the Taiwan **question** with other **issues** related to China-US relations.

Example 4.8 (adapted from Wang & Feng 2018: 257)

Chinese ST: 中国 经济 发生 的 **问题**，说到底，是 结构性 问题、经济 增长 方 式 问题 和 体制 问题……

PY: zhōng guó jīng jì fā shēng de wèn tí, shuō dào dǐ, shì jié gòu xìng wèn tí jīng jì zēng zhǎng fāng shì wèn tí hé tǐ zhì wèn tí

IG: China economy arise SUB **problem**, after all, be structural problem economy growth mode problem and institution problem

BT: The problems arise in China's economy, after all, are structural problems, problems of economic growth mode, and institutional problems...

English TT: The **problems** we face in China's economy can all boil down to structural problems, the mode of growth pattern and institutional problems.

In terms of **museum and tourist texts**, Jiang (2010) proposes a model of translation quality assessment of this text type based on SFL. A three-phase methodology is designed, according to which each phase narrows down the level of comparison. Phase I involves the contrastive descriptions of register and genre in the ST and the TT. Phase II identifies the similarities and differences between the ST and the TT in terms of the four metafunctional modes of meaning, but at the same time relating them to the contextual parameters of field, tenor, and mode. Phase III deals with the effectiveness of the TT, targeting its success or failure in different aspects. Based on the comparison of the ST and the TT in Example 4.9, Jiang (2010) comments on the acceptability and informativity of the TT, and points out the imbalance of information between the ST and the TT. In the ST, '夜色' (PY: yè sè; IG: night view), which functions as the modifier of the nominal group '深堂 廊庑' (PY: shēn táng láng wǔ; IG: deep hall corridor), is replaced by 'beautiful scenery' in the TT. Besides, descriptions about the corridor in the ST are rephrased as 'a moonlight evening' in the TT. We also find the addition of 'beautiful' in the TT, which indicates the translator's positive evaluation of the painting.

Example 4.9 (adapted from Jiang 2010: 123)

Chinese ST: 绘 夜色 掩映 的 深堂 廊庑……
PY: huì yè sè yǎn yìng de shēn táng láng wǔ
IG: depict night view set off SUB deep hall corridor
BT: The painting depicts the deep hall and the corridor set off by the night view…
English TT: This work reflects the **beautiful** scenery of an imperial garden on **a moonlit evening**…

4.3.3 Recommending Texts in Systemic Functional Translation Studies

Both recommending and enabling processes are geared towards social processes. In other words, they lead to the process of doing. For **recommending** texts, they are aimed either at advising the addressees to take a certain action or to prompt them to buy certain types of goods-&-services. Like enabling texts, recommending texts are oriented towards tenor, and can be explored from perspectives such as institutional terms, status roles, power roles, familiarity, contact, and sociometric goals.

Advertisements are primarily characterized as recommending texts. The translation of such texts has to be oriented towards the target culture. Thus, the translator is required to communicate in the target culture, and the crucial role of the translation is whether it will elicit the potential customers' response or not. Seminal studies on recommending texts have been conducted by Steiner (e.g. 1997, 1998a, 1998b, 2001a, 2004a), who examines the translations and registerial variation of the advertisements of Rolex watches. He analyses texts selected from magazines like *Newsweek*, *Time International*, and *Der Spiegel*, where the German TTs are systematically different from the English ST. Example 4.10 shows how the German TT differs from the English ST in terms of the unintended agent metaphor. In the ST, 'its' means the 'Rolex Oyster's', which serves as the agent in a typologically characteristic way, and the semantic process of 'help' is here nominalized. In the German TT, the translator avoids using 'Hilfe' – the literal translation of 'help', but chooses 'Unterstützung' – a noun associated with the process of 'unterstützen' (IG: support) and retains the agent metaphor. Steiner (1998b) comments that 'Zuverlässigkeit' (IG: dependability) is another lexical choice to avoid the agent metaphor, but it does not sound natural in German.

Example 4.10 (adapted from Steiner 1998b: 311)

English ST: In the middle of the ocean its help is indispensable.
German TT: Mitten auf dem Ozean ist die Unterstützung einer Rolex Oyster unabdingbar.
IG: middle of the ocean is the support a Rolex Oyster indispensable
BT: In the middle of the ocean the support of a Rolex Oyster is indispensable.

In her study on the translations of perfume advertisements, Qian (2007) examines four 'unfaithful' translations by using the appraisal framework (Martin & White 2005).

Example 4.11 is an advertisement of Boss perfume for men. One can easily observe that the Chinese TT is much longer than the English ST. In the ST, only one lexical choice of appraisal is found, i.e. 'masculine', which is characterized as appreciation, and depicts the unique smell of the perfume. In the TT, however, the translator not only includes descriptions of the 'top note', 'middle note', and 'low note', but also adds six lexical choices of appraisal, especially those of judgement and appreciation (highlighted in bold). The object of the evaluation also shifts from the perfume in the ST to designer, male character, and smell. As commented by Qian (2007), 'masculine' in the ST represents the Westerner's aesthetic standards of male, while the added qualities such as 'freshness' and 'self-confidence' in the TT indicate the Chinese value orientation.

Example 4.11 (adapted from Qian 2007: 60)

English ST: Launched in 1986, Boss is a distinctly **masculine** fragrance that combines citrus and tangy apple with woody tones of sandalwood.

Chinese TT: 这款香水的设计灵感源自于1986年同名的男装品牌。Boss **成功**表达男人的**自信**与**品味**，前味由香柠檬、柑橘、蜂蜜组成，中味含有胡荽、琥珀及苔藓，后味由檀香、皮革与雪松组合而成。气味**清新**而充满男人的**简洁**与**自信**。

PY: zhè kuǎn xiāng shuǐ de shè jì líng gǎn yuán zì yú 1986 nián tóng míng de nán zhuāng pǐn pái. Boss chéng gōng biǎo dá nán rén de zì xìn yǔ pǐn wèi, qián wèi yóu xiāng níng méng gān jú fēng mì zǔ chéng, zhōng wèi hán yǒu hú suī hǔ pò jí tái xiǎn, hòu wèi yóu tán xiāng pí gé yǔ xuě sōng zǔ hé ér chéng. qì wèi qīng xīn ér chōng mǎn nán rén de jiǎn jié yǔ zì xìn.

IG: this MEAS perfume SUB design inspiration originate in 1986 year same name SUB men's clothing brand. Boss **successfully** express men SUB **self-confidence** and **taste**, top note by bergamot citrus honey compose, middle note include coriander amber and moss, low note by sandalwood leather and cedar compose. smell **fresh** and fill with men SUB **succinctness** and **self-confidence**.

BT: The inspiration for designing this perfume originates from the men's clothing with the same name in 1986. Boss **successfully** expresses men's **self-confidence** and **taste**. The top note is composed by bergamot, citrus and honey. The middle note includes coriander, amber and moss. The low note is composed by sandalwood, leather and cedar. The smell is **fresh** and fills with men's **succinctness** and **self-confidence**.

Both TTs in Example 4.10 and 4.11 are 'free' translations, which are less constrained by their STs. One can note that, in translating recommending texts, the translators' overriding concern is to produce a text that fits the target context of culture and context of situation optimally based on the awareness of the goals of the ST. In the case of advertisement, the goal is to promote and to sell the products. By contrast, in recreating texts, adaptation to the context of the target language is not highly prioritized.

4.3.4 Expounding Texts in Systemic Functional Translation Studies

Expounding texts are concerned with building up knowledge. The goal of the expounding process is to create field, i.e. to orient towards field itself. Of the nine studies in the database, there are five on **scientific writing** (e.g. Veroz 2017), three on **academic writing** (e.g. Ventola 1995, see Example 3.4 in Section 3.1), and one on **philosophy** (Wang 2018).

Veroz (2017) conducts a quantitative analysis of European parliament **technological texts** in three languages, i.e. English, Spanish, and French, and explores how ideational meaning is construed in the data. In terms of process type, a predominance of material processes is found, especially actions related to the administrative, economic, and legal affairs. As seen in Example 4.12, the material process in English is re-construed equivalently in the Spanish and the French TTs, thereby resulting in a large number of material processes in the ST and the TTs.

Example 4.12 (adapted from Veroz 2017: 29–30)

English ST: The first phase of this agreement **was established** in Council Regulation (EC) No 617/2009…

Spanish TT: La primera fase del acuerdo **se estableció** mediante el Reglamento (CE) n° 617/2009 del Consejo…

IG: the first phase of the agreement be established through the regulation (CE) n° 617/2009 of the council

BT: The first phase of this agreement **was established** through the Council Regulation (EC) No 617/2009…

French TT: La première phase de cet accord **a fait l'objet** du règlement du Conseil (CE) n° 617/2009…

IG: the first phase of this agreement be established the regulation the council (CE) n° 617/2009…

BT: The first phase of this agreement **was established** through the Council Regulation (EC) No 617/2009…

Veroz (2017) also notes the occurrences of mental and verbal processes. For instance, mental processes of perception are especially found in the final reports, as a result of the use of enacting clauses, which are realized by short phrases that introduce main provisions of a law. In Example 4.13, we find mental processes that inform readers about the source from which the law builds on its authority.

Example 4.13 (adapted from Veroz 2017: 30)

English ST: **Having regard** to Article 148(2) of the Treaty on the Functioning of the European Union…

Spanish TT: **Visto** el artículo 148, apartado 2, del Tratado de Funcionamiento de la Unión Europea…

IG: seen the article 148, paragraph 2, the treaty of functioning of the European Union,
BT: Having seen Article 148, Paragraph 2 of the Treaty on the Functioning of the European Union
French TT: **Vu** l'article 148, paragraphe 2, du traité sur le fonctionnement de l'Union européenne...
IG: see article 148, paragraph 2, the treaty on the functioning of the European Union...
BT: Having seen Article 148, Paragraph 2 of the Treaty on the Functioning of the European Union...

In terms of the participants within the transitivity structure, Veroz (2017) finds that most participants are institutions, followed by legal documents and humans. As shown in Example 4.14, there is an equivalent re-construal of Agent in the three texts.

Example 4.14 (adapted from Veroz 2017: 33)

English ST: On 11 July 2006 the **Council** (Agent) **authorized** (Process: material) the Commission to open negotiations with the Republic of Croatia.
Spanish TT: El 11 de julio, el **Consejo** (Agent) **autorizó** (Process: material) a la Comisión a iniciar las negociaciones con la República de Croacia.
IG: the 11 of July, the council authorized to the commission to start the negotiations with the republic of Croatia
BT: On the 11 of July, the Council authorized the Commission to start negotiations with the Republic of Croatia.
French TT: Le 11 juillet 2006, le **Conseil** (Agent) a **autorisé** (Process: material) la Commission à ouvrir des négociations avec la République de Croatie.
IG: the 11 July 2006, the council authorized the commission to open the negotiations with the republic of Croatia
BT: On 11 July 2006, the Council authorized the Commission to open negotiations with the Republic of Croatia.

4.3.5 Exploring Texts in Systemic Functional Translation Studies

With **exploring** texts, people explore societal views, public values, and positions via reviews and/or arguments. The speakers or writers can adopt a professional role, such as reviewer, critic, or opinion leader; alternatively, they may be members of the public who express their opinions through different channels, including traditional platforms like print media, radio, and TV or newly established online-based media channels.

Many texts that are highly valued throughout history have exploring components, such as *The Analects* by Confucius and the *Platform Sutra* dedicated to Zen master Huineng. However, we note that there are other text types combined in these texts. They are thus categorized as hybrid texts (see Section 4.3.8). In total, six studies in the database are classified as exploring texts, including three on **speeches** or **addresses** (see Section 3.2 for Munday's 2018 study on the US inaugural address), two on **legal**

interpreting of courtroom discourse (e.g. Teng, Burn, & Crezee 2018), and one on an **argumentative essay**, namely Francis Bacon's *Of Studies* (Liu & Yang 2013).

In their study that analyse Bacon's *Of Studies* and its 11 Chinese translations, Liu and Yang (2013) quantify the various patterns of thematic progression, investigating how messages are re-presented from the perspective of Theme and Rheme. Example 4.15 identifies the similarities of thematic pattern in the ST and the Chinese TT translated by Wang Zuoliang. The quantitative analysis reveals that the English ST favours the T_2R_1 type of thematic progression ($T_1=T_2, R_1 \neq R_2$) (see Zhu 1995). Conversely, the T_2R_1 type (T_1-R_1, $T_2(=R_1)$-R_2) is more commonly found in the Chinese TT, which is not only a reflection of the linguistic principle of economy in Chinese, but is also a result of the convention of word order and parallel structures in Chinese.

Example 4.15 (adapted from Liu & Yang: 277–279, with Themes being underlined)

English ST:
1. <u>Studies</u> serve for delight, for ornament, and for ability. T_1-R_1
2. <u>Their chief use for delight</u>, is in privateness and retiring; $T_2(=R_1)$-R_2
3. <u>for ornament</u>, is in discourse; $T_3(=R_1)$-R_3
4. <u>and for ability</u>, is in the judgment, and disposition of business. $T_4(=R_1)$-R_4

Chinese TT:
1. <u>读书</u> 足以 怡情，（足以）傅彩，（足以）长才。 T_1-R_1
PY: dú shū zú yǐ yí qíng, (zú yǐ) fù cǎi, (zú yǐ) zhǎng cái.
IG: read book enough delight enough ornament enough ability
BT: Reading books is enough for delight, for ornament and for ability.
2. <u>其 怡情 也</u>，最 见 于 独处 幽居 之 时； $T_2(=R_1)$-R_2
PY: qí yí qíng yě, zuì jiàn yú dú chǔ yōu jū zhī shí;
IG: its delight MOD best seen in solitude seclusion SUB time
BT: The delight is best seen in the time of solitude and seclusion;
3. <u>其 傅彩 也</u>，最 见 于 高谈阔论 之 中； $T_3(=R_1)$-R_3
PY: qí fù cǎi yě, zuì jiàn yú gāo tán kuò lùn zhī zhōng;
IG: its ornament MOD best seen in eloquence SUB in
BT: the ornament is best seen in eloquence;
4. <u>其 长才 也</u>，最 见 于 处世 判事 之 际。 $T_4(=R_1)$-R_4
PY: qí zhǎng cái yě, zuì jiàn yú chǔ shì pàn shì zhī jì.
IG: its ability MOD best seen in disposition judgment SUB time
BT: the ability is best seen in disposition and judgment.

4.3.6 Enabling Texts in Systemic Functional Translation Studies

As a field of activity potentially leading to the doing field, **enabling** field enables people to take certain actions by either instructing or regulating. **Public notice** is primarily one type of enabling field, as it often requires readers to take some action; however, other fields or text types may also be interwoven in the data of enabling texts (see Section 4.3.8).

All four studies in the database are concerned with **regulatory texts**, such as **legal documents** of different kinds. For instance, Espindola and Wang (2015) discuss how tenancy agreements regulate the readers' behaviour in terms of modality choices, and point out similarities and differences in the use of modality. Example 4.16 shows how 'shall' is translated as '不得' (PY: bù dé; IG: must not), both being modalities of obligation that assess the validity of the agreement and assign the modal responsibility to the tenant.

> Example 4.16 (adapted from Espindola & Wang 2015: 116)
>
> English ST: The Tenant **shall not** make any alteration and/or additions to the Premises without the prior written consent of the Landlord.
> Chinese TT: 租客 在 没有 业主 书面 同意 前 **不得** 对 该物业 作 任何改动 及 / 或 加建。
> PY: zū kè zài méi yǒu yè zhǔ shū miàn tóng yì qián bù dé duì gāi wù yè zuò rèn hé gǎi dòng jí/huò jiā jiàn.
> IG: tenant CV not have landlord written consent before **must not** to the premise make any alteration and or addition
> BT: The Tenant **must not** make any alteration and/or addition to the Premise before having the Landlord's written consent.

One can also note that the type and value of obligation can be changed in the TT. As shown in Example 4.17, 'shall' is translated as '将' (PY: jiāng; IG: will), involving not only a shift from obligation to probability, but also a change from high to median value. Hence, an interpersonal meaning of positive probability, which is not found in the ST, is ascribed to the proposition in the TT. Despite these changes, the rhetorical force that regulates the tenant to assume specific responsibilities is not weakened.

> Example 4.17 (adapted from Espindola & Wang 2015: 116)
>
> English ST: All costs, expenses and other outgoings so incurred by the Landlord in relation to such action **shall** be a debt owed by the Tenant to the Landlord.
> Chinese TT: 而 由此 而 引起 的 一切 费用 及 开支 **将** 构成 租客 所欠 业主 的 债项。
> PY: ér yóu cǐ ér yǐn qǐ de yí qiè fèi yòng jí kāi zhī jiāng gòu chéng zū kè suǒ qiàn yè zhǔ de zhài xiàng.
> IG: but therefrom yet cause SUB all cost and outgoing **will** constitute tenant own landlord SUB debt
> BT: But all incurred costs and outgoings **will** constitute the Tenant's debts to the Landlord.

4.3.7 Sharing Texts in Systemic Functional Translation Studies

Sharing texts deal with personal experiences and values. In terms of tenor, they aim at building up interpersonal relationships and can target addressees with different relationships, ranging from stranger to intimate. In terms of mode, they are not restricted to face-to-face communication, as they have been integrated with technological developments and involve various channels of communication, such as telegraph, telephone, computer software, and cellphone application. In our database, only two studies of sharing texts are found, both of which deal with the analysis of Steve Jobs' **love letter** and its Chinese translations (Lin 2015; Zhang & Zheng 2016). Written to his wife, Jobs' love letter is collected in his biography. Its published Chinese translation is frequently criticized by Chinese readers for being unimpressive and unromantic. Consequently, various netizens have provided their own translations of the love letter – some in prose style, others in the style of modern or classical poetry.

Lin (2015) assesses the quality of the Chinese translations of the love letter based on the analysis of process type. As illustrated in Example 4.18, the ST, written for Jobs' wife, provides narrative accounts of the wedding. TT1 is a literal translation, which retains the relational process type of the major clause. TT2 changes the process type to a mental one by personifying the snowflakes and successfully expresses the delight in the ST. TT3 renders the prose to a poem, alternating 'got married' to '执 子 之 手' (PY: zhí zǐ zhī shǒu; IG: hold you SUB hand) that has been extracted from *The Book of Songs* in classical Chinese literature, and omitting the circumstance 'at the Ahwahnee' in the ST.

Example 4.18 (adapted from Lin 2015: 79)

English ST: It was snowing when we got married at the Ahwahnee.
Chinese TT1: 当 我们 在 阿瓦尼 举行 婚礼 时 天 在 下雪。
PY: dāng wǒ mén zài ā wǎ ní jǔ xíng hūn lǐ shí tiān zài xià xuě.
IG: when we CV Ahwahness hold wedding ceremony time sky CV snow
BT: When we hold the wedding ceremony at the Ahwahnee, it was snowing.
Chinese TT2: 阿瓦尼 的 漫天 雪花 见证 了 我们的 海誓山盟。
PY: ā wǎ ní de màn tiān xuě huā jiàn zhèng le wǒ mén de hǎi shì shān méng.
IG: Ahwahnee SUB boundless snowflake witness ASP our solemn vow
BT: The boundless snowflakes at the Ahwahnee witnessed our solemn vows.
Chinese TT3: 执 子 之 手, 白 雪 为 鉴。
PY: zhí zǐ zhī shǒu, bái xuě wéi jiàn.
IG: hold you SUB hand, white snow be witness
BT: Holding your hand, white snow will be our witness.

Zhang and Zheng (2016) analyse the same data from the perspective of intertextuality. They conduct a quantitative survey and point out the genres of the TTs, following Hatim and Mason's (1990) classification. For instance, in Example 4.19, the prose genre of TT1 is equivalent to that of the ST. Both TT2 and TT3 are in classic style. Specifically, TT2 is a poem with seven characters in a line and TT3 models on the 'ci' (词) style popular in Song Dynasty. The authors further analyse the data in accordance with the contextual parameters. The change of tenor in the TTs is identified, which involves a shift of target readers from Jobs' wife to the current netizens who are dissatisfied with the prose translation. Thus, reader-oriented methods of translation tend to be adopted to make the text appealing to readers and to dialogue with them.

Example 4.19 (adapted from Zhang & Zheng 2016: 80–82)

English ST: We didn't know much about each other twenty years ago.
Chinese TT1: 20 年 前，我们 相遇，彼此 陌生……
PY: èr shí nián qián, wǒ men xiāng yù, bǐ cǐ mò shēng
IG: twenty year ago, we meet, each other unknown
BT: Twenty years ago, we met, and were unknown to each other…
Chinese TT2: 二十 年 前 初 相识，
PY: èr shí nián qián chū xiāng shí,
IG: twenty year ago first meet
BT: Twenty years ago, we first met.
Chinese TT3: 浮生 若 梦 二十 春，
PY: fú shēng ruò mèng èr shí chūn,
IG: life be like dream twenty spring
BT: After twenty springs, life is like a dream

4.3.8 Hybrid Texts in Systemic Functional Translation Studies

In our database, some texts share the features of different text types and do not fall within a single type in the register typology (see Matthiessen & Teruya 2016 for investigations on registerial hybridity). If the texts they translate instantiate conventional registers, the registerial 'routines' will be easy for translators to access, some preparatory translation can even be carried out (cf. Matthiessen 2021). However, since it is difficult to characterize the texts into one category, it is likely that they pose challenges to translators.

Twenty-two texts are categorized as hybrid texts. They include **The Analects** by Confucius (exploring & reporting) (see e.g. Huang 2014, 2016, Example 3.21), **The Platform Sutra** – a collection of Master Huineng's personal conversations and public sermons (exploring & reporting) (e.g. Yu & Wu 2016, 2017a, 2017b; Yu 2019; see Example 3.5), **public notices** (enabling, exploring, & reporting) (e.g. Zhang 2009; Zhang & Pan 2015), **medical consultation** (exploring, expounding, reporting, & doing) (e.g. Tebble 1999, 2014), and **court decisions** (enabling & reporting) (e.g. Poon 2006).

In their study of **The Platform Sutra** and its English translations, Yu and Wu (2017a) examine the system of PERSONAL PRONOUN, and relate these lexical choices to the recreation of the different images of Huineng. As seen in the TT of Example 4.20, the use of inclusive personal pronouns, i.e. 'we', 'us', and 'our' help Huineng to build up a closer tenor relationship with his listeners, thus creating a non-authoritative image of Huineng as an intimate mentor rather than a solemn master. Besides, 'you' – another personal pronoun – is used alternatively with 'we', reflecting a transition from the inclusive 'we' to the addressee, and indicating Huineng's authority.

Example 4.20 (adapted from Yu & Wu 2017a: 73)

Chinese ST: 善知识 菩提 般若 之 智， 世人本自有之，
PY: shàn zhī shí pú tí bō rě zhī zhì, shì rén běn zì yǒu zhī,
IG: charitable person Bodhi Prajna SUB wisdom, common people originally self have it
BT: Charitable person, common people originally have the wisdom of Bodhi Prajna.
只缘心迷，不能自悟，须假大善知识，示导见性。
PY: zhǐ yuán xīn mí, bù néng zì wù, xū jiǎ dà shàn zhī shí, shì dǎo jiàn xìng.
IG: only because mind confuse, NEG can self enlighten, need use great learned people, guide see nature
BT: It is only because their minds are confused and cannot enlighten themselves. There need great learned people to guide them and to see the Buddha nature.
当知愚人智人，佛性本无差别。
PY: dāng zhī yú rén zhì rén, fó xìng běn wú chā bié.
IG: should know foolish people wise people, Buddha nature originally have NEG difference
BT: They should know that for foolish people and wise people, their Buddha nature has no difference.
English TT: Learned Audience, the Wisdom of Enlightenment is inherent in every one of **us**. It is because of the delusion under which **our** mind works that **we** fail to realize it ourselves, and that **we** have to seek the advice and the guidance of enlightened ones before **we** can know **our** own essence of mind. **You** should know that so far as Buddha-nature is concerned, there is no difference between an enlightened man and an ignorant one.

However, in another TT (see Examples 4.21), the translator uses no personal pronoun when translating Huineng's account of the meeting with his master, but retains the lexical choices of 'Hui Neng' (the interactant's name), 'your disciple' (a humble term used to refer to the interactant), and 'the Master' (an honorific term used to refer to the interactant's master) in the ST. In this way, a different image of Huineng is created, who speaks to his disciples in a detached and alienated manner.

Example 4.21 (adapted from Yu & Wu 2017a: 74)

Chinese ST: 惠能 对曰：
PY: huì néng duì yuē:
IG: Huineng reply
BT: Huineng replied
弟子 是 岭南 新州 百姓， 远 来 礼 师，
PY: dì zǐ shì lǐng nán xīn zhōu bǎi xìng, yuǎn lái lǐ shī.
IG: disciple be Lingnan Xinzhou civilian, afar come respect teacher,

BT: I am (Your disciple is) a civilian from Xinzhou in Lingnan, I come afar to show respect to my teacher,
惟求作佛，不求余物。
PY: wéi qiú zuò fó, bù qiú yú wù.
IG: only seek be Buddha, NEG seek other thing
BT: I only seek to be a Buddha, I do not seek other things.
English TT: **Hui Neng** replied, '**Your disciple** is a commoner from Hsin Chou in Ling Nan and comes from afar to bow to **the Master**, seeking only to be a Buddha, and nothing else'.

Zhang (2009) illustrates the hybridity of text types in her analysis of the translations of **public notices** in Macao. As discussed in Section 4.3.6, public notices are typical examples of enabling texts. The imperative clause in the Chinese version in Example 4.22 aims at instructing readers to buy tickets; hence, the text is categorized as enabling. The English version of this notice also serves the purpose of appealing to the reader.

Example 4.22 (adapted from Zhang 2009: 146)

Chinese version: 观众购票请往售票处
PY: guān zhòng gòu piào qǐng wǎng shòu piào chù
IG: audience buy ticket please go to ticket office
BT: Audiences please go to ticket office to buy tickets.
English version: Visitors please go to ticketing for admission fee.

However, public notices can also be classified as reporting or exploring texts or a combination of several text types. Example 4.23, as a reporting text, aims to inform the teachers and students about the new plan of the university, and has no information that regulates the behaviour of readers or instructs them. The English version also provides ample information about the referential content.

Example 4.23 (adapted from Zhang 2009: 145)

Chinese version: 由2003年9月开始，以下4个学术单位办公室将推行服务承诺计划，给予您最佳的服务。
PY: yóu èr líng líng sān nián jiǔ yuè kāi shǐ, yǐ xià sì gè xué shù dān wèi bàn gōng shì jiāng tuī xíng fú wù chéng nuò jì huá, gěi yǔ nín zuì jiā de fú wù.
IG: from 2003 year 9 month start, following 4 MEAS academic unit office will implement performance pledge plan, give you (HON) best service
BT: Starting from September 2013, the following 4 offices of academic units will implement the Performance Pledge Plan, to give you the best service.
English version: Starting from September 2003, the following 4 academic units will implement the Performance Pledge Plan so as to provide the best service to you.

Examples 4.24 is an exploring text that expresses the opinion and stance of Macao via sending a friendly message to tourists. The English version is similar in its expression of this message. In Zhang's (2009) study, these texts in Examples 4.23, 4.24, and 4.25 are characterized as operative, informative, and expressive types respectively based on Reiss's (1971) typology.

Example 4.24 (adapted from Zhang 2009: 145)

Chinese version: 澳门 欢迎 您！
PY: ào mén huān yíng nín!
IG: Macao welcome you (HON)
BT: Macao welcomes you!
English version: Macao Welcomes You.

Example 4.25, a notice posted on the gate of St Francis Xavier Catholic Church in Macao, is a combination of exploring and enabling text types. The initial part of the Chinese version expresses the friendly attitude of the church, marked by the verbal group of '欢迎' (PY: huān yíng; IG: welcome), while the latter part regulates the visitors' behaviour and demands their cooperation. The English version is more concise than the Chinese version, but their text types are the same.

Example 4.25 (adapted from Zhang 2009: 147)

Chinese version: 欢迎 参观 在 圣堂 内 请 勿 喧哗 出 入 关 门 多谢 合作
PY: huān yíng cān guān zài shèng táng nèi qǐng wù xuān huá chū rù guān mén duō xiè hé zuò
IG: welcome visit CV holy hall in please do not make noise exit enter close door thank cooperation
BT: Welcome to visit. In the holy hall, please do not make noises. Close the door when exit and enter. Thank you for your cooperation.
English version: Welcome. Thank you for showing respect in this place of worship.

In this chapter, we discussed the role that register and text type played in SFTS. Two kinds of text typology are introduced, i.e. Reiss's (1971) typology that leads to various works in German functionalism and Matthiessen's (2014c, 2015c, 2015d) context-based typology that characterizes texts based on the contextual parameter of field in SFL. Moreover, we introduce studies that explore the different registers, summarize their findings, and present the challenges that translators may come across when dealing with different registers. In SFL, register is located along the cline of instantiation between the instance pole and the potential of the cline. With certain knowledge of the conventional registers, translators can then access the registerial 'routines' and do not have to move all the way up to the overall meaning potential. They can even carry out some automated preparations and will improve the quality of the target texts, as proved by researches on registers (or sublanguages) in the area of machine translation (see Kittredge & Lehrberger 1982). In Chapter 5, we will further explore the relationship between machine translation and SFTS and meanwhile introduce more research that is based on technological development.

Chapter 5

Technology-based Approaches in Systemic Functional Translation Studies

In this chapter, we introduce some approaches in SFTS that are based on the development of translation-oriented language technology. Three topics will be addressed, i.e. machine translation, corpus-based approaches, and the tools for investigating translation process. In Section 5.1, we provide a historical sketch of machine translation in SFTS and outline some important studies. Section 5.2 focuses on three strands of work that apply corpus-based methodology to SFTS research, including the CroCo and GECCo corpora built by Erich Steiner and his group, Juliane House's newly updated model of translation quality assessment, and Jeremy Munday's model for descriptive translation studies. Section 5.3 ends this chapter by discussing methods used in translation process research and highlighting the integration of product-based and process-based approaches.

5.1 Machine Translation and Systemic Functional Translation Studies

Machine translation represented one of the earliest attempts by scholars to apply computational techniques to the processing of natural human language. It became a research area in the 1940s after the invention of computer. Specifically, it was Warren Weaver, Nobert Wiener, and A.D. Booth who first proposed using computers for translation in 1947 (see Hutchins 2003; Ke 2009 for general overviews and historical developments of machine translation). Defined as 'computerized systems responsible for the production of translations with or without human assistance' (Hutchins 2003: 501), machine translation grew out of the early applications of computer for military code-breaking. Thus, language was in this context considered as 'code', and what one needed was 'the appropriate codebook to be converted into various forms' (Bateman & O'Donnell 2015: 454). By adopting this view of language, the early applications were not successful.

5.1.1 M.A.K. Halliday and Machine Translation

In SFTS, researches on machine translation started with **Michael Halliday**'s engagement with machine translation early in his career. In the 1950s, when Halliday had just completed his PhD on Chinese language at Cambridge University (Halliday 1955, 1959), he joined Cambridge Language Research Unit – a research group led by **Margaret Masterman** (e.g. 1957, 1965). By then, computational linguistics had not really been formulated as a discipline, and machine translation was still named mechanical translation. As a member of this group, Halliday worked with scholars from different backgrounds, involving linguists and mathematicians alike, such as Arthur Frederick Parker-Rhodes, Richard Richens, Yorick Wilks, Martin Kay, and Karen Sparck-Jones, many of whom have played significant roles in the institutionalization of computational linguistics.

The group was influenced by linguistic notions, especially those of J.R. Firth (Masterman 1965). Also, Firth attended the first project meeting held at King's College London, and presented his seminal paper 'Linguistic Analysis and Translation' (Firth 1968a). Firth's influence was evident in two ways. Firstly, the group attached importance to the context of situation, with which texts can be translated properly. Secondly, meaning was regarded as a valuable component in language description. In contrast to the dominant dictionary-based word-for-word or syntactic-structure-mapping approaches, the team adopted a meaning-based approach towards machine translation. They first derived sets of concepts from the source sentence, and then generated them in the target text in accordance with the context. Also, they adopted two dominant approaches, i.e. 'one involving a language-neutral interlingua' and 'a thesaurus to organize a language's different word senses in a manner analogous to that of Roget's thesaurus' (Bateman & O'Donnell 2015: 456).

Halliday produced two papers on machine translation in this period. In Section 1.3, we have regarded both of them as the early works along the timeline of SFTS. At the beginning of the first paper – **'The Linguistic Basis of a Mechanical Thesaurus'** – Halliday (1956a) highlights the importance of linguistic analysis and states the futility of one-to-one translation equivalent in machine translation. He suggests that '[t]he translation process presupposes an analysis ... of the source and target languages; and it is a commonplace that a one-to-one translation equivalence of categories ... does not by itself result in anything which on contextual criteria could be called translation' (p. 81). Meanwhile, the need for describing the languages involved in machine translation is emphasized.

The initial ideas of SFL are spelled out in this paper. Firstly, Halliday (1956a: 83) discusses the relationship between lexis and grammar by stating that 'we cannot use grammar to determine the lexis because grammar will only determine the grammatical features of the lexis'. He also notes the advantage of lexis over grammar in machine translation, as lexis reflects context more directly. Secondly, Halliday (1956a) has been aware of the paradigmatic organization in language description by viewing lexis systemically as a resource (cf. Matthiessen 2015c). Thirdly, the notion of making choices in the system was seen in Halliday's (1956a) thesaurus method of machine translation. In this sense, a thesaurus is different from a dictionary in that when using a thesaurus one can explore the different options available, while in a dictionary one has to look up the words through entries organized according to alphabet, radicals, and so on.

'**Linguistics and Machine Translation**' (Halliday 1962) appeared one year after the very first publication of SFL – 'Categories of the Theory of Grammar' (Halliday 1961), in which scale and category theory – the early version of SFL – was proposed. Halliday (1962) offers an attempt to apply his overall linguistic theory to machine translation, involving aspects like 'level', 'unit', 'structure', 'form', and 'rank'. He associates translation equivalence with the rank scale in lexicogrammar, and distinguishes three steps in the translation process:

> First, there is the selection of the 'most probable translation equivalent' for each item at each rank, based on simple frequency. Second, there is the conditioning effect of the surrounding text in the source language on these probabilities: here grammatical and lexical features of the unit next above are taken into account and may (or may not) lead to the choice of an item other than the one with highest overall probability. Third, there is the internal structure of the target language, which may (or may not) lead to the choice of yet another item as a result of grammatical and lexical relations particular to that language: these can be viewed as brought into operation similarly by step-by-step progression up the rank scale.
>
> (Halliday 1962: 153)

Here we find the importance of context and the need to move into higher rank scales when making choices in the target language. Such ideas are similar to the environments of translation (Matthiessen 2001), which is the principle of 'contextualization' (see Chapter 2). In larger environments, like context, translation equivalence is more likely to be maintained, and the translation strategies tend to be free rather than literal.

After Halliday (1962), the overall application of SFL theory to translation continued, notably in Halliday, McIntosh, and Strevens (1964), and Catford (1965), as well as Matthiessen (2001). Decades have now passed since the publication of Halliday's (1956a, 1962) early work on machine translation, and computer technology has changed drastically. However, the ideas proposed in these two papers, including choice-making, rank, and stratification are not outdated, and will continue to be influential. They have been applied to translation studies since Catford (1965) and are still seen in various seminal works such as Matthiessen (2001, 2014b, 2021) and Halliday (2009, 2010). An introduction to the overall application of these Hallidayan ideas can be found in Chapter 2 of this book. The reason that they are still relevant today is that SFL is developed by way of building on its immediate predecessors (including the earlier versions of SFL) rather than discarding the earlier versions of the theory (see Matthiessen 2015a).

5.1.2 Erich Steiner and Machine Translation

In 1966, the US government believed that machine translation was no longer feasible and stopped the government funding for machine translation projects, thus stalling the development of work in this area. However, the 1980s witnessed the revival of machine translation when linguistic theory became sophisticated and computer technology became more advanced. It was under this circumstance that the **Eurotra project** of European translation was started (see Durand et al. 1991 for an outline of the Eurotra system).

In those days, Eurotra, which attempted to cover all the working languages of the European Union, was one of the major projects on machine translation. The aim of the project was to build a system of machine translation, which would be able to translate any language pair involved. With the application of linguistic theories, the project adopted the symbol-processing approach towards machine translation, which represented the trend. Feature-based linguistic theories provided solid foundations for Eurotra, involving formal theories such as Function Unification Grammar, Generalized Phrase Structure Grammar, and Head-driven Phrase Structure Grammar that were applied to notate the linguistic information in the system.

The SFL input to Eurotra came from the German team, where **Erich Steiner** (e.g. Steiner 1986; Steiner et al. 1988) had been a member since 1985. Steiner built a model of clause types and participant roles, which had components of the clause grammar and semantics in SFL. For instance, one of the applications of the model was to constrain the mapping of predicate and argument structures across language pairs in terms of participant roles and grammatical functions. At a later stage of the project, Steiner started to interact with the Penman Group at the Information Sciences Institute (ISI) in Los Angeles, who modelled the computational process of text generation and developed the Nigel grammar (e.g. Mann 1985; Mann & Matthiessen 1985; Matthiessen 1985; Bateman et al. 1990; Matthiessen & Bateman 1991).

From 1989 to 1990, Steiner left the Eurotra project and worked in Darmstadt at the Institute for Integrated Publication and Information Systems (IPSI), which was then one of the institutes of the German Federal Research Centre for Applied Mathematics and Computer Science (Gesellschaft für Mathematik und Datenverarbeitung GMD). He continued his work on machine translation by adopting a functional/semantic approach (e.g. Steiner 1992, 1993). For example, in Steiner (1992), he proposes solutions for dealing with problems in translating constructions with differences in phrase structure and in translating lexical versus structural transfer. After comparing the existing solutions, he highlights the functional approach to machine translation, which 'attempts to characterize a suitable level for translation as a level, at which functions of language are represented, rather than merely syntactic information' (p. 607). He further suggests the use of grammatical system networks on different ranks in order to generalize multi-lingual grammar fragments.

5.1.3 Other Studies and Beyond

In the early 1990s, **Graham Wilcock** (1993) made another attempt at applying SFL to machine translation in his master thesis. After attributing the unsatisfactory translation quality of machine translation systems to the restriction to syntactic and semantic factors, he suggests the extraction of other factors such as the pragmatic and discourse ones from the ST and then transferring them to the TT. Therefore, to generate the TT, one requires factors that are unable to be found in the ST. He argues that SFL has two advantages to be applied to machine translation. Firstly, it includes the necessary wider range of factors. Secondly, it is organized paradigmatically as choices in the system, with emphasis being given to such factors. In this regard, part of a prototype system of machine translation is produced, which incorporates factors needed in generating English modal and auxiliary verbal groups.

Later in the mid-1990s, the group of scholars from ISI who worked on natural language processing became founding members of the **Pangloss project**. This project aimed to build an example-based machine translation system which did not rely on knowledge of language structure, but instead on a large parallel corpus and a bilingual dictionary. At an earlier stage, the interlingua of the system adopted the Penman Upper Model of experiential semantics to generate sentences into English. Statistic-based methods were later applied in place of the Penman generation system (Nirenburg 1995; O'Donnell & Bateman 2003).

Some recent developments of machine translation in SFTS are found in the work led by **Ekaterina Lapshinova-Koltunski** (e.g. Lapshinova-Koltunski & Pal 2014; Lapshinova-Koltunski & Vela 2015; Lapshinova-Koltunski & Zampieri 2018), who applies a register-based statistical approach to language comparison, with the aim of improving the quality of statistic-based machine translation. In the literature, there are some previous investigations into the area of statistical machine translation evaluation, which focus on the errors found in translation (e.g. Irvine et al. 2013). However, the types of errors are only examined at the level of lexis and only the parameter of domain (one genre parameter to reflect the topic of the text) is studied, with the rest of the settings of a genre being ignored. In some studies, the value of genre in statistical machine translation is mentioned (e.g. Santini et al. 2010; Irvine & Callison-Burch 2014), but components of register or genre are still missing in these systems of statistical machine translation. Lapshinova-Koltunski's studies have made up for the deficiency. For instance, Vela and Lapshinova-Koltunski (2015) conduct an experiment to compare texts produced from machine translation, texts translated by human, and comparable originals in the same language. The lexicogrammatical features of certain registers are pointed out. From the perspective of registerial features, they find similarities between machine-translated and human-translated texts, regardless of the translation methods involved. Based on their findings, they suggest that registerial features be included in the machine translation quality evaluation process.

Since the 1990s, dramatic changes had taken place, leading to the popularity of statistic-based and example-based approaches in machine translation (Somers 2003). There had also been substantial input from machine learning, which was essentially statistic-based and originated from computer science and more innovative drives of neuro-network technologies. Since then, linguistic or symbol-processing approaches had never played a major role in machine translation. In other words, machine translation had moved far away from linguistic theories. The impact of SFL on machine translation was also very small. As commented by O'Donnell and Bateman (2003: 346), the follow-up investigations of machine translation in SFTS 'have been and continued to be seriously hampered by the difficulties of achieving full-scale systemic analysis components'. The well-known Google Translate, which is a free machine translation service developed by Google, also applies a statistic-based engine.[1] Its method of translation is based on statistical analysis instead of traditional rule-based analysis as provided by SYSTRAN. Instead of translating to the target language directly, Google Translate will first translate the ST into English, which is treated as a bridge language, and then generate the TT in the target language. Google Translate will also look for the most appropriate patterns of the translation based on statistics, including documents that are translated by human translators.

SFL, as a linguistic theory, is currently not being used in machine translation. However, the paradigmatic insights in SFL are unique among the various linguistic theories. Hence, there is still the possibility for SFL to be applied to machine translation no matter how advanced the technology that has been developed. That said, SFL itself will also continue to evolve as it is being developed by scholars around the world and to suit different needs of applications. Therefore, it will continue to be a comprehensive and appliable linguistic theory. As a holistic theory of language as a resource for making meaning in context, systemic functional theory makes it possible for researchers to outline the architecture of language both locally in terms of axis, rank scale, and delicacy as well as globally in terms of the hierarchy of stratification, the cline of instantiation, and the spectrum of metafunction. These theoretical perspectives all have the potential to be applied to machine translation.

5.2 Corpus-based Approaches and Systemic Functional Translation Studies

Corpus-based translation studies is a research area that adopts the methodologies developed in corpus linguistics to study translation (see Olohan 2004; Laviosa 2013). Corpus here refers to a collection of texts used in linguistic or literary studies. With the help of computer technology, large bodies of texts made of vast quantities of words are included in the corpora in electronic form. Also, there is corpus-processing software that made large-scale automated analysis possible.

The application of corpora significantly changed translation studies and translation practice in the past decades. The sub-discipline of corpus-based translation studies was initiated in the 1990s notably by **Mona Baker** (e.g. 1993, 1995, 1996, 2001), who had a linguistic orientation and was influenced by **John Sinclair** (e.g. 1987a, 1987b, 1990) from the University of Birmingham. Nowadays, it is widely acknowledged that corpus is very helpful for the investigation of equivalence through empirical works, especially when the corpus is composed of translations by a variety of translators (see House 2018).

In SFL, there has been a long tradition of using texts as data and corpus-based methodology for studying language and language use (see Wu 2009 for an introduction to corpus-based research in SFL). The application of corpus can be even traced to Halliday's (e.g. 1956b, 1957, 1959, 1992b) early work on the description of Chinese during his days of working as a research assistant for Professor Wang Li in collecting his data of Cantonese in the Pearl River Delta as well as his work on the intonation of English (e.g. Halliday 1967, 1970).

We can associate corpus with the cline of instantiation, and locate it at the instance end of the cline. A corpus is then a collection of texts as instances. In corpus-based studies, it is possible to move along the cline of instantiation. Firstly, we can approach register or text type from the instance end of the cline by making generalizations about the instances. Also, we can associate the instance with the linguistic systems and the overall systemic potential. For instance, in their pioneering study, Halliday and James (1993) examine the system of POLARITY by using a corpus of 18 million words, thus revealing the power of the paradigmatic organization and attaching probability with the system network of POLARITY. According to their research, the probabilities for the two choices in the system – positive and negative – are 0.9 and 0.1 respectively.

To use a large corpus, one needs automated analysis. Computational tools will thus be of great help. Teich (2009) summarizes three reasons that explain the relevance of such tools in SFL. Firstly, unlike formal theories, SFL has an interest in dealing with natural occurring data, and computational tools make it possible for SFL to engage with large data. Secondly, for some studies, such as those on lexical cohesion (e.g. Halliday & Hasan 1976; Hoey 1991), computational tools are essential for carrying out an accurate analysis. Thirdly, some central tenets of SFL, such as language as a probability system (Halliday 1991a), can only be modelled with the help of computational tools.

In the following sub-sections, we will introduce three strands of corpus-based works in SFTS, including those by Erich Steiner and his group, Juliane House, and Jeremy Munday.

5.2.1 Corpus and Erich Steiner's Group

Erich Steiner and his group in Saarbrücken started to build corpora for research on translation and contrastive linguistics from 2009. Before then, they had already done some preliminary work on translation, register, and corpus, such as Teich (2002, 2003), Steiner (2004a), and Neumann (2008).

In their book, *Cross-linguistic Corpora for the Study of Translations: Insights from the Language Pair English-German*, **Hansen-Schirra, Neumann, and Steiner** (2012) provide a detailed introduction to **CroCo (Cross-linguistic Corpus for the Study of Translation)** and its applications. They describe the architecture of CroCo, explaining various annotation and querying techniques, illustrating how CroCo can function as a resource for research in various areas. They also present the empirical findings of their studies based on CroCo, and discuss the implications of the findings for translation.

CroCo, the first family of corpora built by the team, was created for empirical studies on translation, specifically to examine the typical linguistic properties of translations in comparison with the originals in the language pair of English–German, to identify systemic variations between languages, and to study texts from similar registers that were interlingually comparable. It is based on the following theoretical assumptions: 'properties of translations must be seen as systematic, recurring features that can only be accounted for empirically and more concretely with a quantitative approach' (Neumann & Hansen-Schirra 2012: 25). CroCo is suitable for studies in the following three areas: (i) language contrasts/typology, (ii) register contrasts, and (iii) processing effort during translation (cf. Steiner 2001b).

The methodology adopted is not restricted to the traditional system-based comparison, in which 'real-text excerpts or constructed examples are used as mere illustrations of assumptions and claims' (Steiner 2012a: 2). Instead, the following empirical research methods are involved:

> the structured data (the sub-corpora and their relationships to each other, annotated and aligned on various theoretically motivated levels of representation), the formation of hypotheses and their operationalizations, statistics on the data, critical examinations of their significance, and interpretation against the background of system-based comparisons and other independent sources of explanation for the phenomena observed.
>
> (ibid.)

The project is empirical in that 'the information, knowledge and understanding are gathered through experience and direct data collection' (Black 1999: 3). In this way, the empirical method allows systematic observations with the goal of producing replicable studies.

The design of CroCo is guided by various criteria. Firstly, the size of the corpus is large enough to allow 'generalisable statements, balance as well as comparability across languages' (Neumann & Hansen-Schirra 2012: 25; cf. Neumann & Hansen-Schirra 2005). Secondly, a range of texts from different registers are included in the corpus, as registerial variation has played a significant role in the specific characters of translations. Thirdly, texts in both translation directions are included to 'distinguish phenomena that are related to the translation direction from those that apply in general' (Neumann & Hansen-Schirra 2012: 25–26).

The core corpora are divided into four sub-corpora, including English originals (EO), German translations (GTrans), German originals (GO), and English translations (ETrans). Three kinds of bidirectional corpora are included (see Figure 5.1): (i) parallel corpus (including originals and their matching translations in the target language), (ii) monolingually comparable corpus (including originals and translations within one language),

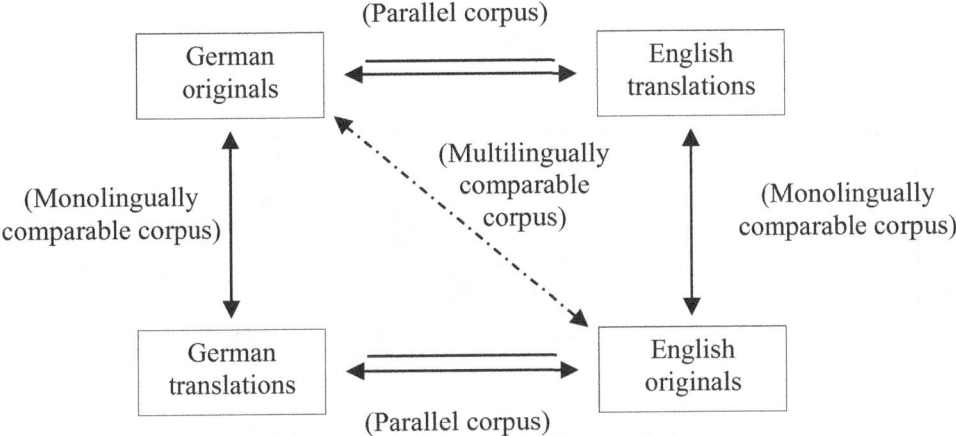

Figure 5.1 Bidirectional translation corpus in the CroCo Project (adapted from Neumann & Hansen-Schirra 2012: 27)

and (iii) multilingually comparable corpus (including originals in both languages). In total, the corpora contain around one million words, and are modelled on the English–Norwegian Parallel Corpus (Johansson 2007).

Each sub-corpus contains texts selected from eight registers. These texts are translated into both English and German, and fall into the following categories: 'political essays (ESSAY), fictional texts (FICTION), instructional texts (INSTR), popular-scientific writings (POPSCI), shareholder communication (SHARE), prepared speeches (SPEECH), tourism leaflets (TOU) and websites (WEB)' (Neumann & Hansen-Schirra 2012: 27). In addition, two small reference corpora in English and German (ER and GR) are constructed to complement the core corpus, 'each containing 2000-word samples of original texts from 17 different registers' (Neumann & Hansen-Schirra 2012: 31–32). The two reference corpora are designed to 'level out register-specific peculiarities by representing a wide range of registerial spread' (Neumann & Hansen-Schirra 2012: 32). All corpora are annotated at different layers, including word, chunk, clause, and sentence, involving annotations of various kinds, such as tokenization, POS (part of speech) tagging, sense relations, phrase structure, and grammatical functions.

Figure 5.2 provides an overview of the complete design of CroCo and the two reference corpora. It also highlights the different types of contrast to be investigated, as summarized by Steiner (2012b: 72–73) as follows:

- *Contrast C1* (reference corpora, cross-register) between the English reference corpus (ER) and the German reference corpus (GR). Contrasts under C1 yield a cross-register profile for original texts in the languages English and German.

- *Contrast C2* (register controlled) between the registers of ESSAY, FICTION, INSTR, POPSCI, SHARE, SPEECH, TOU, WEB for each of English originals

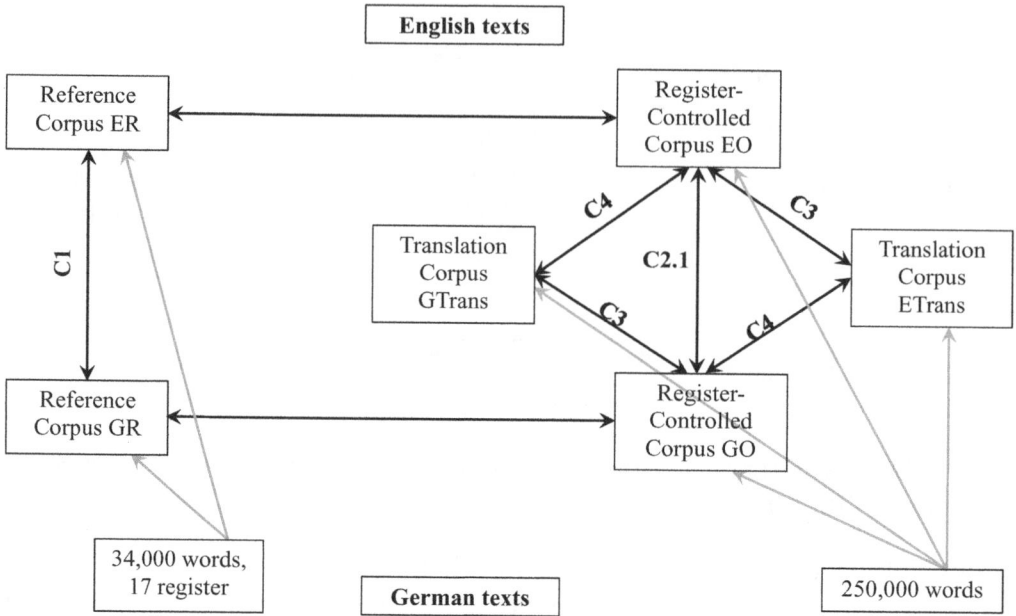

Figure 5.2 The design of CroCo corpus and the different types of contrast (adapted from Steiner 2012b: 72)

(EO), German originals (GO), English translations (ETrans), and German translations (GTrans). The translations are all translations of the samples of matching originals. Within this contrast, we can separately investigate
- *Contrast C2.1* (within one register, between languages, differentiated into eight sub-contrasts by register EO vs. GO, and theoretically also ETrans vs. GTrans), and
- *Contrast C2.2* (between registers, within each of the languages English and German, yielding eight contrasts within each of the corpora EO, GO, ETrans, GTrans).

- *Contrast C3* (translations vs. originals within each of the two languages): EO vs. ETrans and GO vs. GTrans, yielding either one contrast per language globally, or, if intersected by register, eight contrasts between originals and translations for each of the languages.

- *Contrast C4* (originals and their translations across languages, i.e. EO vs. GTrans and GO vs. ETrans); this contrast is the only one between originals and their translations. We differentiate this into Sub-corpora (and texts) as wholes (without alignment) and Aligned corpora, i.e. explicitation by translation units, and we investigate translations between English and German in both directions.

CroCo offers an approach to investigate the properties of translated texts, such as grammatical metaphor (cf. Steiner 2002a, 2002b) and language comparison (Kunz & Steiner 2012; Steiner 2015c), in particular explicitation (cf. Steiner 2008; Hansen-Schirra, Neumann, & Steiner 2007), which is assumed to be one of the properties of translated texts. The CroCo project focuses on the examination of explicitation empirically, which is one of the motivations for building the corpus.

Explicitation, which is postulated as a property of translated texts and suggests that the translated texts are more explicit than the originals, is identified as properties of lexicogrammatical constructions, cohesive structures and configurations. Steiner (2012c: 59) further provides the following discussions:

> We assume explicitation if a translation (or language-internally one text in a pair of register-related texts) realizes meanings (not only ideational, but including interpersonal and textual) more explicitly than its source text – more precisely, meanings not realized in the less explicit source variant but implicitly present in a theoretically-motivated sense. The resulting text is more explicit than its counterpart.

Steiner (2012c) operationalizes explicitation into a set of linguistic features, and derives various indications and operationalizations for explicitation. Table 5.1 illustrates the ways of measuring lexicogrammatical explicitation with respect to metafunction, grammatical systems, and the proportionalities between explicit and implicit indicators. For instance, ideational/experiential explicitness can be measured through realizations of transitivity, and can be operationalized by investigating the number of explicit and implicit functions per unit. By following such approaches, explicitation can be studied

Table 5.1 Operationalizing explicitation as linguistic features according to metafunctions (adapted from Steiner 2012c: 66)

Metafunction		Grammatical system	Operationalization
Ideational	Experiential	TRANSITIVITY	Number of explicit functions: Number of implicit functions (per unit)
	Logical	TAXIS	Number of explicit functions: Number of implicit functions (per unit)
Interpersonal		MOOD	Number of explicit mood-markers: Number of implicit mood-markers (per unit)
		MODALITY	Number of explicit modality-markers: Number of implicit modality-markers (per unit)
Textual		THEME	Number of auto-semantic Themes: Number of syn-semantic (phoric) Themes (per unit)

with the help of large data and rigorous linguistic analysis before being claimed as a translation universal (see Section 6.2.2; cf. House 2008; Becher 2010, 2011).

GECCo (German–English Contrasts in Cohesion) was the second family of corpora built by Erich Steiner and his group. As an extension of CroCo, GECCo includes both written and spoken texts, and contains 1.3 million tokens. Kunz et al. (2017: 279) provide a detailed account of the sub-corpora in GECCo:

> The whole corpus contains ... six subcorpora: English and German originals and their translations (extracted from CroCo; Hansen-Schirra et al. 2012), as well as two spoken subcorpora: German written originals (GO), English written originals (EO), English spoken originals (EO-SPOKEN) and German spoken originals (GO-SPOKEN), translations of German written originals into English (ETRANS) and translations of English written originals into German (GTRANS). The two written subcorpora (EO and GO) consist of texts from eight registers: popular-scientific texts (POPSCI), tourism leaflets (TOU), prepared speeches (SPEECH), political essays (ESSAYS), fictional texts (FICTION), corporate communication (SHARE), instruction manuals (INSTR) and corporate websites (WEB). The two spoken subcorpora contain academic speeches (ACADEMIC) and interviews (INTERVIEW).

The annotation of the corpora includes information on 'tokens, lemmas, morpho-syntactic features (e.g. case, number), parts-of-speech, grammatical chunks along with their syntactic functions, clauses, and sentence boundaries' (Kunz et al. 2017: 280). For the written sub-corpora, the annotation is largely imported from CroCo; while for the spoken sub-corpora, both the Stanford Parser and the Stanford POS Tagger are applied. The annotation provides additional information on the different types of cohesion. For coreference and conjunctive relations, the annotation centres on 'morpho-syntactic preferences of antecedents and anaphors, position of coordinating conjunctions and conjunctive adverbials in a clause' (ibid.). Also, the annotation contains information of the cohesive devices and their sub-categories, involving the functional and structural sub-types of coreference, conjunction, substitution, ellipsis, and lexical cohesion. Table 5.2 lists the categories of cohesion annotated in GECCo.

Semi-automatic procedures are adopted during the process of annotation, involving both rule-based tagging of cohesive candidates and the post correction carried out manually. In this way, cohesive categories are first annotated by following an iterative extraction-annotation process based on the methods from YAC chunker (see Kermes 2003). Then, annotations are corrected by human annotators with the help of MMAX2 (Müller & Strube 2006), which visualizes the annotations and the options for the human annotators to decide. In addition, the manual correction process helps to solve problems during the automatic analysis. For instance, in terms of substitution, there are more borderline cases in German than in English, the categories of the cohesive relations are thus blurred. As shown in Example 5.1, the verbal substitution – 'done so' in the English ST is translated as a combination of a demonstrative reference (das), a comparative reference (so), and as a verb (verhalten), and the 'so' in the German TT is on the borderline

Table 5.2 The cohesive categories being annotated in GECCo
(adapted from Kunz et al. 2017: 276)

Categories of cohesion	Realizational types
coreference	personal head, personal modifier, demonstrative head, demonstrative modifier, demonstrative local, demonstrative temporal, pronominal adverbs, definite articles
coreference chain	number of antecedents, number of anaphors, number of chains, chain length
comparative reference	comparative general, comparative particular
substitution	nominal, verbal, clausal
ellipsis	nominal, verbal, clausal
conjunctive relations	additive connects, additive adverbials, adversative connects, adversative adverbials, causal connects, causal adverbials, temporal adverbials, modal adverbials
lexical cohesion	general nouns

between reference and substitution. According to Kunz et al. (2017: 278), 'so' is here annotated as comparative reference, 'because of its remaining "manner"-meaning'.

Example 5.1 (adapted from Kunz et al. 2017: 277)

English ST: He thought he recognized the twisted thorn trees, and might indeed have **done so**.
German TT: Es wollte ihm scheinen, als erkenne er die krummen Weißdornbäume wieder, und **das** möchte sich durchaus **so verhalten**
IG: it will him seem, as recognize he the (ACC) twisted thorn trees again, and that think himself completely so behave
BT: It seems to him that he recognizes the twisted thorn trees, and that he thought he behaved so.

It can also be noted that manual procedures are used for the annotation of coreference chains since human annotators can manually identify antecedents and associate them to the anaphors that have been automatically tagged by the system (see Lapshinova-Koltunski & Kunz 2014 for a detailed introduction to the semi-automatic procedures of coreference, substitution, and conjunctive relations).

As the name of GECCo (German–English Contrasts in Cohesion) suggests, the corpora are primarily used to compare texts from various registers in English and German in terms of cohesion. The following research questions are raised in the GECCo project:

(i) How cohesive are the texts in the corpus?

(ii) How strong are the cohesive relations?

(iii) Which semantic relations are generally expressed and which relations are preferred over others?

(iv) How much cohesive variation is there in one language as compared to the other? How much difference is there between (written and spoken) registers?

These questions are relevant in shedding light on the contrasts of cohesion between the two languages. Such knowledge will influence the local and possibly global translation strategies adopted by translators when they choose the strategies consciously to adhere to the conventions in the target language and to establish textuality, coherence, or thematic progression. Kunz et al. (2017: 270) give the following suggestions to help translators make their decisions:

(i) Generally explicitate textual relations which are left implicit in the source text by inserting cohesive devices in the target text.

(ii) Move a textual relation that is preferred in the source text into the background in the target text by implicitating particular meaning relations and explicitating others.

(iii) Make a vague cohesive relation stronger by using a more specific cohesive device or by using more cohesive devices in one cohesive chain.

(iv) Use more different cohesive devices to mark one conceptual type of cohesive relation.

The various papers based on GECCo (e.g. Kunz et al. 2017; Menzel, Lapshinova-Koltunski, & Kunz 2017; cf. Steiner 2015c) have pointed out the differences of cohesive patterns between German and English in quantitative terms, and suggested the preferred cohesive patterns, such as preference for logico-semantic relations in German, and preference for coreference relations and general nouns in English. Moreover, the importance of register is highlighted while examining the differences between English and German. Currently, a book that summarizes the findings based on GECCo is yet to be published. Also, suggestions for future research are put forward, such as further investigations in researches on translationese. One of the contributions of the GECCo project lies in the production of a corpus for contrastive linguistic work from the perspective of textual cohesion.

The corpora are credited for their coverage of a wide range of registers, their inclusion of spoken and written language, and their complicated way of annotation. Following methodologies of empirical studies, the empirical results are statistically refined and evaluated, and the statistical evaluation techniques have presented new models in corpus-based empirical work. In this way, the cohesive contrasts between German and English are summarized in terms of degree, strength, semantic type, and variation of cohesive devices and chains. In addition, works based on GECCo shed light on three areas of application. Firstly, the findings provide more discourse-oriented methodologies in the area of language teaching. Secondly, the studies feed into the teaching of translation and suggest the production of target-culture-adapted texts. Thirdly, findings from GECCo are influential on linguistic engineering and machine translation by illustrating how improved control of text cohesion can improve linguistic engineering in various perspectives.

5.2.2 Corpus and Juliane House's Model of Translation Quality Assessment

In **Juliane House**'s (e.g. 2015, 2018) latest version of the model of translation quality assessment (see Figure 5.3), she recognizes the significance of corpus, and integrates findings from corpus-based studies into her model. According to House (2018), corpus studies can extend an evaluator's view of an individual text to a large number of texts in the same genre, providing more information about translation quality assessment, and

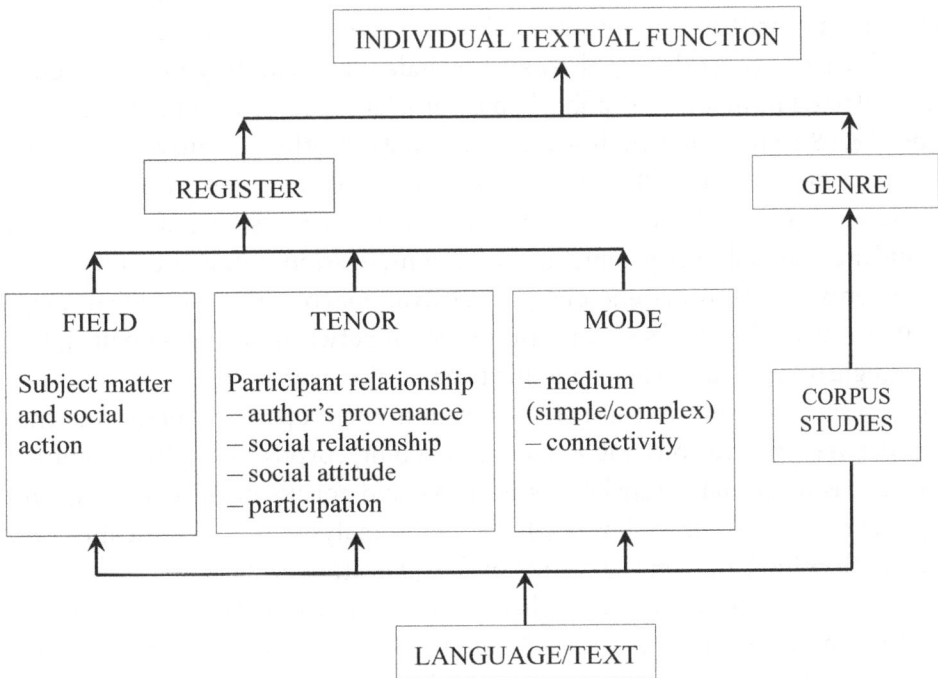

Figure 5.3 A revised scheme for analysis and comparing originals and translation texts (adapted from House 2018: 97; cf. Figure 1.5)

paying special attention to genre. As proved by studies by House and her team, with the help of corpus, it is possible to observe how English has influenced German based on the use of certain lexical choices and the linguistic structures in German translations and comparative texts (see Becher, House, & Kranich 2009). In this way, the 'genre analysis' component in the model is made more concrete. The notions of norms and conventions are also taken into consideration during the evaluation of the quality of a translated text. Further, the corpus-based approach in the model and her notion of cultural filter are complementary.

House (2015) confirms the usefulness of corpus in translation as a tool of scientific inquiry. To illustrate her point, she reports on the findings in the project of 'Verdecktes Übersetzen – Covert Translation' conducted at the German Science Foundation's Research Centre on Multilingualism in Hamburg from 1999 to 2011 (see Becher, House, & Kranich 2009; Kranich, House, & Becher 2012). In this corpus-driven project, the qualitative analysis based on House's (e.g. 1997, 2015) model is integrated with corpus-based methods by combining the lexicogrammatical and contextual analyses and the quantitative investigation of certain lexical choices and linguistic structures. It is hypothesized that the dominance of the English language has led to changes in indigenous communicative norms in German in terms of both German original texts and covert translations from English to German.

Becher, House, and Kranich (2009) select texts in registers that have particularly been influenced by Anglophone dominance, such as popular science and business. The multilingual corpora consist of 650 texts of English–German originals and translations, with French and German control texts also being included. Texts in the genre of 'popular science' are selected from journals published by official organizations (including *Scientific American*, *New Scientists*, and their satellite journals in other languages) in two timeframes, i.e. 1978–1982 and 1999–2002, on general social and political topics. The word count is around 700,000. Texts in the genre of 'economic texts' include around 300,000 words, and are selected from product presentations, mission statements, visions, corporate statements, letters to shareholders, as well as annual reports from global companies from 2002 to 2006. The reverse translation relation between German–English, French/Spanish–English in the genre of 'economic texts' is also examined.

Figure 5.4 sketches the structure of the corpus in the project, and marks out the relationship between the various sub-corpora, including corpus of English original texts (E-ORI), corpus of German translations (G-TRA), and corpus of German original texts (G-ORI). The project has three phases: (i) qualitative analyses, (ii) quantification, and (iii) re-contextualization based on the results of the quantitative analyses.

The qualitative analyses of the English popular science texts have shown that the texts are person-oriented, with readers being 'invited' to locate the person depicted in the text through linguistic resources. Mental processes are used to build a personal relationship between the author and the reader. Also, simulated dialogues, repetition, structural parallelism, as well as various devices are used to personalize and dramatize

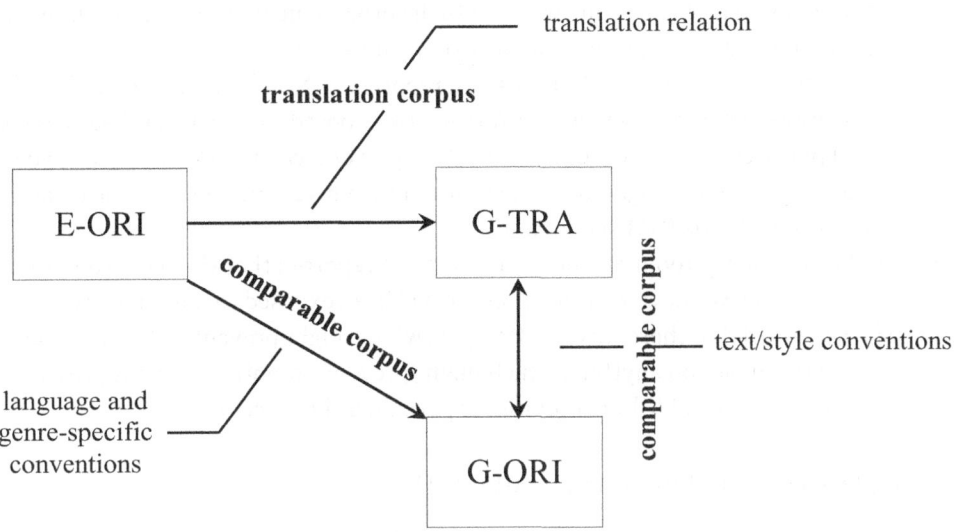

Figure 5.4 Translation corpus and comparable corpus in the 'Verdecktes Übersetzen – Covert Translation' project (adapted from Kranich, House, & Becher 2012: 331)

the scientific topics. However, the German popular science texts are found to be less person-oriented, more technological, and serious. Uses of mental processes are rarely seen. Didactic interventions are frequently found, as producers of the texts who assume that the readers need more knowledge tend to make the texts informative. Moreover, there is the assumption that readers want to be instructed rather than entertained at work.

Example 5.2 is selected from an article on HIV infection in *Scientific American* and *Spektrum der Wissenschaft*. It reveals the differences between the ST and the TT in terms of addressee involvement by changing the scene of the interior of a hospital in the English ST to the exterior of a hospital. In this way, readers of the German TT are no longer required to engage with the story being told. In Example 5.3, we find additions of information about the treatment and the risks in the German TT, by which the translator of the German TT makes the TT more explicit.

Example 5.2 (adapted from House 2015: 110)

English ST: Suppose **you** are a doctor in an emergency room and a patient tells **you** she was raped two hours earlier. She is afraid she may have been exposed to HIV, the virus that causes AIDS but has heard that there is a 'morning-after pill' to prevent HIV infection. Can **you** in fact do anything to block the virus from replicating and establishing infection?

German TT: In der Notfallaufnahme eines Krankenhauses berichtet eine Patientin, sie sei vor zwei Stunden vergewaltigt worden und nun in Sorge, AIDS-Erregern ausgesetzt zu sein, sie habe gehört, es gebe eine „Pille danach", die eine HIV-Infektion verhüte. Kann

der Arzt überhaupt etwas tun, was eventuell vorhandene Viren hindern würde, sich zu vermehren und sich dauerhaft im Körper einzunisten?
IG: in the (DAT) emergency a (GEN) hospital reported a (NOM) patient, she be before two hours raped get and now in worry, AIDS-cause exposed to be, she has heard, it gives a (ACC) pill after, which a (ACC) HIV-infection prevent. can the (NOM) doctor whatever something do, what might available viruses prevent get, oneself to replicate and oneself continue in the (DAT) body nest?
BT: In the emergency room of a hospital, a patient reported that she had been raped two hours ago and was now worrying that she had been exposed to the AIDS virus. She said she had heard that there was an 'after-pill', which might prevent an HIV infection. Can the doctor in fact do anything which might prevent potentially existing viruses from replicating and establishing themselves permanently in the body?

Example 5.3 (adapted from House 2015: 111)

English ST: Treatment may reduce the chance of contracting HIV infection after a risky encounter.
German TT: Eine sofortige Behandlung nach Kontakt mit einer Ansteckungsquelle verringert unter Umständen die Gefahr, dass sich das Human- Immunschwäche-Virus im Körper festsetzt. Gewähr gibt es keine, zudem erwachsen eigene Risiken.
IG: a (NOM) immediate treatment after contact with a (DAT) infection source reduce under circumstance the danger, that oneself the (NOM) human-immunodeficiency-virus in the (GEN) body establish. guaranty there is NEG, to the (GEN) grow particular risk.
BT: Immediate treatment after contact with a source of infection reduces under certain circumstances the danger that the human immuno-deficiency-virus establishes itself in the body. There is no guarantee for this; moreover, new risks arise.

After qualitative analyses, quantitative analyses are carried out to verify the results of the qualitative analyses. With the help of corpus, the preferred linguistic choices used to express subjectivity and addressee orientation, the collocation and co-occurrence patterns, as well as the syntactic and textual position vis-à-vis the organization of information are pointed out. Table 5.3 presents the findings of the quantitative contrastive analyses in the following aspects: (i) personal pronoun 'we' and 'wir'; (ii) sentence initial 'and' and 'und'; (iii) sentence initial 'but' and 'aber/doch'; and (iv) epistemic modal markers.

Furthermore, the quantitative analyses are associated with the shining-through phenomenon in English–German translations (see Table 5.4). House (2015) identifies three evidences from the four phenomena investigated, i.e. the use of personal pronoun 'we' and 'wir', the use of sentence-initial 'but' and 'aber/doch', and the use of epistemic modal markers. It is thus concluded that the German translations are more interactional than texts originally produced in German. Also, the analysis of sentence-initial concessive conjunctions, i.e. 'but' and 'aber/doch', supports the hypothesis that German original popular science texts have increasingly absorbed certain conventions from English

Table 5.3 Comparisons between English and German original popular scientific texts seen from the frequency of selected linguistic items (adapted from House 2015: 113)

	Personal pronoun 'we' 'wir'	Sentence-initial 'and' 'und'	Sentence-initial 'but' 'aber/doch'	Epistemic modal markers
English originals	27.5	3.1	32.6	22.8
German originals	17.7	0.9	9.0	7.1
Conclusions	English texts are more personal.	English texts simulate spoken interaction more.	English texts simulate spoken interaction more.	English texts are more dialogic.

Table 5.4 Shining-through and contact-induced changes in translated and non-translated German popular science texts (adapted from House 2015: 114)

	Personal pronoun 'we' wir	Sentence-initial 'and' und	Sentence-initial 'but' aber/doch	Epistemic modal markers
Shining-through effects in translation	√	Unclear	√	√
Impact on German originals	×	×	√	×
Conclusions	German original texts become more personal, but change is not due to translations.	German original texts become more interactional, but the reason is unclear.	German original texts become more interactional as authors adopt Anglophone usage patterns from translations.	German original texts do not become more dialogic.

(see also Becher 2011). Over time, the English–German translations of popular science texts have a tendency of allowing more importations of conventions and norms from the source texts in English. These features are even seen in the non-translated texts produced in German. House then suggests that the English–German translations have paved the way for the overall change in the conventions of German popular science texts.

5.2.3 Corpus and Jeremy Munday's Systemic Model for Descriptive Translation Studies

Munday (e.g. 1997, 2002) also highlights the corpus-based methodology in his model, which combines SFL, corpus linguistics, and the analysis of the cultural and social context. Munday (2002) adopts Toury's (1995) methodology of descriptive translation studies, which draws on Even-Zohar's (e.g. 1979) polysystem theory by locating the target text in the target culture and the sociocultural system. The methodology includes three phases (Toury 1995): (i) to locate the target text in the target culture and examine how the target text has been accepted, (ii) to compare the source text and the target text, to observe the translation shifts, and to identify how the segments of the ST and the TT are related, (iii) to generalize the findings on the underlying concept of translation. It is further argued that to describe the norms in translation, phases (i) and (ii) have to be repeated to analyse similar texts, to enlarge the corpus, and to build up a profile of translations in accordance with author, period, genre, etc.

Munday (2002: 78) regards his model as 'specific, systematic and replicable'. Four interrelated steps are included (see Figure 5.5). The first step is to locate the ST within its sociocultural system. Then, the profile of the ST is built in terms of how it is received in its culture. Similarly, the profile of the TT is built and compared with that of the ST. Finally, linguistic shifts are expected to be observed, with the impact of such shifts being evaluated on the cultural level.

The model has three components, i.e. SFL, corpus linguistics, and contextual interpretation. Firstly, the SFL analysis includes the analysis of the metafunctional modes of meaning, which is expected to point out the lexicogrammatical features of the text, and to identify the important aspects related to translation shift. Secondly, the corpus linguistic tools are capable of providing information about the concordances of any search word or phrase, including 'total text length (the number of "tokens"), the number of different word forms ("types"), type-token rations (which give some indication of variety of language), word frequency lists, and so on' (Munday 2002: 80). There are two advantages of incorporating corpus methodology: (i) the corpus-based tools can reveal phenomena that may not be observed during the manual analysis; (ii) the process of the automated analysis is faster and more reliable. Thirdly, the results revealed by the previous two steps are to be examined in a wider political and sociocultural context. The contextual consideration is based on the organizing principle of stratification in SFL as well as the cline of instantiation between context of culture and context of situation.

After illustrating the model by analysing Gabriel García Márquez's essay in Spanish and its English translations, Munday (2002: 91) has confirmed that the corpus linguistic

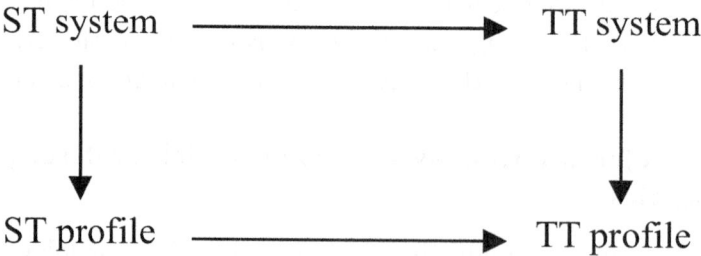

Figure 5.5 Four areas of analysis in Munday's systemic model for descriptive translation studies (adapted from Munday 2002: 78)

tools can 'enable rapid manipulation of text and an uncovering of trends that may not be obvious to manual analysis'. He further states that the model is adaptable in that 'adjustments can be made when analysing languages that are differently structured' (ibid.). Munday (2002) also believes that his model is replicable and results of the analysis are set in the sociocultural and political context of texts, so as to enable 'conclusions to be drawn as to the norms at work in the translation process' (ibid.).

As illustrated in Example 5.4, a translation shift in terms of transitivity structure is found in the first clause complex; thus, the responsibility of causing the accident is removed from the organizers of the trip in the ST to an agentless passive ('was dismantled') in the TT. In addition, the cohesive structure in the second and third clause complexes is changed in the TT. The ST written by García Márquez is characterized with the frequent use of the conjunction 'y' (IG: and) according to the corpus-based analysis. However, the 'y' (IG: and) in the ST is changed to a full stop in the TT – a stronger break. It is also noted that the textual transition of 'sin embargo' (IG: for all that) – a discourse marker that guides the readers – in the ST is omitted by the translator; as a result, such transition is left implicit and readers of the TT have to infer the textual transition on their own. Finally, the paratactic relation marked by 'y' (IG: and) in the last clause complex of the ST is changed to hypotactic relation marked by 'causing' in the TT. Munday (2002) suggests that changes in such a pattern in the TT is a dislocation of the style of García Márquez.

Munday (2002) relates the translation shifts to his contextual interpretation. Several possibilities are summarized, e.g. (i) the translator followed a non-systematic strategy when doing translation, which leads to a distorted TT, (ii) changes in punctuation may be done by a copy-editor, (iii) some omissions in the TT may due to the constraints of space in the magazine, and (iv) some anti-US discussions in the ST are omitted on purpose due to ideological reasons.

> Example 5.4 (adapted from Munday 2002: 89)
>
> Spanish ST: Según ellos, a la medianoche del 22, **los responsables del viaje des montaron el motor desahuciado** y lo tiraron en el mar para aligerar la carga. Pero la barca, descompensada, dio una voltereta de costado y todos los pasajeros cayeron al agua. **Sin embargo**, una suposición de expertos es que la voltereta pudo haber roto las frágiles soldaduras de los tubos de alumnio, y la barca se hundió.
> IG: according to they, at the midnight from 22, they responsibility via travel give Montaron the engine dismantel and the throw into the sea to reduce the load. but the boat, destabilized, give a roll of side and all the passengers fall in the water. however, a suspect of experts is that the capsize can have broken the fragile soldering of the tube of aluminium, and the boat itself sink.
> BT: According to them, at the midnight of the 22nd, those who were responsible of travel in Montaron dismantled the engine and threw it into the sea to lighten the load. But the boat was destabilized and turned over to its side and all the passengers fell into

the water. However, one suspect from experts is that the capsize can have broken the fragile soldering of the aluminium tube, and the boat sank.

English TT: At midnight on the first day out, **the engine – a write off – was dismantled** and thrown into the sea to lighten the load. But the boat was destabilized and turned over on to its side. All the passengers fell into the water. Experts suspect that the capsize may have broken the fragile soldering on the aluminium tube, **causing** the boat to sink.

Based on the analysis, Munday (2002) acknowledges the appliability of SFL, highlights the need to balance automated and manual analysis, and recognizes the importance of data size and comprehensiveness of analysis (cf. Matthiessen 2014a). However, as criticized by Matthiessen (see Matthiessen, Wang, & Ma 2017b), when different theories are put together in an eclectic way, the researcher runs the risk of creating 'a Frankenstein's monster'. The different components may not fit, and it may prove difficult to explain how the components are related to each other. With the help of a linguistic theory like SFL, one does not in fact need to combine the framework with descriptive translation studies to increase its credibility, as SFL itself is powerful enough to relate the findings to the sociocultural context.

According to Matthiessen (see Matthiessen, Wang, & Ma 2017b), if we would like to integrate the works on descriptive translation studies by the Israeli group of scholars (e.g. Even-Zohar 1979; Toury 1995), we can ground their methodology in the SFL tradition. For instance, instead of merely locating the target text within the target culture system and conducting a separate analysis from the perspective of polysystem theory or DTS, we can return to insights from SFL. Examples include Malinowski's (e.g. 1923, 1935) studies on context, Firth's (e.g. 1957b) further development of context of culture and context of situation, as well as Halliday's (1978) conception of context as a higher-order semiotic system. Based on these, we can re-interpret polysystem theory and DTS in SFL terms. Indeed, Toury (2004) also welcomes SFL by adopting Halliday's (1991a, 1991b) notion of probability in his description of translation universals or laws within the DTS framework.

5.3 Technologies in Translation Process Research and Systemic Functional Translation Studies

Studies on translation process attempt to examine what goes on in the heads of the translators while they are translating, i.e. the 'black box' in their heads (House 2018: chapter 8; Wang & Ma 2015). Early studies on translation process tend to adopt methods of introspective and verbal report, such as Ericsson and Simon's (1984) think-aloud protocol (TAP). However, TAP has limitations because the phenomenon of translation process is affected when a translator is asked to think aloud. To remedy this limitation, more recent studies in this area involve various experimental methods such as keystroke logging (keylogging), eye tracking, and screen recording.

The method of **keystroke logging** is expected to record the translators' operations on the computer, including deletions, cutting and pasting, up and down scrolling, switches between mouse and keyboard, as well as pauses. *Translog* is a software designed especially for researches of translation process (Jakobsen 2011; Carl, Bangalore, & Schaefer 2015). It records the uses of keyboard and mouse during the translation process, and then produces a log file to be analysed systematically. Keystroke logging is suitable for investigating various questions, including 'Is there evidence for the existence of "units of translation"? What is the difference between expert and novice translators? Do expert translators use the keyboard differently from novice translators?' (House 2018: 105). Moreover, *Translog* can record the computer screen, providing more information for translators to reflect on what has happened during the translation process. The data obtained from screen recording is suitable for integration with other methods, such as think-aloud protocol, retrospective interview, questionnaire, and keystroke logging.

The method of **eye tracking** records the information on the translators' eye movement by using camera and infrared light. During the translation process, the translators' eyes make different kinds of movements, either rapid movements – also known as saccades, or longer sweeping movements. The forward and backward saccades are often seen in reading and writing activities; while the longer sweeping movements signal attention shifts between the ST and the TT, and are used to detect the difficult parts in the ST as well as to differentiate monolingual reading and 'reading for translation' (Jensen 2008). Also, eye tracking equipment can record measures that are indicative of cognitive effort, including fixations and pupil dilation. For instance, in translation process research, fixations are used to examine how expert and novice translators solve translation problems differently.

On the one hand, with the help of the technologies, we can now track eye movements, log keystrokes and even scan the translator's brain, and translation process is in this way studied as a material phenomenon. The SFL-based studies are, on the other hand, within the semiotic order of systems (see Section 1.1). According to the SFL theory, texts unfolding in their contexts of situation are modelled as ongoing choices in the system networks that represent the potential or sub-potential of a language. Therefore, one fascinating challenge for scholars, as suggested by Matthiessen (2021), is to relate these findings on translation as a material process to the interpretations of translation as process within the semiotic order of systems.

Though SFTS centres on product-based research, it can be integrated with process-based studies to reveal more interesting findings. Around 2010, the group headed by **Fabio Alves** (e.g. Alves 2003; Alves, Pagano, & da Silva 2011; Alves et al. 2016) in Brazil cooperated with **Erich Steiner**'s group in Germany, leading to a collaboration between process-based and product-based researches.

In the research conducted by Alves et al. (2010), they integrate the corpus-based and process-based methodologies to identify translation units and their associations with cognitive efforts during several translators' performances of one translation task. The methodologies include corpus-based approach (see Section 5.2.1), key logging, eye tracking, and retrospective verbalizations. In an exploratory study, two participants, whose mother tongue is German, were asked to translate a 318-word excerpt from a company website. No time limit was set, and the participants were allowed to have access to the internet, except for the company website where the text was selected. The study has two goals: firstly, to identify indicators of segmentations of translation units; secondly, to find evidence of the grammatical (de)metaphorization strategies.

In the product-based analysis, they focus on the translation of grammatical metaphor and observe how the two translators adopt different patterns of metaphoricity in their translations. As shown in Example 5.5, different strategies are adopted to translate 'sich widersprechen' in the ST. In TT1, 'sich widersprechen' is translated by the English equivalent as a verb. In TT2, the verb in the ST is translated as a copula (are) and an adjective functioning as Complement. Such a translation shift involves a further shift of process type from relational (identifying) in the ST and TT1 to relational (attributive) in TT2. By doing so, the translator of TT2 removes the main semantic burden from the verb and makes the representation of the meaning in the clause more static. However, the product-based analysis of the ST and TT2 does not reflect any motivation for such a shift. Explanations therefore have to be obtained from the process-based analysis.

> Example 5.5 (adapted from Alves et al. 2010: 127)
>
> German ST: Wir sind davon überzeugt, dass erfolgreiche Unternehmensführung und soziale Verantwortung **sich nicht widersprechen.**
> IG: we be thus convince, that successful business management and social responsibility oneself not contradict
> BT: We thus believe that successful business management and social responsibility do not contradict each other.
> English TT1: We firmly believe that business success and social responsibility do not necessarily **contradict** each other.
> English TT2: We are convinced that successful management and social responsibility **are** not **contradictory**.

The process-oriented analysis helps to retrieve indicators of translation unit segmentation. As suggested by Alves and Vale (2009), a translation unit starts with a pause registered by key logging, it evolves continuously during the production phase until it is interrupted by another pause. The pauses may occur for two purposes, either for planning (internal support) or consultation (external support). Micro and macro TUs are further distinguished by Alves et al. (2010: 129):

> A micro TU [translation unit] is defined as the flow of continuous TT production – which may incorporate the continuous reading of source and TT segments – separated by pauses during the translation process, as registered by key logging and/or eye tracking software.

It can be correlated to a ST segment that attracts the translator's focus of attention at a given moment. A macro TU is defined as a collection of micro TUs that comprises all the interim text productions that follow the translator's focus on the same ST segment from the first tentative rendering to the final output that appears in the TT. Thus, a macro TU incorporates all the text production segments (revisions, deletions, substitutions, etc.) in the unfolding of the process which correspond to the initial focus of attention that triggered a given micro TU.

To log the keystrokes of the translators, *Translog* software was used. As shown in Figure 5.6, the second translator has more than 20 pause intervals (marked by *) during the translation process, which is a much higher amount compared to that of the first translator. This indicates that the second translator has used more effort. While translating 'sich widersprechen' in the ST (see Example 5.4), the drafting process is broken down into four sequential micro translation units, including the insertion of 'do not contract' and the follow-up deletions. It is also found that the nine minor translation

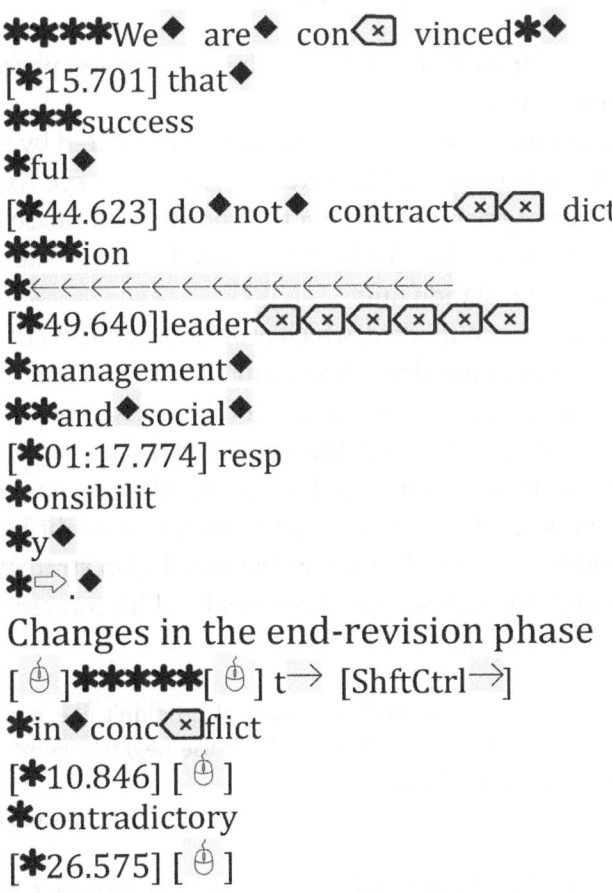

Figure 5.6 Illustration of micro translation unit giving rise to a macro translation unit during the translation process of the second translator (adapted from Alves et al. 2010: 131)

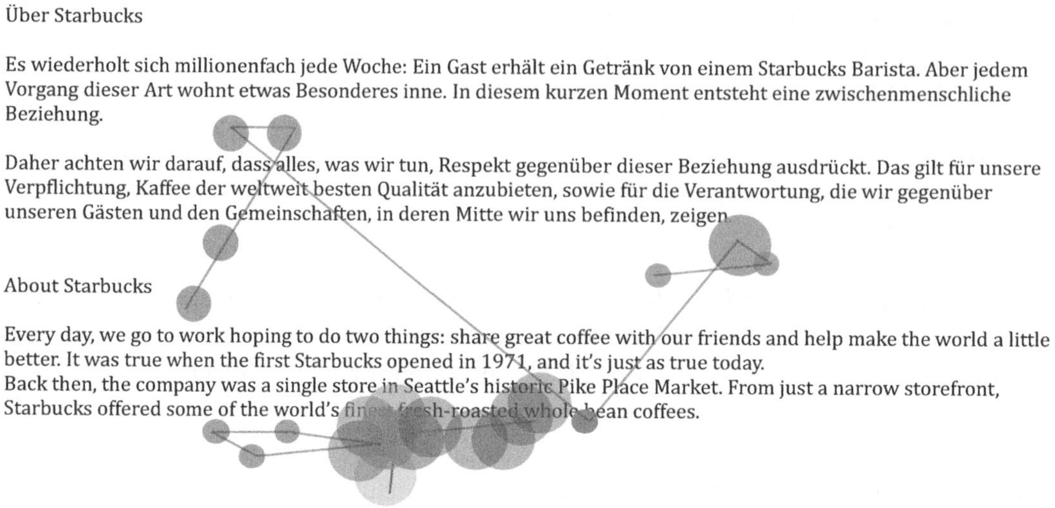

Über Starbucks

Es wiederholt sich millionenfach jede Woche: Ein Gast erhält ein Getränk von einem Starbucks Barista. Aber jedem Vorgang dieser Art wohnt etwas Besonderes inne. In diesem kurzen Moment entsteht eine zwischenmenschliche Beziehung.

Daher achten wir darauf, dass alles, was wir tun, Respekt gegenüber dieser Beziehung ausdrückt. Das gilt für unsere Verpflichtung, Kaffee der weltweit besten Qualität anzubieten, sowie für die Verantwortung, die wir gegenüber unseren Gästen und den Gemeinschaften, in deren Mitte wir uns befinden, zeigen.

About Starbucks

Every day, we go to work hoping to do two things: share great coffee with our friends and help make the world a little better. It was true when the first Starbucks opened in 1971, and it's just as true today.
Back then, the company was a single store in Seattle's historic Pike Place Market. From just a narrow storefront, Starbucks offered some of the world's finest fresh-roasted whole bean coffees.

Figure 5.7 Eye fixations by the second translator while translating 'sich widersprechen' in the drafting phase (adapted from Alves et al. 2010: 134)

units, i.e. four in the drafting phase and five in the end-revision phase, have given rise to the macro translation unit.

Furthermore, the analysis of keystroke logging is triangulated by eye tracking, with the help of Tibii T60 eye tracker. As illustrated by Figure 5.7, eye fixations reflect the effort in translating this segment. Data from the end-revision phase then reveals how the second translator made his decision by internal and external support as well as the emergence of the macro translation unit.

In addition, interviews are conducted, which provide accounts of the translators' own retrospections on what they have done. According to Shreve (2006: 29), these observations are regarded as metacognitive components of the translation tasks. It is the translation metacognition that 'assumes that the translator has an explicit knowledge and awareness of the mental processes involved in the translation, where active control is required, and, most importantly, what conscious strategies might be applied at these conscious control points'. When reflecting on the translation strategy of choosing the adjective 'contradictory', the second translator admitted his awareness of the register by making the following remarks:

> I mentioned that before … I was in conflict (laughter) … I didn't like 'conflict' because it seemed too (?) for a corporate text … they wouldn't use negative words … that's why I changed it back to 'contradictory' I think.
>
> (Alves et al. 2010: 136)

The integration of product-based and process-based approaches not only identifies the translation units and interprets the process of (de)metaphorization in the translation process, but also illustrates the importance of triangulation of product and process-based data. Alves et al.'s (2010) study successfully demonstrates the power of the technology-based methods introduced in this chapter, such as corpus tool, keystroke logging, and eye tracking. However, it must be noted that this is only an exploratory attempt. We hope more in-depth investigations can be made in this area, including the introduction of more advanced technologies, as well as the examination of several different kinds of texts and translators from various backgrounds (see Section 6.2.3).

In this chapter, we introduced three strands of researches that are related to the development of translation-oriented language technology, including machine translation, corpus-based studies, and some tools used in the investigation of translation process. We associate all the three approaches to SFTS. For machine translation, we discussed the application of SFL in Halliday's (1956a) early attempts, in the Eurotra project in the 1980s, and in the recent developments in Saarbrücken. For corpus-based researches, we selected the works by three influential researchers in SFTS and illustrated how corpus tools were integrated with SFL in their studies. Finally, we introduced researches that apply methods of keystroke logging and eye tracking, and discussed how process-based studies can be integrated with product-based studies. Chapter 5 is based on the various key concepts of SFL introduced in the previous chapters and it reveals the integration of SFL theory with the technological development. In the next chapter, we will disucss the trends in SFTS and make some suggestions for future research.

Chapter 6

Current Situation and Future Direction of Systemic Functional Translation Studies

Chapter 6 discusses the current issues and limitations in SFTS, and makes suggestions for future researches.[1] Section 6.1 presents the limitations of some researches on SFTS in general. In Section 6.2, we discuss some possibilities for future research in this area.

6.1 Limitations of Some Researches in Systemic Functional Translation Studies

6.1.1 Complementarity between Manual and Automated Analysis

According to Matthiessen (2014a), to achieve great reliability in the analysis, we have to face with the trade-offs between the comprehensiveness of the analysis and the volume of text analysed (see Figure 6.1). Comprehensiveness can only be a matter of degree, as there are various intermediate points situated along the cline of fully comprehensive (exhaustive) analysis and highly selective analysis. By considering the volume of text to be analysed, a differentiation can be made between minimally reliable analysis and maximally reliable analysis. Thus, when we either try to involve a wide range of systems

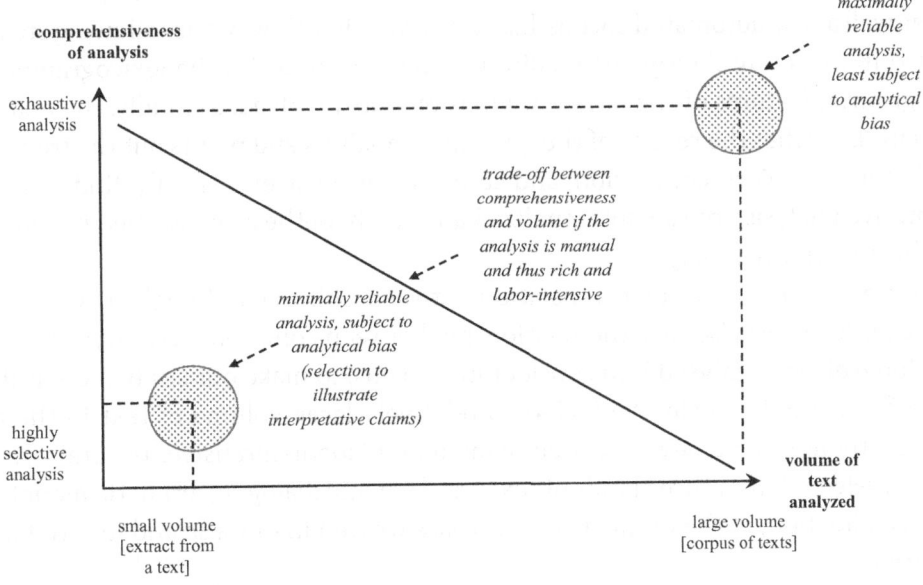

Figure 6.1 Relationship between comprehensiveness of analysis and volume of text analysed (adapted from Matthiessen 2014a: 189)

or increase the volume of texts analysed, we need to choose whether to do the analysis manually or automate the analysis by using computational tools.

On the one hand, the lexicogrammatical analysis in SFL has to be carried out manually rather than automatically by a computer despite the various developments in computational linguistics (cf. Bateman & O'Donnell 2015), and manual analysis requires a lot of efforts from researchers. Alternatively, if a large team of analysts are hired to do the analysis, the result of the analysis may be inconsistent and unreliable. On the other hand, the automated analysis tends to be restricted to lower 'levels' – in terms of both strata and ranks within a stratum (see Teich 2009; Wu 2009). The concordance lists obtained from computational tools are mainly based on graphological or orthographic patterns. In lexicogrammar, tools like word class (POS) tagger only work at lower ranks such as word and morpheme. While at a higher rank like that of the clause, parsers based on either dependency tree or constituency tree will work; this is an area without systemic functional component and thus in order to advance needs the work of SFL. In other words, if we expect semantic patterns or lexicogrammatical patterns at ranks that are higher than morpheme or word, then the concordance programmes can presently give us very little information.

The best solution, as suggested by Matthiessen (2014a: 191), is 'to develop a two-pronged approach based both on manual "high-level" analysis of small samples of texts and on automated analysis of large samples of text'. In this way, we can complement manual and automated analysis by combining both the techniques of discourse analysis and the techniques of corpus linguistics. As previously shown in Section 5.2.2, House's (2015) study is based on a corpus of 700,000 words (see also Becher et al. 2009). It combines the manual analysis based on House's (2015) model of translation quality assessment as well as the automated corpus-based analysis. In this way, the following steps are included in the study. Firstly, the qualitative analysis identifies the lexicogrammatical and registerial features of the different kinds of texts involved. Secondly, the quantitative analysis verifies the results of the qualitative analysis and points out the frequently used linguistic choices, collocation, and co-occurrence patters. Thirdly, findings of the quantitative analysis are re-contextualized and the hypothesis is testified by evidence from the quantitative analysis.

In our own study on drama translation between Chinese and English (Wang & Ma 2018, 2019, 2020), we also take the relationship between comprehensiveness of analysis and volume of text analysed into consideration. Thus, to make our study more reliable, trade-offs have to be made. We include a relatively large volume of text in the analysis, even though the analysis will be manual and labour-intensive. In total, we analyse texts selected from three kinds of text, i.e. dramatic dialogue, dramatic monologue, and stage direction, in the drama titled *Teahouse* written in Chinese and its two English translations.

In terms of the analytical framework, we try to make our analysis comprehensive by involving a selective number of systems rather than being exhaustive. With the help of a

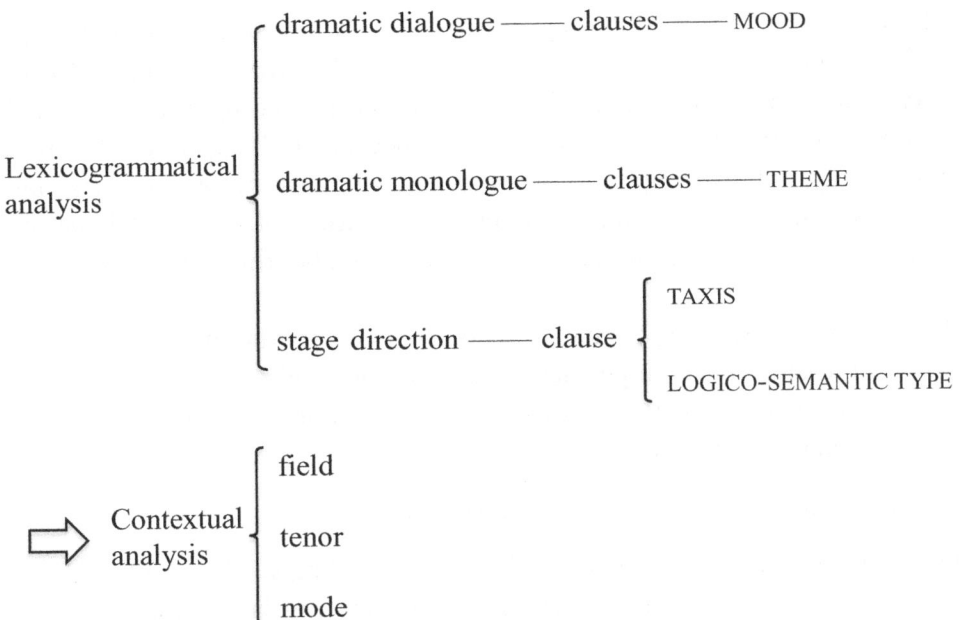

Figure 6.2 Analytical framework in Wang and Ma (2020)

pilot study involving a relatively small number of clauses, we select the lexicogrammatical systems that tend to reveal more differences between the ST and the TTs (see Figure 6.2). As a result, the analysis of dramatic dialogue will focus on the systems of MOOD, with considerations of the semantic system of SPEECH FUNCTION. The analysis of dramatic monologue will be based on the choices in the system of THEME. The analysis of stage direction will report on the analysis in the systems of TAXIS and LOGICO-SEMANTIC TYPE. Taken together, these selected systemic analyses are capable of offering a revealing account of how the discourse of *Teahouse* is organized to effectively function in its context of situation and context of culture.

6.1.2 Divergence of Models in Systemic Functional Linguistics

Within SFL, there are currently three different models, including the Hallidayan or the 'IFG model' (named after Halliday's [1985b] *Introduction to Functional Grammar*), the 'Sydney model' (named after Sydney University where James R. Martin and his colleagues worked), and the 'Cardiff model' (named after Cardiff University where Robin Fawcett and Gordon Tucker worked) (see Bartlett & O'Grady 2017, which brings together the three strands of SFL).

The 'Hallidayan model' is represented by the various works by Michael Halliday and Christian Matthiessen, such as the different versions of Halliday's *Introduction to Functional Grammar* (IFG) (Halliday 1985b, 1994; Halliday & Matthiessen 2004, 2014). When Halliday (e.g. 1961, 1966b) began to develop his theories in the early 1960s, linguistics was preoccupied with the Chomskyan theories of language. Although coming from the same generation as Chomsky, Halliday already had his questions on language clearly framed before Chomsky came on the scene, and he never attempted to answer Chomsky's questions about language rising from Western philosophy and epistemology. Despite encountering various obstacles in his early years, Halliday succeeded in developing his theory and realizing his vision of appliable linguistics (Matthiessen, Wang, & Ma 2019b). Matthiessen has summarized some contributions of Michael Halliday and his theory as follows (see Matthiessen et al. forthcoming; cf. Matthiessen 2007):

(i) As a generalist (still possible for scholars of his generation), contributing to different areas of linguistics and developing a holistic theory of language in context (ranging from phonology to semantics) – SFL as a kind of appliable linguistics;

(ii) Describing Chinese and English in particular;

(iii) Contributing to different areas of linguistic studies, such as child language development, educational linguistics, translation studies, and ecolinguistics.

Both the 'Sydney model' and the 'Cardiff model' share the same historical roots and are based on the basic concepts of language proposed by Halliday. The 'Sydney model' is especially known for the works on educational linguistics (e.g. Martin 1984; Rose & Martin 2012), appraisal framework (e.g. Martin & White 2005), positive/critical discourse analysis (e.g. Martin 2004), and the stratified model of context (e.g. Martin 1998). The 'Cardiff model' or 'Cardiff Grammar' (see Fawcett 2008) is a cognitive-interactive version of systemic functional grammar that enables a researcher to analyse texts in terms of functional syntax, words, intonation, and meanings.

The three models of SFL, like three 'dialects' or 'registers' (cf. Hasan et al. 2007), share similarities, and are all aimed at a scientific description or model of language in context. In terms of their application to translation, we find that most researches in SFTS are based on the 'Hallidayan model'. There are various applications of the appraisal framework and the notion of re-instantiation from the Sydney model to translation, but few applications of 'Cardiff Grammar'.

As a result of the divergence of schools in SFL, researchers may be perplexed by the differences between the models. For instance, Martin's (e.g. 1992) stratified model of context is different from Halliday's (e.g. 1992a) model of stratification (see Section 2.2). The difference is that ideology, genre, and register in Martin's model are all regarded as contextual planes, which are related to each other in terms of realization. Register, which is located in the semantics stratum in the 'Hallidayan model', has been moved to context in the 'Sydney model' (see Figure 6.3).

The two models may confuse researchers who are not fully aware of the differences mentioned above. For instance, while introducing the Hallidayan stratificational model

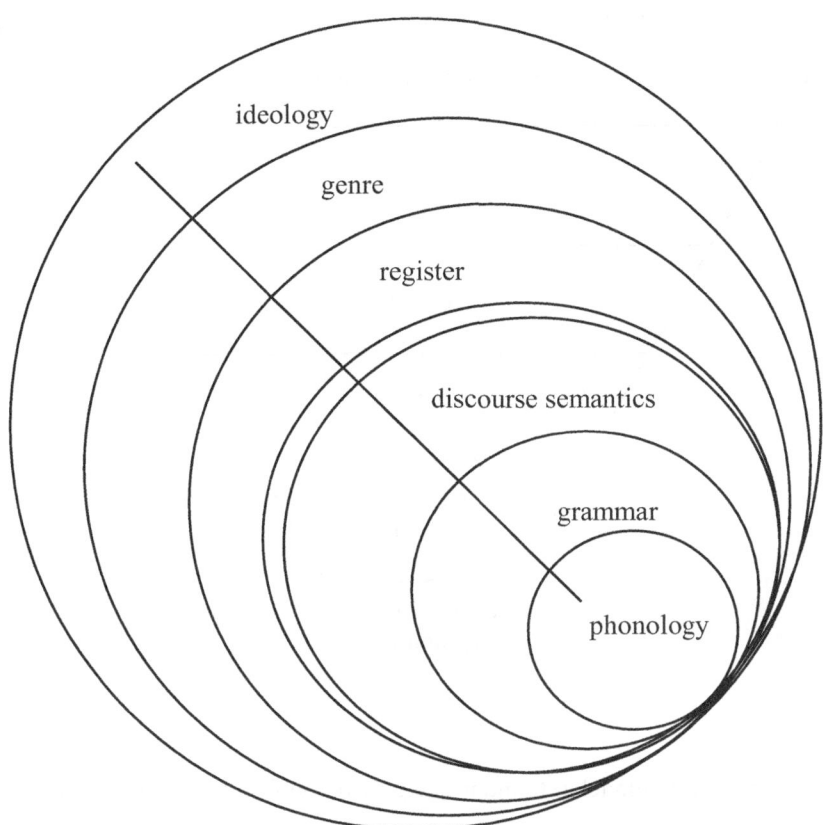

Figure 6.3 Martin's stratified model of context (adapted from Martin 1992: 496)

of language, Munday (2001, 2016) combines the 'Hallidayan model' with 'Martin's model'. As shown in Figure 6.4, 'semantics' in the 'Hallidayan model' is labelled as 'discourse semantics', while 'register and genre' are presented as stratified levels of context. It can also be noted that Munday has added two extra levels of context, namely 'discourse' and 'sociocultural environment', which can be considered as 'ideology' in Martin's model.

Instead of relating the strata by way of realization, Munday (e.g. 2016) holds that the strata influence one and another by following a top-down order. The 'sociocultural environment' is at the highest level, which conditions the 'genre' stratum. 'Genre' then determines the 'register' stratum, which is linked to field, tenor, mode, and the three metafunctions. The 'register' stratum is further linked to 'discourse semantics', which in turn influences the lexicogrammatical choices in the target text. Munday's (e.g. 2016) model helps researchers and students in the field of translation studies to become acquainted with Halliday's model. However, the relationship of determination between the strata are very different from realization in stratification, and is in fact no longer Hallidayan. Moreover, it would also be useful if other dimensions are introduced alongside stratification, such as instantiation, rank, and axis, also with an emphasis on the paradigmatic axis over the syntagmatic one.

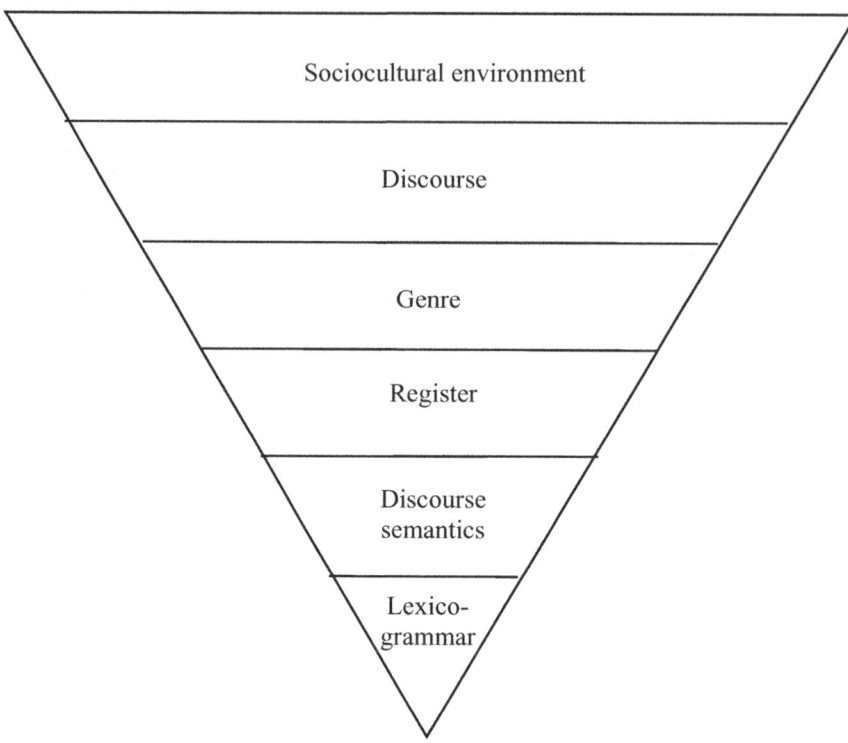

Figure 6.4 The 'Hallidayan' model in Munday's (e.g. 2016) book (adapted from Munday 2016: 143)

6.2 Some Possibilities for Future Research

In this book, we conduct a survey on SFTS to ascertain how systemic functional linguistics, as a linguistic theory, theorizes and models translation. Even though the survey is not exhaustive, we hope it is instructive. It is not the first of its kind (see e.g. Newmark 1987, 1991; Taylor 1993; Steiner 2005, 2015b, 2019; Kunz & Teich 2017 for previous overviews of SFTS), but it is one of the first book-length introductions to this emerging research area. In this final section, we suggest some possibilities for future research and propose some ways of advancing the field.

6.2.1 Development of Multilingual Studies

According to Matthiessen, Teruya, and Wu (2008), multilingual studies is a new field of investigation and application that connects the different areas, including *language typology, language description, translation* (including *interpreting*), *translator education, translation studies, foreign/second language teaching, multilingual lexicography* (including *multilingual term banks for translation*), and *multilingualism*. These areas have been developed over the last half of the 20th century and tend to be drifting apart owing to the institutionalization of the disciplines. However, if we relate them with each other, we will find their connections; for example, translation can draw insights from works on language comparison and typology and vice versa. Also, some areas already have a history of being integrated; for instance, *translation* used to be a method of *language teaching* before it went out of fashion.

The different areas within multilingual studies can be related along the cline of instantiation and the hierarchy of stratification (see Figure 6.5 and Table 6.1). Figure 6.5 visualizes the relationship between the different areas and the number of languages involved along the cline of instantiation. At the instance pole of the cline, we can observe multilinguality instantiated in texts unfolding in contexts. *Translation studies* is located here, dealing with the production of text first in one language and then in another. 'Code switching' and 'code mixing' can also be found here, because the meaning potential of languages is instantiated in the same text. Also, translators and interpreters' re-instantiation of 'a text in one language as a text in another language' is included, which keeps 'the meaning potentials of these two languages distinct in textual instantiation' (Matthiessen, Teruya, & Wu 2008: 149; cf. Matthiessen 2018). At the potential pole of the cline, we find areas of *comparative linguistics*, *contrastive linguistics*, and *language*

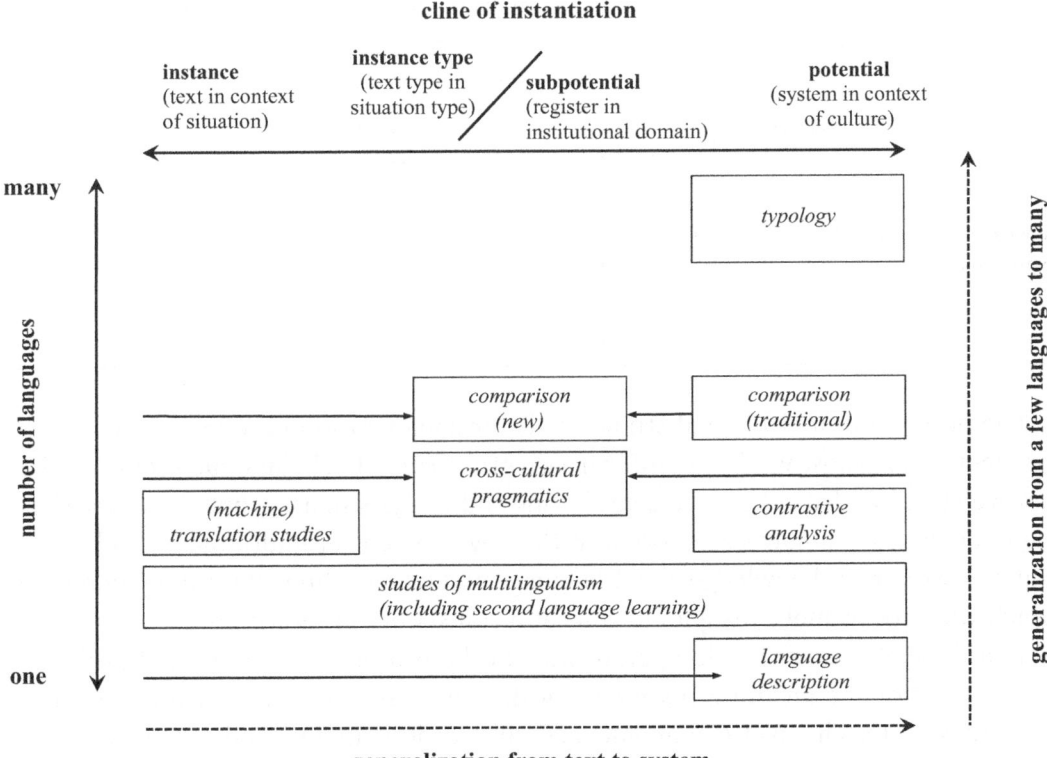

Figure 6.5 Phenomenal realm explored in multilingual studies differentiated in terms of the number of languages in focus and in terms of the cline of instantiation (adapted from Matthiessen, Teruya, & Wu 2008: 149)

typology. In the intermediate regions of the cline, there is *cross-cultural pragmatics*, which is related to the different registers in data selection.

In Table 6.1, another dimension – the hierarchy of stratification – is added. *Translation studies* is located at the stratum of semantics, as it is concerned with the different aspects of meaning. *Comparative linguistics* and *language typology* tend not to explore the strata above lexicogrammar given their emphasis on the strata below semantics. They are thus located on the strata of lexicogrammar, phonology, and phonetics.

Table 6.1 Areas of multilingual studies in relation to the cline of instantiation and the hierarchy of stratification (adapted from Matthiessen, Teruya, & Wu 2008: 154)

		Potential (system)	Sub-potential/instance type	Instance (text in context of situation)
Context				• translation studies (target-oriented)
Language: content	semantics		• contrastive rhetoric with a register-focus; • cross-cultural pragmatics [speech functions and ...	• translation studies (typical)
	lexicogrammar	• typology, comparison	... their grammatical realizations in different languages]	
Language: expression	phonology	• typology, comparison		
	phonetics	• typology, comparison		

The proposal of multilingual studies calls for collaboration between scholars from different areas, whose works can inform each other. For SFL scholars, such collaboration can even be extended not only to data sharing and analysis sharing, but also to the sharing of analytical frameworks. Moreover, the development of multilingual studies will equip us with more knowledge about language and its multilingual meaning potential, which will give us more insights into what a translator, an interpreter, or a bilingual or multilingual speaker would operate with in the process of translation. Developing descriptions of the meaning potentials of different languages will also be useful in explaining various linguistic phenomena, such as code switching and code mixing (e.g. Marasigan 1983; Muysken 2000).

Further, within the broad area of multilingual studies, Matthiessen (2001) regards detailed descriptions of the patterns that logogenetic acts create as one of the most pressing tasks for SFTS. Translation, in the first instance, is a logogenetic act – 'an act in the creation of meaning that takes place as a text unfolds' (p. 115). It is also a process located at the semantic stratum and the instance pole of the cline of instantiation. In SFTS, the clause (complex) is regarded as the 'unit of translation'. Hence, detailed lexicogrammatical analysis of both source texts and target texts will provide us with a lot of information about translation.

The lexicogrammatical analysis can be carried out along all six environments of translation (see Chapter 2). For instance, it can be approached from above in the environment of stratification, such as from the vantage point of context by taking different fields of activity or registers into consideration (see Section 4.2). In doing so, we can build up a text archive and categorize texts according to the eight primary fields of activity (cf. Taylor 1998). This not only enables us to use register to decode the challenges translators meet, but also gives translators a clearer sense of the meaning at risk in the source language and the target language while translating texts in different registers. In translation practice or translator training, this will help translators to build up their multilingual meaning potential, to know about the challenges of translating texts in different registers, and to strengthen their mastery of the foreign language and the mother tongue.

The lexicogrammatical analysis can involve more language pairs. Given that there are thousands of languages spoken in the world today (cf. Lewis, Simons, & Fennig 2015), there will naturally be a large number of language pairs, many of which have not yet been studied. For some language pairs, the differences between the two languages may be tremendously large with respect to various parameters. However, they can still be compared, as long as they both have lexicogrammatical systems, even though the contextual distance between them are likely to be large, as they operate within different contexts of culture.

We can compare texts in languages that are typologically distant with respect to the lexicogrammatical systems. When discussing translation between languages as such, Pawley (1987: 331) draws on Grace's (1981, 1981–1983) anthropological works and makes the following observation:

> If languages have markedly different resources for the characterization of situations, i.e. if their grammars require them to report the same bits of observed reality in very different ways, it may be that translation between such reports is impossible – at least, accurate translation. Grace concludes that what he calls 'isomorphic' or 'quasi-isomorphic' translation is rarely possible between languages that are genetically unrelated or associated with radically different cultures. In an isomorphic translation the source text and its translation specify the same conceptual situation ... Usually, the best one can hope to achieve is that kind of matching which Grace refers to as 'paraphrastic' translation – in which the speaker's communicative intent is more or less accurately captured. What is being translated in such cases is not the linguistic meaning or the conceptual situation specified by the source text; rather, it is the translator's reconstruction of the speaker's pragmatic meaning or communicative purpose.

Pawley (1987) takes English and Kalam as two tremendously different languages. From a systemic functional point of view, 'the most fundamental difference between the two languages seems to be in the division of labour between the two ideational modes of construal – the logical and the experiential' (Matthiessen 2001: 67; see Halliday & Matthiessen 1999: 317–318 for more discussions). Therefore, when construing the flow of goings-on, English relies more on the experiential mode by using one single clause, while Kalam relies more on the logical mode by combining clause simplexes into clause complexes. As shown in Example 6.1, the clause complex in the Kalam ST consists of four clause simplexes, representing a sequence of events. We find four processes realized by four verbal groups, including 'd', 'yokek', 'amb', and 'yowp', showing how Kalam draws on the logical metafunction to link the four clause simplexes into one clause complex. In the English TT, only one process is used, i.e. 'threw', while the logical mode of meaning functions to construe a prepositional phrase complex – 'over the fence into the garden', which is a circumstance of Location.

Example 6.1 (adapted from Matthiessen 2001: 68; cf. Pawley 1987: 354)

Kalam ST: B monday **d yokek** waty at **amb** wogmgan **yowp**
IG: man stick **hold he-displaced-different subject** fence above **it-went** garden-inside **it-fell**
BT: The man took hold of the stick, he threw it, it flies over the fence, it fell into the garden.
English TT: The man **threw** a stick over the fence into the garden.

At the same time, as suggested by Matthiessen (2001: 116), we should be aware that our analysis needs to 'operate at a high degree of semiotic abstraction to handle translation differences'. Thus, we need to operate at the stratum of semantics and point out the semantic motifs being constantly treated across different languages. Martin's (1983) attempt at tracking discourse referents provides one example of this kind. These motifs are likely to be found in the mid-region along the cline of instantiation as strategies for specific registers.

6.2.2 Arguments on the Existence or Non-existence of Translation Universals

Translation universals are also referred to as universal tendencies of the translation process, laws of translation, or norms of translation. Previous studies have identified various so-called universals, including explicitation, simplification, levelling out, conventionalization, disambiguation, avoidance of repetition, standardization, over-or-under-representation of source or target language elements, and the general manifestation of a 'third code' (e.g. Blum-Kulka 1986; Baker 1993; Laviosa-Braithwaite 1998; Mauranen & Kujamäki 2004; Mauranen 2008).

According to House (2008: 10), during the search of translation universals, scholars like Toury (2004) 'have largely relied on case studies and impressionistic qualitative work, involving informed intuition and richly contextualised pen and paper analysis'. Conversely, scholars like Baker (1993) have 'relied on, and copiously praised the methodological advantages of, corpus-based qualitative and quantitative work' (ibid.). Further, House (2008) points out the futility of looking for translation universals, suggesting five reasons to refute the claims of the existence of translation universals. Empirical case studies in SFTS can substantiate these reasons.

Firstly, House (2008) confirms that linguistic theories can help find universals of language. Since translation is primarily a linguistic act, these universals can certainly be applied to translation. In our studies such as Wang (2017) and Wang and Ma (2020), we adopt SFL as the theoretical basis, and discover some typological features that operate both in Chinese and English, which can be universals, such as similarities in the basic choices in the systems of THEME, MOOD, MODALITY, TAXIS, and LOGICO-SEMANTIC TYPE. More linguistic analyses between the two languages are likely to reveal more shared features, which are capable of being applied to translation practice. However, whether these features are universals or not can be established by conducting researches on a larger number of languages. Even if they are universals of language, they are not universals of translation per se, but rather universals of language being applied to translation.

Secondly, House (2008) locates the acts of translation at the instance end of the cline of instantiation, i.e. as acts of performance or parole, and emphasizes that translation is dependent on the language pairs involved. The translation universals found in some language pairs may not work in others. Therefore, claims like 'explicitation' should be made based on ample linguistic evidence (e.g. Hansen-Schirra, Neumann, & Steiner 2012). In Ma's (2018) study on poetry translation, she finds that not all translation shifts make the target texts more explicit, such as omissions of different Theme choices, omissions of various process types, and omissions of lexical realizations of processes such as '像' (PY: xiàng; IG: be like) and '如' (PY: rú; IG: be like) in the TTs. Moreover, even additions will not necessarily related to explicitness. For instance, Ma (2018) also finds that additions of conjunctions as textual Themes are due to typological differences rather than the existence of translation universals.

Thirdly, House (2008) draws our attention to the notion of directionality in translation, which is closely related to the issue of language-pair specificity. For instance, some procedures of explicitation found in translations from Chinese to English will not work in the opposite direction. In Wang's (2017) analysis, he finds that, in translating the dramatic monologue back from English to Chinese, many conjunctions that function as textual Themes in English have to be left out and translated implicitly in the Chinese translation (see also Wang & Ma 2018). On the one hand, the use of fewer conjunctions in Chinese is consistent with findings in various studies on language description and typology (e.g. Chao 1968; Li & Thompson 1981). On the other hand, more conjunctions are found in English, and this is not surprising because the Chinese data are written to be spoken, and conjunctions will thus be redundant.

Fourthly, House (2008) takes the universals in translation as genre-specific. In some texts tendencies of certain universals will be found, while in others the case will be different. In our study of a Chinese drama titled *Teahouse* and its English translations (e.g. Wang 2017; Wang & Ma 2018, 2019, 2020), we have analysed three kinds of text, i.e. dramatic dialogue, dramatic monologue, and stage direction. Shifts of mood type are frequently found in dramatic dialogue, involving various examples of mood substitution. However, in the data of dramatic monologue and stage direction, the mood choices remain equivalent in general. Most of the clauses are declaratives and are often translated equivalently.

Fifthly, the diachronic development of texts that belong to a certain genre is also taken into consideration: translations develop dynamically and 'may be critically influenced by the status of the language of the source text genre which in turn may influence the nature of the translation text genre and also the nature of comparable texts in the same genre' (House 2008: 12). Evidence is found in Ma's (2018) analysis of the four different Chinese translations of Rabindranath Tagore's *Stray Birds* in English. The four translations are in the form of either modern poetry or classical Chinese poetry. The translation in the style of classical poetry is heavily influenced by the nature of its genre. Its style is unique in the use of circumstances as marked topical Themes, which is a writing skill in ancient Chinese poems used to foreground the situation of the poems, and is not found in the translations in the form of modern poetry.

Thus, we should be sceptical about the existence of translation universals. Instead of discussing translation universals, we should be aware that many language pairs have not yet been examined. In studies by Grace (e.g. 1981, 1981–1983) and Pawley (1987), we find that the languages often studied in translation are, in fact, not really that far apart. On the one hand, if we take English and Chinese on a global scale, we find that they are not so different, both having very long histories of written and standard languages, and both being adapted to the registers of the modern nation state. On the other hand, there are still languages that operate under very different cultural conditions, such as English and Kalam, that need to be studied systematically. We hope that studies on translation universals can be carried out by adopting an empirical and typological approach with the help of technological possibilities of corpus methodology. Also, the notion of multilingual studies (Matthiessen, Teruya, & Wu 2008; see Section 6.2.1), which connects the different strands of researches engaging with multilingual phenomena, is capable of providing further input to researches on translation universals.

6.2.3 Development of Technology-based Approaches

As previously discussed, the development of technology has enhanced research in SFTS. Future studies can benefit from further technological advancement. In Section 5.3, we have reported on studies that adopt methods used in translation process research, such as keystroke logging and eye tracking. We have also highlighted the integration of product-based and process-based approaches headed by Fabio Alves's group from Brazil and Erich Steiner's group from Germany. Funded by the Brazilian and the German academic exchange service, the project lasted for five years. Such investigations of integrating process-based and product-based studies are still going on. In Brazil, the group around **Fabio Alves** and **Adriana Pagano** is very active in pursuing this line of research (e.g. Alves, Pagano, & da Silva 2011; Pagano, da Silva, & Alves 2013). In Germany, **Stella Neumann** and **Silvia Hansen-Schirra** have also produced a whole range of works combining process-based and product-based studies of translated texts (e.g. Heilmann et al. 2019 for investigation on the length of the source text as well as its effect on translation process and translation product). Various titles in the book series of 'Translation and Multilingual Natural Language Processing' have been published by Language Science Press (e.g. Hansen-Schirra & Grucza 2016; Czulo & Hansen-Schirra 2017; Hansen-Schirra, Czulo, & Hofmann 2017; Hansen-Schirra, Neumann, & Čulo 2017; Menzel, Lapshinova-Koltunski, & Kunz 2017). On the one hand, these research methods have encouraged data triangulation and innovation in research by bridging the gaps between different disciplines, such as applied linguistics, translation studies, computational linguistics, and cognitive science. On the other hand, by using ideas from SFL as a modelling background, these studies have presented new areas in SFTS, and have inspired scholars in SFTS to look at translation process or what translators actually do when they translate. These works push the boundaries of SFL as a theoretical framework, ensuring SFL to suit the needs of being applied in translation process research.

In addition, the development of corpus tools will help researchers in SFTS. One example is **SysConc**, a concordance programme developed by **Wu Canzhong** (2000, 2009). Like other concordance programmes, it 'allows us to search for lexical items, collocational patterns and so on' (Wu 2009: 137). However, it also differs from other concordance programmes from theoretical and implementational perspectives. Wu (2009: 137) has summarized the differences as follows:

> Theoretically, SysConc is geared towards systemic functional research, and is an integral part of the SysAm system; for instance, concordance analysis can be carried out according to the systemic types or some other hierarchical features, and the valid results can be fed into SysFan for manual analysis. Implementationally, SysConc, like other components of SysAm, was developed in Java, a powerful programming language built to be cross-platform and international. This can not only maintain SysConc's integrity, but also integrate SysConc with the other components of SysAm as well as other applications. In addition, the capabilities in Java such as networking and database access would certainly open new grounds for SysConc; for example, SysConc can be used to search the vast amount of information available on the web, or the annotated or analysed databases, to just name a few.

We find various studies in SFTS that analyse texts by using SysFan or SysConc, leading to findings in different aspects, such as theme, mood, and process type (Wu & Fang

2006), cohesion and coherence (Li & Wu 2017), mood and modality (Yu & Wu 2016), personal pronoun (Yu & Wu 2017a), as well as grammatical intricacy and lexical density (Yu & Wu 2017b).

6.3 Epilogue

One of the questions that remains unanswered so far is whether there is a future for theoretically grounded approaches in SFTS to be applied to different domains. To answer this question, we are not going to make predictions but would rather highlight some advantages of SFL – the theoretical basis of SFTS.

At the beginning of this book (see Section 1.1), we emphasize that translation is in the first instance a linguistic phenomenon. Meanwhile, translation is complicated and involves different ordered typology of systems operating within different phenomenon realms. With SFL, it becomes possible to theorize translation as a linguistic phenomenon and to locate translation within an ordered typology of systems (see Table 6.2). Therefore, translation, like other linguistic phenomena, is semiotic primarily, enacted socially, embodied biologically, and ultimately manifested physically. It is also for this reason that translation studies has been approached from different vantage points

Table 6.2 Properties and organizational features of the four orders of system (adapted from Matthiessen 2021: 521)

	Systemic order		Properties	Translation	Translator
immaterial	4th order: semiotic	+meaning	stratified systems: content — expression	translation as recreation of meaning in context — *text (discourse) analysis, descriptions of multilingual meaning potentials*	translator as multilingual meaner — *think aloud protocols (a kind of meta-discourse about translation choices)*
	3rd order: social	+value	role networked systems	translation as social behaviour — (professional) service — *questionnaires, ethnographic interviews, focus groups*	translator as professional person — *questionnaires, ethnographic interviews, focus groups*
material	2nd order: biological	+life	individuation, self-replication, evolution, natural selection	translation as neural activity (in the first instance) related to sensory and motor systems	translator as biological organism — *eye tracking, keystroke logging, brain scanning*
	1st order: physical		subject to 'laws of nature', extended in space-time	translation in (physical) workspace	translator in habitat — affordances of workspace

and examined from various perspectives, eventually leading to the emergence of various 'turns' in translation studies and the institutionalization of translation studies (Matthiessen 2021). In SFL, the study of translation is treated as a component of multilingual studies not separated from the related disciplines or research areas (see Section 6.2.1), so that translation can be constantly in dialogue with its neighbouring areas like language typology, language comparison, second language learning, and machine translation (see Matthiessen, Teruya, & Wu 2008).

SFTS is empowered by SFL, which is a unique linguistic theory that is capable of providing resources for developing a well-rounded understanding of and engagement with translation. The fact that SFL is a holistic theory of language makes it possible for us to relate SFL to eye tracking, keystroke logging, social network analysis, text analysis (discourse analysis), and analysis of context of culture, thus revealing the complementarity between them.

The uniqueness of SFL is also seen in its organization of language in context in terms of a number of semiotic dimensions, which are all unique type of relations. The overall organization of language is determined by the global semiotic dimensions, which include the hierarchy of stratification, the cline of instantiation, and the spectrum of metafunction. These three global dimensions are in turn organized in terms of the local semiotic dimensions, including axis and rank scale. In Chapter 2, we have defined these dimensions as the environments of translation and formulate the principle of the environments as follows: 'the wider the environment of translation, the higher the degree of translation equivalence' (see Matthiessen 2001: 74–75; see also Matthiessen 2021). In all, these aspects of the holistic systemic functional theory of language in contexts are all relevant to the engagement of translation studies.

Notes

Chapter 1

1   This assumes that the languages involved have to be systematically and adequately described and compared.

Chapter 2

1   Following Firth (e.g. 1951), a text has meanings in all strata of language. Meaning is thus not restricted to the stratum of semantics.
2   The complete poem can be found at https://www.dasungemach.de/texte/der-werwolf/.
3   See https://www.un.org/en/universal-declaration-human-rights.

Chapter 3

1   The term 'mode' in 'mode of meaning', though confusable with the contextual parameter of 'mode', here refers to the 'different kinds of meaning associated with different metafunctions' (Matthiessen, Teruya, & Lam 2010: 164). The term 'mode of meaning' is also seen in Matthiessen's (2001, 2014b, 2021) various works that conceptualize translation as recreation of meaning in context.
2   There are also suggestions for taking analysis of all meanings into consideration, such as House's (e.g. 2015) model of translation quality assessment.
3   Figure refers to the configuration of elements, i.e. a process, the participants involved in the process, and the circumstances. Figure is located in semantics and is realized by clause in lexicogrammar.

Chapter 5

1   Before Google launched its own technology to machine translation in 2006, Google Translate used SYSTRAN – a hybrid rule-based technology (see also https://en.wikipedia.org/wiki/Google_Translate#Method_of_translation).

Chapter 6

1   Of course there will sometimes be challenges and oppositions to SFTS, especially from scholars in other fields of research. Some criticism can even be based on bias or ignorance. For instance, Wang Dongfeng from Sun Yat-sen University criticized SFL as a theory not suitable

to study literary translation, simply because in his view SFL does not have a 'poetic function'. Obviously he did not understand the differences between 'metafunction' and 'language use' (cf. Table 1.1). On the same occasion, he also refused to admit that SFL is a holistic theory of language in context by saying that SFL is only capable of studying grammar, thus denying the other strata along the hierarchy of stratification (cf. Section 2.2).

Bibliography

Alves, Fabio (ed.). 2003. *Triangulating translation: Perspectives in process oriented research*. Amsterdam & Philadelphia: John Benjamins.

Alves, Fabio & Daniel Vale. 2009. 'Probing the unit of translation in time: Aspects of the design and development of a web application for storing, annotating, and querying translation process data.' *Across Languages and Cultures* 10(2): 251–273.

Alves, Fabio, Adriana Pagano, & Igor L. da Silva. 2011. 'Modelling (un)packing of meaning in translation: Insights from effortful text production.' *Copenhagen Studies in Language* 41: 153–164.

Alves, Fabio, Adriana Pagano, Stella Neumann, Erich Steiner, & Silvia Hansen-Schirra. 2010. 'Units of translation and grammatical shifts: Towards an integration of product- and process-based research in translation.' In Gregory Shreve & Erik Angelone (eds.), *Translation and cognition*. Amsterdam & Philadelphia: John Benjamins. 109–142.

Alves, Fabio, Karina Sarto Szpak, José Luiz Conçalves, Kyoto Sekino, Marceli Aquino, Rodrigo Araújo e Castro, Arlene Koglin, Norma B. de Lima Fonseca, & Bartolomé Mesa-Lao. 2016. 'Investigating cognitive effort in post-editing: A relevance-theoretical approach.' In Silvia Hansen-Schirra & Sambor Grucza (eds.), *Eyetracking and applied linguistics*. Berlin: Language Science Press. 109–142.

Austin, J.L. 1962. *How to do things with words*. Oxford: Clarendon Press.

Baines, Roger. 2015. 'Subtitling taboo language: Using the cues of register and genre to affect audience experience?' *Meta* 60(3): 431–453.

Baker, Mona. 1992. *In other words: A coursebook on translation*. London & New York: Routledge.

Baker, Mona. 1993. 'Corpus linguistics and translation studies: Implications and applications.' In Mona Baker, Gill Francis, & Elena Tognini-Bonelli (eds.), *Text and technology: In honour of John Sinclair*. Amsterdam & Philadelphia: John Benjamins. 233–250.

Baker, Mona. 1995. 'Corpora in translation studies: An overview and some suggestions for future research.' *Target* 7(2): 223–243.

Baker, Mona. 1996. 'Corpus-based translation studies: The challenges that lie ahead.' In Harold Somers (ed.), *Terminology, LSP and translation: Studies in language engineering in honour of Juan C. Sager*. Amsterdam & Philadelphia: John Benjamins. 175–186.

Baker, Mona. 2001. 'Towards a methodology for investigating the style of a literary translator.' *Target* 12(2): 241–266.

Baker, Mona. 2018. *In other words: A coursebook on translation*. 3rd edition. Abingdon & New York: Routledge.

Bartlett, Tom & Gerard O'Grady (eds.). 2017. *The Routledge handbook of systemic functional linguistics*. Abingdon & New York: Routledge.

Bassnett, Susan & André Lefevere (eds.). 1990. *Translation, history and culture*. London: Pinter.

Bateman, John A. 2008. *Multimodality and genre: A foundation for the systematic analysis of multimodal documents.* London & New York: Palgrave Macmillan.

Bateman, John & Mick O'Donnell. 2015. 'Computational linguistics: The Halliday connection.' In Jonathan J. Webster (ed.), *The Bloomsbury companion to M.A.K. Halliday*. London & New York: Bloomsbury. 453–466.

Bateman, John A., Robert Kasper, Johanna D. Moore, & Richard A. Whitney. 1990. *A general organization of knowledge for natural language processing: The Penman Upper Model.* Information Sciences Institute, University of Southern California.

Becher, Viktor. 2010. 'Abandoning the notion of "translation-inherent" explicitation: Against a dogma in translation studies.' *Across Languages and Cultures* 11: 1–28.

Becher, Viktor. 2011. *Explicitation and implicitation in translation: A corpus-based study of English-German and German-English translations of business texts.* PhD thesis, University of Hamburg, Hamburg, Germany.

Becher, Viktor, Juliane House, & Svenja Kranich. 2009. 'Convergence and divergence of communicative norms through language contact in translation.' In Kurt Braunmüller & Juliane House (eds.), *Convergence and divergence in language contact situations*. Amsterdam: John Benjamins. 125–152.

Bell, Roger. 1991. *Translation and translating: Theory and practice.* London & New York: Longman.

Bernstein, Basil. 1971. *Class, codes, and control (volume 1): Theoretical studies towards a sociology of language.* London: Routledge and Kegan Paul.

Bernstein, Basil (ed.) 1973. *Class, codes, and control (volume 2): Applied studies towards a sociology of language.* London: Routledge and Kegan Paul.

Biber, Douglas & Edward Finegan. 1989. 'Styles of stance in English: Lexical and grammatical marking of evidentiality and affect.' *Text* 9(1): 93–124.

Black, Thomas R. 1999. *Doing quantitative research in the social sciences: An integrated approach to research design, measurement and statistics.* London: Sage.

Blum-Kulka, Shoshana. 1986. 'Shifts of cohesion and coherence in translation.' In Juliane House & Shoshana Blum-Kulka (eds.), *Interlingual and intercultural communiation: Discourse and cognition in translation and second language acquisition*. Tübingen: Gunter Narr. 17–35.

Bourdieu, Pierre. 1984. *Distinction: A social critique of the judgement of taste* (Richard Nice, trans.). London: Routledge.

Bresnan, Joan, Ash Asudeh, Ida Toivonen, & Stephen Wechsler. 2016. *Lexical-functional syntax.* Chichester, West Sussex: Willey-Blackwell.

Bühler, Karl. 1933. 'Die Axiomatik der Sprachwissenschaft.' *Kant-Studien* 38(1–2): 19–20.

Bühler, Karl. 1934. *Sprachtheorie: Die Darstellungsfunktion der Sprache.* Stuttgart: Gustav Fischer.

Carl, Michael, Srinivas Bangalore, & Moritz Schaefer (eds.). 2015. *New directions in translation process research.* Berlin & New York: Springer.

Catford, J.C. 1965. *A linguistic theory of translation.* London: Oxford University Press.

Chang, Chenguang. 2018. 'Modelling translation as re-instantiation.' *Perspectives: Studies in Translation Theory and Practice* 26(2): 166–179.

Chao, Yuen Ren. 1948. *Mandarin primer.* Cambridge: Harvard University Press.

Chao, Yuen Ren. 1968. *A grammar of spoken Chinese.* Berkeley, Los Angeles, & London: University of California Press.

Chen, Ya-Mei. 2011. 'The translator's subjectivity and its constraints in news transediting: A perspective of reception aesthetics.' *Meta* 56(1): 119–144.

Cheng, Xiaotang [程晓棠] & Liang Shuwen [梁淑雯]. 2008. '及物性理论对英汉翻译中转译的启示' [Implications of the transitivity theory on transformation in translation]. *外语与外语教学* [Foreign Languages and Their Teaching] 12: 42–45.

Choi, Gyung Hee. 2013. 'Translating genre of news stories and the correlated grammar in student translation errors.' *Meta* 58(2): 373–396.

Contreras, Heles. 1976. *A theory of word order with special reference to Spanish*. Amsterdam, Oxford, & New York: North-Holland Publishing.

Cook, Guy. 2010. *Translation in language teaching*. Oxford: Oxford University Press.

Czulo, Oliver & Silvia Hansen-Schirra (eds.). 2017. *Crossroads between contrastive linguistics, translation studies and machine translation*. Berlin: Language Science Press.

Daneš, František. 1974. 'Functional sentence perspective and the organization of the text'. In František Daneš (ed.), *Papers on functional sentence perspective*. The Hague: Mouton. 106–128.

de Beaugrande, Robert. 1993. '"Register" in discourse studies: A concept in search of a theory.' In Mohsen Ghadessy (ed.), *Register analysis: Theory and practice*. London: Pinter. 7–25.

da Cunha, Iria & Mikel Iruskieta. 2010. 'Comparing rhetorical structures in different languages: The influence of translation strategies.' *Discourse Studies* 12(5): 563–598.

de Souza, Ladjane Maria Farias. 2010. *Interlingual re-instantiation: A model for a new and more comprehensive systemic functional perspective on translation*. PhD thesis, Universidade Federal de Santa Catarina, Florianópolis, Brazil.

de Souza, Ladjane Maria Farias. 2013. 'Interlingual re-instantiation – a new systemic functional perspective on translation.' *Text & Talk* 33(4–5): 575–594.

Dik, Simon C. 1997a. *The theory of functional grammar: Part 1, structure of the clause*. Kees Hengeveld (ed.). Berlin: Mouton de Gruyter.

Dik, Simon C. 1997b. *The theory of functional grammar: Part 2, complex and derived constructions*. Kees Hengeveld (ed.). Berlin: Mouton de Gruyter.

Dorr, Bonnie J. 1994. 'Machine translation divergences: A formal description and proposed solution.' *Computational Linguistics* 20(4): 597–633.

Durand, Jacques, Paul Bennett, Valerio Allegranza, Frank van Eynde, Lee Humphreys, Paul Schmidt, & Erich Steiner. 1991. 'The Eurotra linguistic specifications: An overview.' *Machine Translation* 6: 103–147.

Ellis, Jeffrey O. 1966. *Towards a general comparative linguistics*. The Hague: Mouton.

Ericsson, K. Anders & Herbert Simon. 1984. *Protocol analysis: Verbal reports as data*. Cambridge, MA: MIT Press.

Espindola, Elaine. 2010. *Illuminated the analysis of the translation is: Systemic functional linguistics strikes Yoda back*. PhD thesis, Universidade Federal de Santa Catarina, Florianópolis, Brazil.

Espindola, Elaine. 2016. 'A systemic functional analysis of thematic structure: Directing attention to Yoda's linguistic manifestation.' *Word* 62(1): 22–34.

Espindola, Elaine & Yan Wang. 2015. 'The enactment of modality in regulatory texts: A comparative study of tenancy agreements.' *Journal of World Languages* 2(2–3): 106–125.

Even-Zohar, Itamar. 1979. 'Polysystem theory.' *Poetics Today* 1(1–2): 287–310.

Fairclough, Norman. 1995a. *Critical discourse analysis*. London: Routledge.

Fairclough, Norman. 1995b. *Media discourse*. London: Edward Arnold.

Fang, Jing & Canzhong Wu. 2009. 'Exploring shifts in translating English nominal groups modified by embedded clauses: A corpus-based approach.' Paper presented at 2009 ASFLA Conference. Queensland, Brisbane. 1–20.

Fang, Li [方立], Hu Zhuanglin [胡壮麟], & Xu Kerong [徐克容]. 1977. '谈谈现代英语语法的三大体系和交流语法学' [On the three systems in modern English grammar and communicative grammar]. 语言教学与研究 [Language Teaching and Research] 6: 1–28.

Fawcett, Robin. 2008. *Invitation to systemic functional linguistics through the Cardiff grammar: An extension and simplification of Halliday's systemic functional grammar.* London: Equinox.

Firbas, Jan. 1992. *Functional sentence perspective in written and spoken communication.* Cambridge: Cambridge University Press.

Firth, J.R. 1950. 'Personality and language in society.' *The Sociological Review* 42(2): 37–52. Reprinted in J.R. Firth. 1957. *Papers in linguistics 1934-1951.* Glasgow & New York: Oxford University Press. 177–189.

Firth, J.R. 1951. 'Modes of meaning.' In *Essays and studies.* London: The English Association. 177–189. Reprinted in J.R. Firth. 1957. *Papers in linguistics 1934-1951.* Glasgow & New York: Oxford University Press. 190–216.

Firth, J.R. 1957a. *Papers in linguistics 1934-1951.* London: Oxford University Press.

Firth, J.R. 1957b. 'Ethnographic analysis and language with reference to Malinowski's views.' In Raymond William Firth (ed.), *Man and culture: An evaluation of the work of Bronislaw Malinowski.* London: Routledge & Kegan Paul. 93–118. Reprinted in J.R. Firth. 1968. F.R. Palmer (ed.), *Selected papers of J.R. Firth 1952-59.* London & Harlow: Longmans. 137–167.

Firth, J.R. 1968a. 'Linguistic analysis and translation.' In F.R. Palmer (ed.), *Selected papers of J.R. Firth 1952-59.* London & Harlow: Longmans. 74–83.

Firth, J.R. 1968b. 'Linguistics and translation.' In F.R. Palmer (ed.), *Selected papers of J.R. Firth 1952-59.* London & Harlow: Longmans. 84–95.

Firth, J.R. 1968c. 'Linguistic analysis as a study of meaning.' In F.R. Palmer (ed.), *Selected papers of J.R. Firth 1952-59.* London & Harlow: Longmans. 12–26.

Firth, J.R. 1968d. 'Descriptive linguistics and the study of English.' In F.R. Palmer (ed.), *Selected papers of J.R. Firth 1952-59.* London & Harlow: Longmans. 96–113.

Firth, J.R. 1968e. 'A new approach to grammar'. In F.R. Palmer (ed.), *Selected Papers of J.R. Firth 1952-59.* London & Harlow: Longmans. 114–125.

Ghadessy, Mohsen & Gao Yanjie. 2000. 'Thematic organization in parallel texts: Same and different methods of development.' *Text* 20(4): 461–488.

Grace, George W. 1981. *An essay on language.* Columbia: Hornbeam Press.

Grace, George W. 1981-1983. *Ethonolinguistic notes.* Hawaii: Department of Linguistics, University of Hawaii.

Greenberg, J.H. (ed.) 1966. *Universals of language.* 2nd edition. Cambridge, MA: MIT Press.

Gregory, Michael J. 1967. 'Aspects of varieties differentiation.' *Journal of Linguistics* 3: 177–198.

Gregory, Michael. 2001. 'What can linguistics learn from translation?' In Erich Steiner & Colin Yallop (eds.), *Exploring translation and multilingual text production: Beyond content.* Berlin: Mouton de Gruyter. 19–40.

Guo, Jiading [过家鼎]. 2002. '注意外交用词的政治含义' [Political implications should be noted in diplomatic dictions]. 中国翻译 [Chinese Translators Journal] 23(6): 59–60.

Halliday, M.A.K. 1955. *The language of the Chinese secret history of the Mongols*. PhD thesis, Cambridge University, Cambridge, UK.

Halliday, M.A.K. 1956a. 'The linguistic basis of a mechanical thesaurus, and its application to English preposition classification.' *Mechanical Translation* 3: 81-88. Reprinted in M.A.K. Halliday. 2005. Jonathan J. Webster (ed.), *Computational and quantitative studies*. Volume 6 in the *Collected works of M.A.K. Halliday*. London & New York: Continuum. 6-19.

Halliday, M.A.K. 1956b. 'Grammatical categories in Modern Chinese.' *Transactions of the Philological Society* 55(1): 177-224. Reprinted in M.A.K. Halliday. 2005. Jonathan J. Webster (ed.), *Studies in Chinese language*. Volume 8 in the *Collected works of M.A.K. Halliday*. London & New York: Continuum. 209-248.

Halliday, M.A.K. 1957. 'Some aspects of systematic description and comparison in grammatical analysis'. In J.R. Firth (ed.), *Studies in linguistic analysis*. Oxford: Blackwell. 54-67. Reprinted in M.A.K. Halliday. 2002. Jonathan J. Webster (ed.), *On grammar*. Volume 1 in the *Collected works of M.A.K. Halliday*. London & New York: Continuum. 21-36.

Halliday, M.A.K. 1959. *The language of the Chinese secret history of the Mongols*. Oxford: Basil Blackwell. Reprinted in M.A.K. Halliday. 2005. Jonathan J. Webster (ed.), *Studies in Chinese language*. Volume 8 in the *Collected works of M.A.K. Halliday*. London & New York: Continuum. 5-174.

Halliday, M.A.K. 1961. 'Categories of the theory of grammar.' *Word* 17: 241-292. Reprinted in M.A.K. Halliday. 2002. Jonathan J. Webster (ed.), *On grammar*. Volume 1 in the *Collected works of M.A.K. Halliday*. London & New York: Continuum. 37-94.

Halliday, M.A.K. 1962. 'Linguistics and machine translation.' *Zeitschrift für Phonetik, Sprachwissenschaft und Kommunikationsforschung* 15: 145-158. Reprinted in M.A.K. Halliday. 2005. Jonathan J. Webster (ed.), *Computational and quantitative studies*. Volume 6 in the *Collected works of M.A.K. Halliday*. London & New York: Continuum. 20-36.

Halliday, M.A.K. 1964. 'Syntax and the consumer.' In C.I.J.M. Stuart (ed.), *Report of the Fifteenth Annual (First International) Round Table Meeting on Linguistics and Language Study*. Washington, D.C.: Georgetown University Press. 11-24. Reprinted in M.A.K. Halliday & James R. Martin (eds.). 1981. *Readings in systemic linguistics*. London: Batsford. 21-28. Reprinted in M.A.K. Halliday. 2003. Jonathan J. Webster (ed.), *On language and linguistics*. Volume 3 in the *Collected works of M.A.K. Halliday*. London & New York: Continuum. 36-49.

Halliday, M.A.K. 1966a. 'General linguistics and its application to language teaching.' In Angus McIntosh & M.A.K. Halliday, *Patterns of language: Paper in general, descriptive and applied linguistics*. London: Longmans. 1-41.

Halliday, M.A.K. 1966b. 'Some notes on "deep" grammar.' *Journal of Linguistics* 2(1): 57-67. Reprinted in M.A.K. Halliday. 2002. Jonathan J. Webster (ed.), *On grammar*. Volume 1 in the *Collected works of M.A.K. Halliday*, 106-117. London & New York: Continuum. 106-117.

Halliday, M.A.K. 1967. *Intonation and grammar in British English*. The Hague: Mouton.

Halliday, M.A.K. 1967/1968. 'Notes on transitivity and theme in English: Part 1-3.' *Journal of Linguistics* 3(1), 3(2), 4(2). Reprinted in M.A.K. Halliday. 2005. Jonathan J. Webster (ed.), *Studies in English language*. Volume 7 in the *Collected works of M.A.K. Halliday*. London & New York: Continuum. 5-153.

Halliday, M.A.K. 1970. *A course in spoken English: Intonation*. Oxford: Oxford University Press.

Halliday, M.A.K. 1973. *Explorations in the functions of language*. London: Edward Arnold.

Halliday, M.A.K. 1978. *Language as social semiotic: The social interpretation of language and meaning.* London: Edward Arnold.

Halliday, M.A.K. 1979. 'Modes of meaning and modes of expression: Types of grammatical structure and their determination by different semantic functions.' In David J. Allerton, Edward Carney, & David Holdcroft (eds.), *Function and context in linguistic analysis.* Cambridge: Cambridge University Press. 57–79. Reprinted in M.A.K. Halliday. 2002. Jonathan J. Webster (ed.), *On grammar.* Volume 1 in the *Collected works of M.A.K. Halliday.* London & New York: Continuum. 196–218.

Halliday, M.A.K. 1985a. 'Systemic background.' In James D. Benson & William S. Greaves (eds.), *Systemic perspectives on discourse (volume 1): Selected theoretical papers from the 9th International Systemic Workshop.* Norwood: Ablex. 1–15. Reprinted in M.A.K. Halliday. 2003. Jonathan J. Webster (ed.), *On language and linguistics.* Volume 3 in the *Collected works of M.A.K. Halliday.* London & New York: Continuum. 185–198.

Halliday, M.A.K. 1985b. *An introduction to functional grammar.* London: Arnold.

Halliday, M.A.K. 1991a. 'Towards probabilistic interpretations.' In Eija Ventola (ed.), *Functional and systemic linguistics: Approaches and uses.* Berlin & New York: Mouton de Gruyter. 39–61. Reprinted in M.A.K. Halliday. 2005. Jonathan J. Webster (ed.), *Computational and quantitative studies.* Volume 6 in the *Collected works of M.A.K. Halliday.* London & New York: Continuum. 42–62.

Halliday, M. A. K. 1991b. 'Corpus studies and probabilistic grammar.' In Karin Aijimer & Bengt Altenberg (eds.), *English corpus linguistics: Studies in honour of Jan Svartvik.* Harlow: Longman. 30–43.

Halliday, M.A.K. 1992a. 'How do you mean?' In Martin Davies & Louise Ravelli (eds.), *Advances in systemic linguistics: Recent theory and practice.* London: Pinter. 20–35. Reprinted in M.A.K. Halliday. 2002. *On grammar.* Volume 1 in the *Collected works of M.A.K. Halliday.* London & New York: Continuum. 352–368.

Halliday, M.A.K. 1992b. 'A systemic interpretation of Peking syllable finals.' In Paul Tench (ed.), *Studies in systemic phonology.* London & New York: Pinter. 98–121. Reprinted in M.A.K. Halliday. 2005. Jonathan J. Webster (ed.), *Studies in Chinese language.* Volume 8 in the *Collected works of M.A.K. Halliday.* London & New York: Continuum. 294–320.

Halliday, M.A.K. 1994. *An introduction to functional grammar.* 2nd edition. London: Edward Arnold.

Halliday, M.A.K. 1996. 'On grammar and grammatics.' In Ruqaiya Hasan, Carmel Cloran, & David G. Butt (eds.), *Functional descriptions: Theory into practice.* Amsterdam & Philadelphia: John Benjamins. 1–38. Reprinted in M.A.K. Halliday. 2002. Jonathan J. Webster (ed.), *On grammar.* Volume 1 in the *Collected works of M.A.K. Halliday.* London & New York: Continuum. 384–418.

Halliday, M.A.K. 2001. 'Towards a theory of good translation.' In Erich Steiner & Colin Yallop (eds.), *Exploring translation and multilingual text production: Beyond content.* Berlin: Mouton de Gruyter. 13–18.

Halliday, M.A.K. 2002. 'Computing meanings: Some reflections on past experience and present prospects.' In Guowen Huang & Zongyan Wang (eds.), *Discourse and language functions.* Beijing: Foreign Language Teaching and Research Press. 3–25. Reprinted in M.A.K. Halliday. 2005. Jonathan J. Webster (ed.), *Computational and quantitative studies.* Volume 6 in the *Collected works of M.A.K. Halliday.* London & New York: Continuum. 239–267.

Halliday, M.A.K. 2005. 'On matter and meaning: The two realms of human experience.' *Linguistics and the Human Sciences* 1(1): 59–82.

Halliday, M.A.K. 2007. 'Applied linguistics as an evolving theme.' In Jonathan J. Webster (ed.), *Collected works of M.A.K. Halliday (volume 9): Language and education*. London & New York: Continuum. 1–19.

Halliday, M.A.K. 2008. 'Working with meaning: Towards an appliable linguistics.' In Jonathan J. Webster (ed.), *Meaning in context: Implementing intelligent applications of language studies*. London & New York: Continuum. 7–23.

Halliday, M.A.K. 2009. 'The gloosy ganoderm: Systemic functional linguistics and translation.' *Chinese Translators Journal* [中国翻译] 1: 17–26. Reprinted in M.A.K. Halliday. 2013. Jonathan J. Webster (ed.), *Halliday in the 21st century. Volume 11* in the *Collected Works of M.A.K. Halliday*. London & New York: Bloomsbury. 105–126.

Halliday, M.A.K. 2010. 'Pinpointing the choice: Meaning and the search for equivalents in a translated text.' In Ahmar Mahboob & Naomi K. Knight (eds.), *Appliable linguistics*. London & New York: Continuum. 13–24. Reprinted in M.A.K. Halliday. 2013. Jonathan J. Webster (ed.), *Halliday in the 21st century. Volume 11* in the *Collected works of M.A.K. Halliday*. London & New York: Bloomsbury. 143–154.

Halliday, M.A.K. & Ruqaiya Hasan. 1976. *Cohesion in English*. London: Longman.

Halliday, M.A.K. & Ruqaiya Hasan. 1985. *Language, context, and text: A social semiotic perspective*. Victoria: Deakin University Press.

Halliday, M.A.K. & Z.L. James. 1993. 'A quantitative study of polarity and primary tense in the English finite clause.' In John M. Sinclair, Michael Hoey, & Gwyneth Fox (eds.), *Techniques of description: Spoken and written discourse: A festschrift for Malcolm Coulthard*. London: Routledge. 32–66. Reprinted in M.A.K. Halliday. 2005. Jonathan J. Webster (ed.), *Computational and quantitative studies. Volume 6* in the *Collected works of M.A.K. Halliday*. London & New York: Continuum. 93–129.

Halliday, M.A.K. & Christian M.I.M. Matthiessen. 1999. *Construing experience through meaning: A language-based approach to cognition*. London: Pinter.

Halliday, M.A.K. & Christian M.I.M. Matthiessen. 2004. *An introduction to functional grammar*. 3rd edition. London: Edward Arnold.

Halliday, M.A.K. & Christian M.I.M. Matthiessen. 2006. *Construing experience through meaning: A language-based approach to cognition*. London & New York: Continuum.

Halliday, M.A.K. & Christian M.I.M. Matthiessen. 2014. *Halliday's introduction to functional grammar*. 4th edition. London & New York: Routledge.

Halliday, M.A.K. & Edward McDonald. 2004. 'Metafunctional profile of the grammar of Chinese.' In Alice Caffarel, James R. Martin, & Christian M.I.M. Matthiessen (eds.), *Language typology: A functional perspective*. Amsterdam & Philadelphia: John Benjamins. 253–305.

Halliday, M.A.K., Angus McIntosh, & Peter Strevens. 1964. *The linguistic sciences and language teaching*. London: Longman.

Halverson, Sandra. 1997. 'The concept of equivalence in translation studies: Much ado about something.' *Target* 9(2): 207–233.

Hansen-Schirra, Silvia & Sambor Grucza (eds.). 2016. *Eyetracking and applied linguistics*. Berlin: Language Science Press.

Hansen-Schirra, Silvia, Oliver Czulo, & Sascha Hofmann (eds.). 2017. *Empirical modelling of translation and interpreting*. Berlin: Language Science Press.

Hansen-Schirra, Silvia, Stella Neumann, & Oliver Čulo (eds.). 2017. *Annotation, exploitation and evaluation of parallel corpora*. Berlin: Language Science Press.

Hansen-Schirra, Silvia, Stella Neumann, & Erich Steiner. 2007. 'Cohesive explicitness in an English-German translation corpus.' *Languages in Contrast* 7(2): 241–265.

Hansen-Schirra, Silvia, Stella Neumann, & Erich Steiner (eds.). 2012. *Cross-linguistic corpora for the study of translations: Insights from the language pair English-German*. München: Mouton de Gruyter.

Hartley, Anthony & Cécile Paris. 2001. 'Translation, controlled languages, generation.' In Erich Steiner & Colin Yallop (eds.), *Exploring translation and multilingual text production: Beyond content*. Berlin: Mouton de Gruyter. 307–326.

Hasan, Ruqaiya. 1973. 'Code, register and social dialect.' In Basil Bernstein (ed.), *Class, codes and control (volume 2): Applied studies towards a sociology of language*. London: Routledge & Kegan Paul. 253–292.

Hasan, Ruqaiya. 1985. *Linguistics, language and verbal art*. Geelong, Victoria: Deakin University Press.

Hasan, Ruqaiya. 1999. 'Speaking with reference to context.' In Mohsen Ghadessy (ed.), *Text and context in functional linguistics*. Amsterdam: John Benjamins. 219–328.

Hasan, Ruqaiya. 2009. 'The place of context in a systemic functional model.' In M.A.K. Halliday & Jonathan Webster (eds.), *A companion to systemic functional linguistics*. London & New York: Continuum. 166–189.

Hasan, Ruqaiya, Carmel Cloran, Geoffrey Williams, & Annabelle Lukin. 2007. 'Semantic networks: The description of English meaning in SFL.' In Ruqaiya Hasan, Christian M.I.M. Matthiessen, & Jonathan Webster (eds.), *Continuing discourse on language (volume 2)*. London: Equinox. 697–738.

Hatim, Basil & Ian Mason. 1990. *Discourse and the translator*. London: Routledge.

Hatim, Basil & Ian Mason. 1997. *The translator as communicator*. London & New York: Routledge.

Heilmann, Arndt, Tatiana Serbina, Daniel Couto Vale, & Stella Neumann. 2019. 'Shorter than a text, longer than a sentence: Source text length for ecologically valid translation experiments.' *Target* 31(1): 98–124.

Hickey, Leo. 1990. 'The style of topicalization: How formal is it?' In *The pragmatics of style*. London & New York: Routledge. 52–70.

Hoang, Van Van. 2006. *Translation: Theory and practice*. Hanoi: Nhà xuất bản giáo duc.

Hoey, Michael. 1991. *Pattern of lexis in text*. Oxford: Oxford University Press.

Holmes, James S. 1988. *Translated! Papers on literary translation and translation studies*. Amsterdam: Rodopi.

Holz-Mänttäri, Justa. 1984. *Translatorisches Handeln: Theorie und Methode*. Helsinki: Suomalainen Tiedeakatemia.

House, Juliane Marie-Luise. 1976. *A model for translation quality assessment and some implications for foreign language teaching*. PhD thesis, University of Toronto, Canada.

House, Juliane. 1977. *A model for translation quality assessment*. Tübingen: Gunter Narr.

House, Juliane. 1997. *Translation quality assessment: A model revisited*. Tübingen: Gunter Narr.

House, Juliane. 2001. 'How do we know when a translation is good.' In Erich Steiner & Colin Yallop (eds.), *Exploring translation and multilingual text production: Beyond content*. Berlin: Mouton de Gruyter. 127–160.

House, Juliane. 2008. 'Beyond intervention: Universals in translation?' *trans-kom* 1(1): 6–19.

House, Juliane. 2015. *Translation quality assessment: Past, present and future*. Abingdon & New York: Routledge.

House, Juliane. 2016. *Translation as communication across languages and cultures*. Abingdon & New York: Routledge.

House, Juliane. 2018. *Translation: The basics*. Abingdon & New York: Routledge.

Hu, Honghui [胡红辉] & Zeng Lei [曾蕾]. 2012. '《论语》及其英译本中投射语言的人际功能分析' [An interpersonal analysis of projection in *The Analects* and its English translations]. 北京科技大学学报（社会科学版）[Journal of University of Science and Technology Beijing (Social Sciences Edition)], 39(1): 42–51.

Hu, Zhuanglin [胡壮麟], Zhu Yongsheng [朱永生], & Zhang Delu [张德录]. 1989. 系统功能语法概论 [A survey of systemic-functional grammar]. 长沙 [Changsha]: 湖南教育出版社 [Hunan Education Press].

Hu, Zhuanglin [胡壮麟], Zhu Yongsheng [朱永生], Zhang Delu [张德禄], & Li Zhanzi [李战子]. 2008. 系统功能语言学概论（修订版）[Introduction to systemic functional linguistics (revised edition)]. 北京 [Beijing]: 北京大学出版社 [Peking University Press].

Huang, Guowen [黄国文]. 2002a. '《清明》一诗英译文的人际功能探讨' [An interpersonal analysis of Du Mu's *Qingming* and its translated versions]. 外语教学 [Foreign Language Education] 23(3): 34–38.

Huang, Guowen [黄国文]. 2002b. '杜牧《清明》英译文的逻辑功能分析' [A functional analysis of logical meaning in the English version of the poem *Qingming* by Du Mu]. 外语与翻译 [Foreign Languages and Translation] 1: 1–4.

Huang, Guowen [黄国文]. 2002c. '唐诗英译文中的引述现象分析' [An analysis of reported speech in translating ancient Tang poems into English]. 外语学刊 [Foreign Language Research] 3: 1–6.

Huang, Guowen [黄国文]. 2002d. '对唐诗《寻隐者不遇》英译文的功能语篇分析' [A functional discourse analysis of the English version of the Tang poem *Xun Yin Zhe Bu Yu*]. 解放军外国语学院学报 [Journal of the PLA University of Foreign Languages] 5: 67–70.

Huang, Guowen [黄国文]. 2002e. '功能语言学分析对翻译研究的启示——《清明》英译文的经验功能分析' [The enlightenment of functional linguistics to translation studies: A functional analysis of the experiential meaning in the English version of the poem *Qing Ming*]. 外语与外语教学 [Foreign Language and Their Teaching] 5: 1–6, 11.

Huang, Guowen [黄国文]. 2002f. '关于语篇与翻译' [About discourse and translation]. 外语与外语教学 [Foreign Language and Their Teaching] 7: 1–2.

Huang, Guowen [黄国文]. 2003a. '古诗英译文中的时态分析' [An analysis of tense in the translation of ancient Chinese poems]. 四川外语学院学报 [Journal of Sichuan International Studies University] 1: 95–100.

Huang, Guowen [黄国文]. 2003b. '静态和动态在翻译中的表现——柳宗元的《江雪》英译文分析' [The dynamic and static realization in translation: An analysis of the English translation of *Jiangxue* by Liu Zongyuan]. 外语与翻译 [Foreign Languages and Translation] 1: 1–6.

Huang, Guowen [黄国文]. 2003c. '从《天净沙·秋思》的英译文看'形式对等'的重要性' [The importance of formal equivalence: A study of the English version of the poem *Tian Jing Sha Qiu Si*]. 中国翻译 [Chinese Translators Journal] 2: 21–23.

Huang, Guowen [黄国文]. 2004. '翻译研究的功能语言学途径' [A functional linguistic approach to translation studies]. 中国翻译 [Chinese Translators Journal] 5: 15–19.

Huang, Guowen [黄国文]. 2006. 翻译研究的语言学探索——古诗词英译本的语言学分析 [Linguistic explorations in translation studies: Analysis of English translations of ancient Chinese poems and lyrics]. 上海 [Shanghai]: 上海外语教育出版社 [Shanghai Foreign Language Education Press].

Huang, Guowen [黄国文]. 2009. '语法隐喻在翻译研究中的应用' [Grammatical metaphor in translation studies]. 中国翻译 [Chinese Translators Journal] 1: 5–9.

Huang, Guowen [黄国文]. 2011. '《论语》的篇章结构及英语翻译的几个问题' [The textual structure of Confucius *Lun Yu* (*The Analects*) in relation to the English translation of the book title and chapter headings]. 中国外语 [Chinese Translators Journal] 6: 88–95.

Huang, Guowen. 2014. 'Analysing the reporting clause in translating Confucius' *Lun Yu* (*The Analects*).' In Fang Yan & Jonathan J. Webster (eds.), *Developing systemic functional linguistics: Theory and application.* London: Equinox. 256–270.

Huang, Guowen [黄国文]. 2015. '"译意"和"译味"的系统功能语言学解释' [Translating meaning and translating underlying meaning: A systemic functional interpretation]. 外语教学与研究 [Foreign Language Teaching and Research] 47(5): 732–742.

Huang, Guowen. 2016. 'Searching for metafunctional equivalence in translated texts.' In Jonathan J. Webster & Peng Xuanwei (eds.), *Applying systemic functional linguistics: The state of the art in China today.* London & New York: Bloomsbury. 285–306.

Huang, Xiaocong. 2013. 'Transitivity in English-Chinese literary translation: The case of James Joyce's "Two Gallants".' *Babel* 59(1): 93–109.

Hunston, Susan & Geoff Thompson (eds.). 2000. *Evaluation in text: Authorial stance and the construction of discourse.* Oxford: Oxford University Press.

Hutchins, John. 2003. 'Machine translation: General overview.' In Ruslan Mitkov (ed.), *The Oxford handbook of computational linguistics.* Oxford: Oxford University Press. 501–511.

Irvine, Ann & Chris Callison-Burch. 2014. 'Using comparable corpora to adapt mt models to new domains.' In *Proceedings of the Ninth Workshop on Statistical Machine Translation.* Baltimore, Maryland: Association for Computational Linguistics. 437–444.

Irvine, Ann, John Morgan, Marine Carpuat, & D.S. Munteanu. 2013. 'Measuring machine translation errors in new domains.' *TACL* 1: 429–440.

Jakobsen, Arnt Lykke. 2011. 'Tracking translators' keytrokes and eye movements with Translog.' In Cecilia Alvstad, Adelina Hild, & Elisabet Tiselius (eds.), *Methods and strategies of process research.* Amsterdam & Philadelphia: John Benjamins. 37–55.

Jakobsen, Arnt Lykke. 2014. The development and current state of translation process research. In Elke Brems, Reine Meylaerts, & Luc van Doorslaer (eds.), *The known unknowns of translation studies.* Amsterdam: John Benjamins. 65–88.

Jakobsen, Arnt Lykke. 2017. Translation process research. In John W. Schwieter & Aline Ferreira (eds.), *The handbook of translation and cognition.* Hoboken, NJ: Wiley-Blackwell. 19–49.

Jakobson, Roman. 1959. 'On linguistic aspects of translation.' In Reuben A. Brower (ed.), *On translation.* Cambridge: Harvard University Press. 232–239.

Jakobson, Roman. 1960. 'Closing statement: Linguistics and poetics.' In Thomas A. Sebeok (ed.), *Style in Language*. Cambridge: MIT Press. 350–377.

Jensen, Kristian. 2008. 'Assessing eye-tracking accuracy in translation studies.' In Susanne Göpferich, Arnt Lykke Jakobsen, & Inger Mees (eds.), *Looking at eyes: Eye tracking studies of reading and translation processing*. Copenhagen: Samfundslitteratur. 157–174.

Jiang, Chengzhi. 2010. 'Quality assessment for the translation of museum texts: Application of a systemic functional model.' *Perspectives: Studies in Translatology* 18(2): 109–126.

Johansson, Stig. 2007. *Seeing through multilingual corpora*. Amsterdam: John Benjamins.

Károly, Krisztina. 2017. 'Logical relations in translation: The case of Hungarian-English news translation.' *Perspectives: Studies in Translation Theory and Practice* 25(2): 273–293.

Katan, David. 2009. 'Culture.' In Mona Baker & Gabriela Saldanha (eds.), *Routledge encyclopedia of translation studies*. 2nd edition. London & New York: Routledge. 28–31.

Kay, Martin. 1979. 'Functional grammar.' In *Proceedings of the Fifth Annual Meeting of the Berkeley Linguistic Society*. 142–158.

Ke, Ping. 2009. 'Machine translation.' In Mona Baker & Gabriela Saldanha (eds.), *Routledge encyclopedia of translation studies*. 2nd edition. London & New York: Routledge. 162–169.

Kennedy, George A. 1937. 'A minimum vocabulary in modern Chinese.' *The Modern Language Journal* 21(8): 587–592.

Kermes, Hannah. 2003. *Off-line (and on-line) text analysis for computational lexicography*. Doctoral dissertation, Universität Stuttgart, Germany.

Kim, Mira. 2007. *A discourse based study on Theme in Korean and textual meaning in translation*. PhD thesis, Macquarie University, Sydney, Australia.

Kim, Mira. 2011. 'A study on target reader reactions to different Theme choices in two different versions of English translations of a Korean short story.' In Euiyon Cho (ed.), *Translation studies, what does it study: Linguistic, cultural and social approaches*. Seoul: Dongkuk University Press. 53–83.

Kim, Mira & Huang Zhi. 2012. 'Theme choices in translation and target readers' reactions to different Theme choices.' *T & I Review* 2: 79–112.

Kim, Mira & Christian M.I.M. Matthiessen. 2015. 'Ways to move forward in translation studies: A textual perspective.' *Target* 27(3): 335–350.

Kittredge, Richard & John Lehrberger (eds.). (1982). *Sublanguage: Studies of language in restricted semantic domains*. Berlin: Walter de Gruyter.

Koller, Werner. 1979. *Einführung in die Übersetzungswissenschaft*. Heidelberg & Wiesbaden: Quelle & Meyer.

Kranich, Svenja, Juliane House, & Viktor Becher. 2012. 'Changing conventions in English and German translations of popular science texts.' In Kurt Braunmüller & Christoph Gabriel (eds.), *Multilingual individuals and multilingual societies*. Amsterdam: John Benjamins. 315–335.

Kress, Gunter & Theo van Leeuwen. 1996. *Reading images: The grammar of visual design*. London & New York: Routledge.

Kunz, Kerstin & Erich Steiner. 2012. 'Towards a comparison of cohesive reference in English and German: System and text.' *Linguistics and the Human Sciences* 6(1–3): 219–251.

Kunz, Kerstin & Elke Teich. 2017. 'Translation studies.' In Tom Bartlett & Gerard O'Grady (eds.), *The Routledge handbook of systemic functional linguistics*. Abingdon & New York: Routledge. 547–560.

Kunz, Kerstin, Stefania Degaetano-Ortlieb, Ekaterina Lapshinova-Koltunski, Katrin Menzel, & Erich Steiner. 2017. 'English-German contrasts in cohesion and implications for translation.' In Gert de Sutter, Marie-Aude Lefer, & Isabelle Delaere (eds.), *Empirical translation studies: New methodological and theoretical traditions*. Berlin: Mouton de Gruyter. 265–311.

Lambert, José. 2013. 'Prelude: The institutionalization of the discipline.' In Carmen Millán & Francesca Bartrina (eds.), *The Routledge handbook of translation studies*. London & New York: Routledge. 7–28.

Lapshinova-Koltunski, Ekaterina & Kerstin Kunz. 2014. 'Detecting cohesion: Semi-automatic annotation procedures.' Paper presented at Corpus Linguistics, Lancaster, UK, July.

Lapshinova-Koltunski, Ekaterina & Santanu Pal. 2014. 'Comparability of corpora in human and machine translation.' In *Proceedings of the Seventh Workshop on Building and Using Comparable Corpora*. Reykjavik, Iceland. LREC.

Lapshinova-Koltunski, Ekaterina & Mihaela Vela. 2015. 'Measuring "registerness" in human and machine translation: A text classification approach.' In *Proceedings of the 2nd Workshop on Discourse in Machine Translation (DiscoMT)*. Lisbon, Portugal: Association for Computational Linguistics.

Lapshinova-Koltunski, Ekaterina & Marcos Zampieri. 2018. 'Linguistic features of genre and method variation in translation: A computational perspective.' In Dominique Legallois, Thierry Charnois, & Meri Larjavaara (eds.), *The grammar of genres and styles: From discrete to non-discrete units*. Berlin: Mouton de Gruyter.

Lavid, Julia. 2000. 'Cross-cultural variation in multilingual instructions: A study of speech act realization patterns.' In Eija Ventola (ed.), *Discourse and community: Doing functional linguistics: Language in performance*. Tübingen: Gunter Narr. 71–86.

Laviosa-Braithwaite, Sara. 1998. 'Universals of translation.' In Mona Baker (ed.), *Routledge encyclopedia of translation*. London: Routledge. 288–291.

Laviosa, Sara. 2013. 'Corpus linguistics in translation studies.' In Carmen Millán & Francesca Bartrina (eds.), *The Routledge handbook of translation studies*. London & New York: Routledge. 228–240.

Lewis, M. Paul, Gary F. Simons, & Charles D. Fennig. (eds.) 2015. *Ethnologue: Languages of the world*. 18th edition. Dallas: SIL International.

Li, Charles N. & Sandra A. Thompson. 1981. *Mandarin Chinese: A functional reference grammar*. Berkeley, Los Angeles, & London: University of California Press.

Li, Eden Sum-hung. 2007. *A systemic functional grammar of Chinese*. London & New York: Continuum.

Li, Long. 2017. 'An examination of ideology in translation via modality: *Wild Swans* and *Mao's Last Dancer*.' *Journal of World Languages* 4(2): 118–144.

Li, Saihong. 2019. 'A corpus-based multimodal approach to the translation of restaurant menus.' *Perspectives: Studies in Translation Theory and Practice* 27(1): 1–19.

Li, Xi & Canzhong Wu. 2017. 'Coherence in *Hong Lou Meng* and its English translations: An exploratory investigation.' *Functional Linguistics* 4(1): 1–14.

Lin, Guoli [林国丽] 2015. '概念意义的隐性评价功能——"乔布斯情书"英文及汉译本对比分析' [The implicit evaluative functions of ideational meaning – a comparison between Jobs' love letter and its Chinese versions]. 外语学刊 [Foreign Language Research] 5: 77–81.

Liu, Xiangjun & Xiaohu Yang. 2013. 'Thematic progression in English-Chinese translation of argumentative classics: A quantitative study of Francis Bacon's "Of Studies" and its 11 Chinese translations.' *Perspectives: Studies in Translatology* 21(2): 272–288.

Ma, Yuanyi. 2018. *A systemic functional perspective on Rabindranath Tagore's Stray Birds and its Chinese translations*. Doctoral thesis, Hong Kong Polytechnic University, Hong Kong.

Ma, Yuanyi & Bo Wang. 2021. *Translating Tagore's Stray Birds into Chinese: Applying systemic functional linguistics to Chinese poetry translation*. Abingdon & New York: Routledge.

Malinowski, Branislow. 1923. 'The problem of meaning in primitive languages.' In C.K. Ogden & I.A. Richards (eds.), *The meaning of meaning*. London: Kegan Paul. 1–84.

Malinowski, Bronislaw. 1935. *Coral gardens and their magic: A study of the methods of tilling the soil and of agricultural rites in the Trobriand Islands: Volume 2: The language of magic and gardening*. New York: American Book Company.

Malmkjær, Kirsten. 2013. 'Where are we? (From Holmes's map until now).' In Carmen Millán & Francesca Bartrina (eds.), *The Routledge handbook of translation studies*. London & New York: Routledge. 31–44.

Mann, William C. 1985. 'An introduction to the Nigel text generation grammar.' In James D. Benson & William S. Greaves (eds.), *Systemic perspectives on discourse (volume 1)*. Norwood: Ablex. 84–95.

Mann, William C. & Christian M.I.M. Matthiessen. 1985. 'Demonstration of the Nigel text generation grammar.' In James D. Benson & William S. Greaves (eds.), *Systemic perspectives on discourse (volume 1)*. Norwood: Ablex. 50–83.

Marasigan, Elizabeth. 1983. *Code-switching and code-mixing in multilingual societies*. Singapore: Singapore University Press.

Martin, James R. 1983. 'Participant identification in English, Tagalog and Kâte.' *Australian Journal of Linguistics* 3(1): 45–74.

Martin, James R. 1984. 'Types of writing in infants and primary school.' In Len Unsworth (ed.) *Reading, writing, spelling: Proceedings of Fifth Macarthur Reading/Language Symposium*. Sydney: Macarthur Institute of Higher Education. 34–55.

Martin, James R. 1991. 'Intrinsic functionality: Implications for contextual theory.' *Social Semiotics* 1(1): 99–162.

Martin, James R. 1992. *English text: System and structure*. Amsterdam & Philadelphia: John Benjamins.

Martin, James R. 1998. 'Modelling context: A crooked path of progress in contextual linguistics.' In Mohsen Ghadessy (ed.), *Text and context in functional linguistics*. Amsterdam & Philadelphia: John Benjamins. 25–61.

Martin, James R. 2004. 'Positive discourse analysis: Power, solidarity and change.' *Revista Canaria de Estudios Ingleses* 49: 179–200.

Martin, James R. 2009. 'Realisation, instantiation and individuation: Some thoughts on identity in youth justice conferencing.' *D.E.L.T.A.* 25: 549–583.

Martin, J.R. & David Rose. 2007. *Working with discourse: Meaning beyond the clause*. London: Continuum.

Martin, James R. & Peter R.R. White. 2005. *The language of evaluation: Appraisal in English*. London: Palgrave.

Mason, Ian. 2012. 'Text parameters in translation: Transitivity and institutional cultures.' In Lawrence Venuti (ed.), *The translation studies reader*. 3rd edition. London & New York: Routledge. 399–410.

Masterman, Margaret. 1957. 'The thesaurus in syntax and semantics.' *Mechanical Translation* 4(1–2): 35–43.

Masterman, Margaret. 1965. 'Semantic algorithms.' In *Proceedings of the Conference on Computer-Related Semantic Analysis*. Las Vegas, Nevada: Wayne State University. 1–97.

Mathesius, Vilém. 1928. 'On linguistic characterology with illustrations from modern English.' In *Actes du Premier Congrès International de Linguistes à La Haye, du 10-15 Avril, 1928*. Leiden: A.W. Sijthoff. 56–63.

Mathesius, Vilém. 1975. *A functional analysis of present day English on a general linguistic basis*. Berlin: Mouton de Gruyter.

Matthiessen, Christian M.I.M. 1985. 'The systemic framework in text generation: Nigel.' In James D. Benson & William S. Greaves (eds.), *Systemic perspectives on discourse (volume 1)*. Norwood: Ablex. 96–118.

Matthiessen, Christian M.I.M. 1992. 'Interpreting the textual metafunction.' In Martin Davies & Louise Ravelli (eds.), *Advances in systemic linguistics: Recent theory and practice*. London: Pinter. 37–82.

Matthiessen, Christian M.I.M. 1993. 'Register in the round: Diversity in a unified theory of register analysis.' In Mohsen Ghadessy (ed.), *Register analysis: Theory and practice*. London: Pinter. 221–292.

Matthiessen, Christian M.I.M. 1995a. 'THEME as an enabling resource in ideational "knowledge" constructions.' In Mohsen Ghadessy (ed.), *Thematic development in English texts*. London: Pinter. 85–104.

Matthiessen, Christian M.I.M. 1995b. *Lexicogrammatical cartography: English systems*. Tokyo: International Language Sciences Publishers.

Matthiessen, Christian M.I.M. 2001. 'The environments of translation.' In Erich Steiner & Colin Yallop (eds.), *Exploring translation and multilingual text production: Beyond content*. Berlin: Mouton de Gruyter. 41–124.

Matthiessen, Christian M.I.M. 2004. 'Descriptive motifs and generalizations.' In Alice Caffarel, James R. Martin, & Christian M.I.M. Matthiessen (eds.), *Language typology: A functional perspective*. Amsterdam: John Benjamins. 537–674.

Matthiessen, Christian M.I.M. 2007. 'The "architecture" of language according to systemic functional theory: Developments since the 1970s.' In Ruqaiya Hasan, Christian M.I.M. Matthiessen, & Jonathan Webster (eds.), *Continuing discourse on language (volume 2)*. London: Equinox. 505–561.

Matthiessen, Christian M.I.M. 2009a. 'Ideas and new directions.' In M.A.K. Halliday & Jonathan J. Webster (eds.), *Continuum companion to systemic functional linguistics*. London & New York: Continuum. 12–58.

Matthiessen, Christian M.I.M. 2009b. 'Multisemiotic and context-based register typology: Registerial variation in the complementarity of semiotic systems.' In Eija Ventola & Arsenio Jesús Moya Guijarro (eds.), *The world shown and the world told*. Basingstoke: Palgrave Macmillan. 11–38.

Matthiessen, Christian M.I.M. 2013. 'Applying systemic functional linguistics in healthcare contexts.' *Text and Talk* 33(4–5): 437–466.

Matthiessen, Christian M.I.M. 2014a. 'Appliable discourse analysis.' In Fang Yan & Jonathan J. Webster (eds.), *Developing systemic functional linguistics: Theory and application*. London: Equinox. 135–205.

Matthiessen, Christian M.I.M. 2014b. 'Choice in translation: Metafunctional considerations.' In Kerstin Kunz, Elke Teich, Silvia Hansen-Schirra, Stella Neumann, & Peggy Daut (eds.), *Caught in the middle - language use and translation: A festschrift for Erich Steiner on the occasion of his 60th birthday*. Saarbrücken: Saarland University Press. 271–333.

Matthiessen, Christian M.I.M. 2014c. 'Registerial cartography: Context-based mapping of text types and their rhetorical-relational organization.' In *Proceedings of the 28th Pacific Asia Conference on Language, Information and Computation*. 5–26.

Matthiessen, Christian M.I.M. 2015a. 'Halliday on language.' In Jonathan J. Webster (ed.), *The Bloomsbury companion to M.A.K. Halliday*. London & New York: Bloomsbury. 137–202.

Matthiessen, Christian M.I.M. 2015b. 'Halliday's conception of language as a probabilistic system.' In Jonathan J. Webster (ed.), *The Bloomsbury companion to M.A.K. Halliday*. London & New York: Bloomsbury. 203–241.

Matthiessen, Christian M.I.M. 2015c. 'Register in the round: Registerial cartography.' *Functional Linguistics* 2(9): 1–48.

Matthiessen, Christian M.I.M. 2015d. 'Modelling context and register: The long-term project of registerial cartography.' *Letras, Santa Maria* 25(50): 15–90.

Matthiessen, Christian M.I.M. 2018. 'The notion of a multilingual meaning potential: A systemic exploration.' In Akila Sellami-Baklouti & Lise Fontaine (eds.), *Perspectives from systemic functional linguistics*. Abingdon & New York: Routledge. 90–120.

Matthiessen, Christian M.I.M. 2019. 'Register in systemic functional linguistics.' *Register Studies* 1(1): 10–41.

Matthiessen, Christian M.I.M. 2020. 'Trinocular views of register: Approaching register trinocularly.' *Language, Context and Text* 2(1): 3–21.

Matthiessen, Christian M.I.M. 2021. 'Translation, multilingual text production and cognition viewed in terms of systemic functional linguistics.' In Fabio Alves & Arnt Lykke Jakobsen (eds.), *The Routledge handbook of translation and cognition*. Abingdon & New York: Routledge. 517–544.

Matthiessen, Christian M.I.M. & John A. Bateman. 1991. *Text generation and systemic-functional linguistics: Experiences from English and Japanese*. London: Frances Pinter.

Matthiessen, Christian M.I.M. & M.A.K. Halliday. 2009. *Systemic functional grammar: A first step into the theory*. Bilingual edition, with introduction by Huang Guowen. Beijing: Higher Education Press.

Matthiessen, Christian M.I.M. & Kazuhiro Teruya. 2016. 'Registerial hybridity: Indeterminacy among fields of activity.' In Donna R. Miller & Paul Bayley (eds.), *Hybridity in systemic functional linguistics: Grammar, text and discursive context*. Sheffield: Equinox. 205–239.

Matthiessen, Christian M.I.M., Kazuhiro Teruya, & Marvin Lam. 2010. *Key terms in systemic functional linguistics*. London & New York: Continuum.

Matthiessen, Christian M.I.M., Kazuhiro Teruya, & Wu Canzhong. 2008. 'Multilingual studies as a multi-dimensional space of interconnected language studies.' In Jonathan J. Webster (ed.), *Meaning in context: Implementing intelligent applications of language studies*. London & New York: Continuum. 146–220.

Matthiessen, Christian M.I.M., Bo Wang, & Yuanyi Ma. 2017a. 'Interview with Christian M.I.M. Matthiessen: On translation studies (part I).' *Linguistics and the Human Sciences* 13(1–2): 201–217.

Matthiessen, Christian M.I.M., Bo Wang, & Yuanyi Ma. 2017b. 'Interview with Christian M.I.M. Matthiessen: On translation studies (part II).' *Linguistics and the Human Sciences* 13(3): 338–358.

Matthiessen, Christian M.I.M., Bo Wang, & Yuanyi Ma. 2018. 'Interview with Christian M.I.M. Matthiessen: On translation studies (part III).' *Linguistics and the Human Sciences* 14(1–2): 175–187.

Matthiessen, Christian M.I.M., Bo Wang, & Yuanyi Ma. 2019a. 'Expounding register and registerial cartography in systemic functional linguistics: An interview with Christian M.I.M. Matthiessen.' *WORD* 65(2): 1–14.

Matthiessen, Christian M.I.M., Bo Wang, & Yuanyi Ma. 2019b. 'Matthiessen on Halliday: An interview with Christian M.I.M. Matthiessen (part I).' *Language, Context and Text* 1(2): 366–387.

Matthiessen, Christian M.I.M., Bo Wang, Isaac N. Mwinlaaru, & Yuanyi Ma. 2018. 'The "axial rethink" — making sense of language: An interview with Christian M.I.M. Matthiessen.' *Functional Linguistics* 5(8): 1–19.

Matthiessen, Christian M.I.M., Bo Wang, Yuanyi Ma, & Isaac N. Mwinlaaru. forthcoming. *Systemic functional perspective on language and linguistics*. Singapore: Springer.

Mauranen, Anna. 2008. 'Universal tendencies in translation.' In Gunilla Anderman & Margaret Rogers (eds.), *Incorporating corpora: The linguist and the translator*. Clevedon: Multilingual Matters. 32–48.

Mauranen, Anna & Pekka Kujamäki (eds.). 2004. *Translation universals: Do they exist?* Amsterdam & Philadelphia: John Benjamins.

McDonald, Edward. 2020. *Grammar west to east: The investigation of linguistic meaning in European and Chinese traditions*. Singapore: Springer.

McGregor, William B. 2021. *Neo-Firthian approaches to linguistic typology*. Sheffield: Equinox.

Menzel, Katrin, Ekaterina Lapshinova-Koltunski, & Kerstin Kunz (eds.). 2017. *New perspectives on cohesion and coherence: Implications for translation*. Berlin: Language Science Press.

Müller, Christoph & Michael Strube. 2006. 'Multi-level annotation of linguistic data with MMAX2.' In Sabine Braun, Kurt Kohn, & Joybrato Mukherjee (eds.), *Corpus technology and language pedagogy: New resources, new tools, new methods*. Frankfurt am Mein: Peter Lang. 197–214.

Munday, Jeremy. 1997. *Systems in translation: A computer-assisted systemic analysis of the translation of García Márquez*. Doctoral dissertation, University of Bradford, Bradford, UK.

Munday, Jeremy. 2001. *Introducing translation studies: Theories and applications*. London & New York: Routledge.

Munday, Jeremy. 2002. 'Systems in translation: A systemic model for descriptive translation studies.' In Theo Hermans (ed.), *Crosscultural transgressions: Research models in translation studies II: Historical and ideological issues*. Manchester: St Jerome. 76–92.

Munday, Jeremy. 2010. 'Evaluation and intervention in translation.' In Mona Baker, Maeve Olohan, & María Calzada Pérez (eds.), *Text and context: Essays on translation and interpreting in honour of Ian Mason*. London & New York: Routledge. 77–94.

Munday, Jeremy. 2012. *Evaluation in translation: Critical points of translator decision-making*. London: Routledge.

Munday, Jeremy. 2015. 'Engagement and graduation resources as markers of translator/interpreter positioning.' *Target* 27(3): 406–421.

Munday, Jeremy. 2016. *Introducing translation studies: Theories and applications*. 4th edition. London & New York: Routledge.

Munday, Jeremy. 2018. 'A model of appraisal: Spanish interpretations of President Trump's inaugural address 2017.' *Perspectives: Studies in translation theory and practice* 26(2): 180–195.

Munday, Jeremy & Meifang Zhang (eds.) 2017. *Discourse analysis in translation studies*. Amsterdam & Philadelphia: John Benjamins.

Muysken, Pieter 2000. *Bilingual speech: A typology of code-mixing*. Cambridge: Cambridge University Press.

Mwinlaaru, Isaac N. & Winfred Wenhui Xuan. 2016. 'A survey of studies in systemic functional language description and typology.' *Functional Linguistics* 3(8): 1–41.

Neumann, Stella. 2008. *Contrastive register variation: A quantitative approach to the comparison of English and German*. Habilitationsschrift, Universität des Saarlandes, Saarbrücken, Germany.

Neumann, Stella & Silvia Hansen-Schirra. 2005. 'The CroCo project: Cross-linguistic corpora for the investigation of explicitation in translations.' In *Proceedings from the Corpus Linguistics Conference Series* 1(1). http://www.birmingham.ac.uk/Documents/collegeartslaw/corpus/conference-archives/2005-journal/ContrastiveCorpusLinguistics/thecrocoproject.pdf.

Neumann, Stella & Silvia Hansen-Schirra. 2012. 'Corpus methodology and design.' In Silvia Hansen-Schirra, Stella Neumann, & Erich Steiner (eds.), *Cross-linguistic corpora for the study of translations: Insights from the language pair English-German*. München: Mouton de Gruyter. 21–33.

Newmark, Peter. 1987. 'The use of systemic linguistics in translation analysis and criticism.' In Ross Steele & Terry Threadgold (eds.), *Language topics: Essays in honour of Michael Halliday (volume 1)*. Amsterdam & Philadelphia: John Benjamins. 293–303.

Newmark, Peter. 1988. *A textbook of translation*. Oxford & New York: Prentice Hall.

Newmark, Peter. 1991. *About translation*. Clevedon: Multilingual Matters.

Nida, Eugene. 1964. *Towards a science of translation: With special reference to principles and procedures involved in Bible translating*. Leiden: Brill.

Nida, Eugene A. & Charles R. Taber. 1969. *The theory and practice of translation*. Leiden: Brill.

Nirenburg, Sergei (ed.). 1995. 'The Pangloss Mark III Machine Translation System.' Joint Technical Report, Computing Research Laboratory (New Mexico State University), Center for Machine Translation (Carnegie Mellon University), Information Sciences Institute (University of Southern California). CMU technical report CMU-CMT-95-145.

Nord, Christiane. 1991. *Text analysis in translation*. Amsterdam & Atlanta: Rodopi.

Nord, Christiane. 1995. 'Text-functions in translation: Titles and headings as a case in point.' *Target* 7(2): 261–284.

Nord, Christiane. 1997. *Translating as a purposeful activity: Functionalist approaches explained*. Manchester: St Jerome.

Nord, Christiane. 2002/2003. 'Übersetzen als zielgerichtete Handlung.' *Interaktiv: Newsletter der German Language Division der American Translators Associaation* 6(12): 5–10.

O'Donnell, Mick & John Bateman. 2003. 'SFL in computational contexts: A contemporary history.' In Ruqaiya Hasan, Christian M.I.M. Matthiessen, & Jonathan J. Webster (eds.), *Continuing discourse on language: A functional perspective (volume 1)*. London: Equinox. 343–382.

O'Grady, Gerard. 2017. 'Theme and prosody: Redundancy or meaning making.' *English Text Construction* 10(2): 274–297.

Olohan, Maeve. 2004. *Introducing corpora in translation studies*. London & New York: Routledge.

Pagano, Adriana, Igor L. da Silva, & Fabio Alves. 2013. 'Tracing the unfolding of metaphorical processes in translation: Insights from an experimental exploratory study.' *Translation and Meaning* 9: 263–275.

Pan, Hanting. 2015. 'Ideological positioning in news translation: A case study of evaluative resources in reports on China.' *Target* 27(2): 215–237.

Pawley, Adrew. 1987. 'Encoding events in Kalam and English: Different logics for reporting experience.' In Russell S. Tomlin (ed.), *Coherence and grounding in discourse*. Amsterdam & Philadelphia: John Benjamins. 329–361.

Poon, Emily Wai-Yee. 2006. 'The translation of judgments.' *Meta* 51(3): 551–569.

Procházka, Vladimír. 1964. 'Notes on translating technique.' In Paul L. Garvin (ed.), *A Prague school reader on esthetics, literary structure, and style*. Washington, D.C.: Georgetown University Press. 93–112.

Pym, Anthony. 2014. *Exploring translation theories*. 2nd edition. London & New York: Routledge.

Qian, Hong [钱宏]. 2007. '运用评价理论解释'不忠实'的翻译现象——香水广告翻译个案研究' [Investigating unfaithful translations by applying appraisal theory: A case study on perfume ads translation]. 外国语 [Journal of Foreign Languages] 6: 57–63.

Reid, Thomas B.W. 1956. 'Linguistics, structuralism and philology.' *Archivum Linguisticu* 8(1): 28–37.

Reiss, Katharina. 1971. *Translation criticism - the potential and limitations: Categories and criteria for translation quality assessment* (Erroll F. Rhodes, trans.). Manchester: St Jerome.

Reiss, Katharina. 1976. 'Texttypen, Übersetzungstypen und die Beurteilung von Übersetzungen.' *Lebende Sprachen* 22(3): 97–100.

Reiss, Katharina & Hans J. Vermeer. 1984. *Grundlegung einer allgemeinen Translationstheorie*. Tübingen: Niemeyer.

Rose, David & James R. Martin. 2012. *Learning to write, reading to learn: Genre, knowledge and pedagogy in the Sydney school*. Sheffield & Bristol: Equinox.

Santini, Marina, Alexander Mehler, & Serge Sharoff. 2010. 'Riding the rough waves of genre on the web.' In Alexander Mehler, Serge Sharoff, & Marina Santini (eds.), *Genres on the web: Computational models and empirical studies*. Dordrechht: Springer. 3–30.

Shore, Susana. 2001. 'Teaching translation.' In Erich Steiner & Colin Yallop (eds.), *Exploring translation and multilingual text production: Beyond content*. Berlin: Mouton de Gruyter. 249–276.

Shreve, Gregory. 2006. 'The deliberate practice: Translation and expertise.' *Journal of Translation Studies* 9(1): 27–42.

Simeoni, Daniel. 1998. 'The pivotal status of the translator's habitus.' *Target* 10(1): 1–39.

Sinclair, John McH. 1987a. *Collins COBUILD English Language Dictionary*. London & Glasgow: Collins.

Sinclair, John McH. 1987b. 'Collocation: A progress report.' In Ross Steele & Terry Threadgold (eds.) *Language topics: Essays in honour of Michael Halliday (volume II)*. Amsterdam & Philadelphia: John Benjamins. 319–331.

Sinclair, John McH. 1990. *Collins COBUILD English Grammar*. London & Glasgow: Collins.

Somers, Harold. 2003. 'Machine translation: Latest developments.' In Ruslan Mitkov (ed.), *The Oxford handbook of computational linguistics*. Oxford: Oxford University Press. 512–528.

Steiner, Erich. 1986. *Generating semantic structures in Eurotra-D*. Bonn: Universität Bonn, Institut für Kommunikationsforschung und Phonetik.

Steiner, Erich. 1992. 'Some remarks on a functional level for machine translation.' *Language Sciences* 14(4): 623–659.

Steiner, Erich. 1993. 'Producers – users – customers: Towards a differentiated evaluation of research in machine translation.' *Machine Translation* 7: 281–284.

Steiner, Erich. 1997. 'An extended register analysis as a form of text analysis for translation.' In Gerd Wotjak & Heide Schmidt (eds.), *Modelle der Translation: Festschrift für Albrecht Neubert*. Frankfurt am Main: Vervuert Verlag. 235–256.

Steiner, Erich. 1998a. 'How much variation can a text tolerate before it becomes a different text?: An exercise in making meaningful choices.' In Rainer Schulze (ed.), *Making meaningful choices in English: On dimensions, perspectives, methodology and evidence*. Tübingen: Gunter Narr. 235–257.

Steiner, Erich. 1998b. 'A register-based translation evaluation: An advertisement as a case in point.' *Target* 10(2): 291–318.

Steiner, Erich. 2001a. 'Intralingual and interlingual versions of a text – how specific is the notion of translation?' In Erich Steiner & Colin Yallop (eds.), *Exploring translation and multilingual text production: Beyond content*. Berlin: Mouton de Gruyter. 161–190.

Steiner, Erich. 2001b. 'Translations English-German: Investigating the relative importance of systemic contrasts and of the text type "translation".' SPRIKreports 7: 1–49. http://www.hf.uio.no/ilos/forskning/prosjekter/sprik/docs/pdf/steiner.pdf.

Steiner, Erich. 2002a. 'Grammatical metaphor in translation – some methods for corpus-based investigations.' In Hilde Hasselgard, Stig Johansson, Behrens Bergljot, & Cathrine Fabricius-Hansen (eds.), *Information structure in a cross-linguistic perspective*. Amsterdam: Rodopi. 213–228.

Steiner, Erich. 2002b. 'Ideational grammatical metaphor: Exploring some implications for the overall model.' *Languages in Contrast* 4(1): 139–166.

Steiner, Erich. 2004a. *Translated texts: Properties, variants, evaluations*. Frankfurt am Main: Peter Lang.

Steiner, Erich. 2004b. 'Ideational grammatical metaphor: Exploring some implications for the overall model.' *Languages in Contrast* 4(1): 137–164.

Steiner, Erich. 2005. 'Halliday and translation theory – enhancing the options, broadening the range, and keeping the ground.' In Ruqaiya Hasan, Christian M.I.M. Matthiessen, & Jonathan J. Webster (eds.), *Continuing discourse on language: A functional perspective (volume 1)*. London: Equinox. 481–500.

Steiner, Erich. 2008. 'Explicitation: Towards an empirical and corpus-based methodology.' In Jonathan J. Webster (eds.), *Meaning in context: Implementing intelligent applications of language studies*. London & New York: Continuum. 234–277.

Steiner, Erich. 2012a. 'Introduction.' In Silvia Hansen-Schirra, Stella Neumann, & Erich Steiner (eds.), *Cross-linguistic corpora for the study of translations: Insights from the language pair English-German*. München: Mouton de Gruyter. 1–17.

Steiner, Erich. 2012b. 'A characterization of the resource based on shallow statistics.' In Silvia Hansen-Schirra, Stella Neumann, & Erich Steiner (eds.), *Cross-linguistic corpora for the study of translations: Insights from the language pair English-German*. München: Mouton de Gruyter. 71–89.

Steiner, Erich. 2012c. 'Generating hypotheses and operationalizations: The example of explicitness/explicitation.' In Silvia Hansen-Schirra, Stella Neumann, & Erich Steiner (eds.), *Cross-linguistic corpora for the study of translations: Insights from the language pair English-German*. München: Mouton de Gruyter. 55–70.

Steiner, Erich. 2015a. 'Choice as a category of human activity – and some of its contextual constraints.' *Linguistics and the Human Sciences* 11(2-3): 158–177.

Steiner, Erich. 2015b. 'Halliday's contribution to a theory of translation.' In Jonathan J. Webster (ed.), *The Bloomsbury companion to M.A.K. Halliday*. London & New York: Bloomsbury. 412–426.

Steiner, Erich. 2015c. 'Contrastive studies of cohesion and their impact on our knowledge of translation (English-German).' *Target* 27(3): 351–369.

Steiner, Erich. 2017. 'Methodological cross-fertilization: Empirical methodologies in (computational) linguistics and translation studies'. In Oliver Czulo & Silvia Hansen-Schirra (eds.), *Crossroads between contrastive linguistics, translation studies and machine translation*. Berlin: Language Science Press. 65–90.

Steiner, Erich. 2019. 'Theorizing and modelling translation.' In Geoff Thompson, Wendy L. Bowcher, Lise Fontaine, & David Schönthal (eds.), *The Cambridge handbook of systemic functional linguistics*. Cambridge: Cambridge University Press. 739–766.

Steiner, Erich & Colin Yallop (eds.) 2001. *Exploring translation and multilingual text production: Beyond content*. Berlin: Mouton de Gruyter.

Steiner, Erich, Ursula Eckert, Birgit Roth, & Jutta Winter-Thielen. 1988. 'The development of the EUROTRA-D system of semantic relations.' In Erich Steiner, Paul Schmidt, & Cornelia Zelinsky-Wibbelt (eds.), *From syntax to semantics: Insights from machine translation*. London: Pinter. 40–104.

Steiner, Erich, Bo Wang, Christian M.I.M. Matthiessen, & Yuanyi Ma. 2018a. 'Bridging boundaries between systemic functional linguistics and translation studies: An interview with Erich Steiner (part I).' *Linguistics and the Human Sciences* 14(3): 199–217.

Steiner, Erich, Bo Wang, Christian M.I.M. Matthiessen, & Yuanyi Ma. 2018b. 'Bridging boundaries between systemic functional linguistics and translation studies: An interview with Erich Steiner (part II).' *Linguistics and the Human Sciences* 14(3): 218–236.

Taylor, Christopher. 1993. 'Systemic linguistics and translation.' *Occasional Papers in Systemic Linguistics* 7: 87–103.

Taylor, Christopher. 1998. *Language to language: A practical and theoretical guide for Italian/English translators*. Cambridge: Cambridge University Press.

Taylor, Christopher J. 2003. 'Multimodal transcription in the analysis, translation and subtitling of Italian films.' *The Translator* 9(2): 191–205.

Taylor, Chris & Anthony Baldry. 2001. 'Computer assisted text analysis and translation: A functional approach in the analysis and translation of advertising texts.' In Erich Steiner & Colin Yallop (eds.), *Exploring translation and multilingual text production: Beyond content*. Berlin: Mouton de Gruyter. 277–306.

Tebble, Helen. 1999. 'The tenor of consultant physicians.' *The Translator* 5(2): 179–200.

Tebble, Helen. 2014. 'A genre-based approach to teaching dialogue interpreting: The medical consultation.' *The Interpreter and Translator Trainer* 8(3): 418–436.

Teich, Elke. 1999. 'System-oriented and text-oriented comparative linguistic research: Cross-linguistic variation in translation.' *Languages in Contrast* 2(2): 187–210.

Teich, Elke. 2001. 'Towards a model for the description of cross-linguistic divergence and commonality in translation.' In Erich Steiner & Colin Yallop (eds.), *Exploring translation and multilingual text production: Beyond content*. Berlin: Mouton de Gruyter. 41–124.

Teich, Elke. 2002. 'System-oriented and text-oriented comparative linguistic research: Cross-linguistic variation in translation.' *Languages in Contrast* 2(2): 187–210.

Teich, Elke. 2003. *Cross-linguistic variation in system and text: A methodology for the investigation of translations and comparable texts*. Berlin & New York: Mouton de Gruyter.

Teich, Elke. 2009. 'Linguistic computing.' In M.A.K. Halliday & Jonathan J. Webster (eds.), *Continuum companion to systemic functional linguistics*. London & New York: Continuum. 113–127.

Teng, Wei, J.A. Burn, & I.H.M. Crezee. 2018. 'I'm asking you again! Chinese student interpreters' performance when interpreting declaratives with tag questions in the legal interpreting classroom.' *Perspectives: Studies in Translation Theory and Practice* 26(5): 745–766.

Teruya, Kazuhiro & Christian M.I.M. Matthiessen. 2015. 'Halliday in relation to language comparison and typology.' In Jonathan J. Webster (ed.), *The Bloomsbury companion to M.A.K. Halliday*. London & New York: Bloomsbury. 427–452.

Toury, Gideon. 1995. *Descriptive translation studies and beyond*. Amsterdam & Philadelphia: John Benjamins.

Toury, Gideon. 2004. 'Probabilistic explanations in translation studies: Welcome as they are, would they qualify as universals?' In Anna Mauranen & Pekka Kujamäki (eds.), *Translation universals: Do they exist?* Amsterdam & Philadelphia: John Benjamins. 15–32.

Tymoczko, Maria. 2014. 'Why literary translation is a good model for translation theory and practice.' In Jean Boase-Beier, Antoinette Fawcett, & Philip Wilson (eds.), *Literary translation: Redrawing the boundaries*. Hampshire & New York: Palgrave Macmillan. 11–31.

Ure, Jean. N. 1989. *Text type classified by situational factors*. Manuscript.

Ure, Jean N. & Jeffrey Ellis. 1977. 'Register in descriptive linguistics and linguistic sociology.' In Oscar Uribe-Villegas (ed.), *Issues in sociolinguistics*. The Hague: Mouton. 197–244.

Vasconcellos, Muriel Havel de. 2008. 'Text and translation: The role of theme and information.' *Ilha do Desterro: A Journal of English Language, Literature in English and Cultural Studies* 27: 45–66.

Vela, Mihaela & Ekaterina Lapshinova-Koltunski. 2015. 'Register-based machine translation evaluation with text classification techniques.' Presented at Machine Translation Summit XV, Miami, Florida.

Ventola, Eija. 1995. 'Thematic development and translation.' In Mohsen Ghadessy (ed.), *Thematic development in English text*. London & New York: Pinter. 85–104.

Venuti, Lawrence. 2008. *The translator's invisibility: A history of translation*. 2nd edition. London & New York: Routledge.

Vermeer, Hans J. 2012. 'Skopos and commission in translation action.' In Lawrence Venuti (ed.), *The translation studies reader*. 3rd edition. London & New York: Routledge. 191–202.

Veroz, María Azahara. 2017. 'Translation in the European parliament: The study of the ideational function in technical texts (EN/FR/ES).' *Meta* 62(1): 19–44.

Wang, Binhua & Dezheng Feng. 2018. 'A corpus-based study of stance-taking as seen from critical points in interpreted political discourse.' *Perspectives: Studies in Translation Theory and Practice* 26(2): 246–260.

Wang, Bo. 2014. 'Theme in translation: A systemic functional linguistic perspective.' *International Journal of Comparative Literature & Translation Studies* 2(4): 54–63.

Wang, Bo. 2017. *Lao She's Chaguan (Teahouse) and its translations: A systemic functional perspective on drama translation*. Doctoral thesis, Hong Kong Polytechnic University, Hong Kong.

Wang, Bo & Yuanyi Ma. 2015. 'What is going on in the minds of translators?: A review of studies on translation process.' *Sino-US English Teaching* 12(4): 289–293.

Wang, Bo [王博] & Yuanyi Ma [马园艺]. 2016. '译者的选择——《茶馆》粤语译本的翻译策略' [Choice of the translator: Translation strategies for the Cantonese version of *Teahouse*]. 中国外语研究：2015年卷 [Foreign Language Research in China: 2015]. 82–92.

Wang, Bo & Yuanyi Ma. 2018. 'Textual and logical choices in the translations of dramatic monologue in *Teahouse*.' In Akila Sellami-Baklouti & Lise Fontaine (eds.), *Perspectives from systemic functional linguistics*. Abingdon & New York: Routledge. 140–162.

Wang, Bo & Yuanyi Ma. 2019. 'The recreation of Pock-Mark Liu and Wang Lifa in two Chinese translations of *Teahouse*: A systemic functional analysis of mood choices.' In Kumaran Rajandran & Shakila Abdul Manan (eds.), *Discourse of South East Asia: A social semiotic perspective*. Singapore: Springer. 189–207.

Wang, Bo, & Yuanyi Ma. 2020. *Lao She's Teahouse and its two English translations: Exploring Chinese drama translation with systemic functional linguistics*. Abingdon & New York: Routledge.

Wang, Bo & Yuanyi Ma. in prep. *Rhetorical structure theory: Past, present and future*. Sheffield: Equinox.

Wang, Peng [王鹏]. 2007. 《哈利·波特》与其汉语翻译——以系统功能语言学分析情态系统 [Harry Potter and its Chinese translation: Analysis of modality system from the perspective of systemic functional linguistics]. 重庆 [Chongqing]: 重庆大学出版社 [Chongqing University Press].

Wang, Peng [王鹏]. 2008. 'Harry Potter中情态动词CAN和COULD的英译汉分析' [An analysis of CAN and COULD in the Chinese translation of *Harry Potter*]. 外语与翻译 [Foreign Language and Translation] 24(3): 19–23.

Wang, Xi [王汐]. 2018. '实例化、实现化与个体化三维翻译视角——以《道德经》英译为个案' [Realization, instantiation, and individuation as three dimensions of translation: A case study of English translations of *Daodejing*]. 外语教学 [Foreign Language Education] 39 (2): 86–90.

Wang, Yan [王艳]. 2015. *A systemic perspective on the translation of detective stories*. PhD thesis, Hong Kong Polytechnic University, Hong Kong.

Wang, Yan. 2020. *A comparative study on the translation of detective stories from a systemic functional perspective*. Singapore: Springer.

Wang, Zhenhua [王振华]. 2019. '汉语句子中过程动词和参与者的英语翻译：SFL及物性系统视角' [Translating Chinese clause processes and participants into English: A perspective from transitivity system]. 外语研究 [Foreign Languages Research] 4: 59–65, 112.

Wilcock, Graham. 1993. *Interactive Japanese-European text generation - an approach to multilingual export translation based on systemic functional grammar*. MSc thesis, University of Manchester, UK.

Wolf, Michaela & Alexandra Fukari (eds.). 2007. *Constructing a sociology of translation*. Amsterdam & Philadelphia: John Benjamins.

Wong, Mickey. 2018. 'Censorship and translation in mainland China: General practice and a case study.' In Chris Shei & Zhao-Ming Gao (eds.), *The Routledge handbook of Chinese translation*. Abingdon & New York: Routledge. 221–243.

Wu, Canzhong. 2000. *Modelling linguistic resources: A systemic functional approach.* PhD thesis, Macquarie University, Sydney, Australia.

Wu, Canzhong. 2009. 'Corpus-based research.' In M.A.K. Halliday & Jonathan J. Webster (eds.), *Continuum companion to systemic functional linguistics.* London & New York: Continuum. 128–142.

Wu, Canzhong & Jing Fang. 2006. 'The social semiotics of university introductions in Australia and China.' In *Proceedings of the 33 International Systemic Functional Congress.* 568–591.

Wu, Guangjun & Zhang Huanyao. 2015. 'Translating political ideology: A case study of the Chinese translations of the English news headlines concerning South China Sea disputes on the website of www.ftchinese.com.' *Babel* 61(3): 394–410.

Yallop, Colin. 2001. 'The construction of equivalence.' In Erich Steiner & Colin Yallop (eds.), *Exploring translation and multilingual text production: Beyond content.* Berlin: Mouton de Gruyter. 229–246.

Yu, Hailing. 2019. *Recreating the image of Chan master Huineng: A systemic functional approach to translations of the Platform Sutra.* Sheffield: Equinox.

Yu, Hailing & Canzhong Wu. 2016. 'Recreating the image of Chan master Huineng: The roles of MOOD and MODALITY.' *Functional Linguistics* 3(4): 1–21.

Yu, Hailing & Canzhong Wu. 2017a. 'Recreating the image of Chan master Huineng: The role of personal pronouns.' *Target* 29(1): 64–86.

Yu, Hailing & Canzhong Wu. 2017b. 'Text complexity as an indicator of translational style: A case study.' *Linguistics and the Human Sciences* 13(1–2): 179–200.

Zeng, Lei [曾蕾]. 2016. '从投射小句复合体到投射语段——以《论语》原文与译文的对等分析为例' [From projection clause nexus to projection text: A case study of *Lunyu* and its English version]. 现代外语 [Modern Foreign Languages] 39(1): 42–51.

Zhang, Chunyan [张春燕] & Zheng Qingjun [郑庆君]. 2016. '网络翻译语篇互文性的功能语言学研究——以乔布斯情书翻译为例' [A functional linguistic study of intertextuality in online translation discourse: Examples from the translations of Jobs' love letter]. 当代修辞学 [Contemporary Rhetoric] 4: 78–87.

Zhang, Meifang. 2001. '从语篇分析的角度看翻译中的对等' [Translation equivalence from the perspective of discourse analysis]. 现代外语（季刊）[Modern Foreign Language (Quarterly)] 24(1): 78–84.

Zhang, Meifang. 2002. '语言的评价意义与译者的价值取向' [The language of appraisal and the translator's attitudinal positioning]. 外语与外语教学 [Foreign Languages and Their Teaching], 7: 15–18.

Zhang, Meifang [张美芳]. 2005. 翻译研究的功能途径 [Functional approaches to translation studies]. 上海 [Shanghai]: 上海外语教育出版社 [Shanghai Foreign Language Education Press].

Zhang, Meifang. 2009. 'Social context and translation of public notices.' *Babel* 55(2): 142–152.

Zhang, Meifang. 2013. 'Stance and mediation in transediting news headlines as paratexts.' *Perspectives: Studies in Translatology* 21(3): 396–411.

Zhang, Meifang [张美芳]. 2015. 功能途径论翻译：以英汉翻译为例 [Functional approaches to English–Chinese translation]. 北京 [Beijing]: 外文出版社 [Foreign Languages Press].

Zhang, Meifang [张美芳] & Guowen Huang [黄国文]. 2002. '语篇语言学与翻译研究' [A text linguistic approach to translation studies]. 中国翻译 [Chinese Translators Journal] 23(3): 3–7.

Zhang, Meifang & Hanting Pan. 2015. 'Institutional power in and behind discourse: A case study of SARS notices and their translations used in Macao.' *Target* 27(3): 387–405.

Zhu, Chunshen. 1993. *Structure of meaning (SOM): Towards a three-dimensional perspective on translating between Chinese and English*. PhD thesis, University of Nottingham, Nottingham, UK.

Zhu, Chunshen. 1996. 'From functional grammar and speech act theory to structure of meaning: A three-dimensional perspective on translating.' *Meta* 41(3): 338–355.

Zhu, Chunshen [朱纯深]. 2008. *Exploration in translation: Language, text, poetics* [翻译探微：语言•文本•诗学]. Jiangsu [江苏]: Yilin Press [译林出版社].

Zhu, Yongsheng [朱永生]. 1995. '主位推进模式与语篇分析' [Patterns of thematic progression and text analysis]. *外语教学与研究* [Foreign Language Teaching and Research] 27(3): 6–12.

Sources of Some Examples

Case, Francis (ed.). 2008. *1001 foods you must try before you die: A global guide to the best ingredients*. New York: Universe.

Case, Francis [弗朗西斯·凯斯] (ed.). 2012. 有生之年非吃不可的1001种食物 [*1001 foods you must try before you die*] (王博 [Wang Bo] & 马鑫 [Ma Xin], trans.). 北京 [Beijing]: 中央编译出版社 [Central Compilation & Translation Press].

Chao, Yuen Ren [赵元任]. 1980. 语言问题 [*Language problems*]. 北京 [Beijing]: 商务印书馆 [Commercial Press].

Christie, Agatha. 2013a. *The mysterious affair at Styles*. London: Harper Collins.

Christie, Agatha [阿加莎·克里斯蒂]. 2013b. 斯泰尔斯庄园奇案 [*The mysterious affair at Styles*] (郑卫明 [Zheng Weiming], trans.). 北京 [Beijing]: 新星出版社 [New Star Press].

Climo, Liz. 2014. *The little world of Liz Climo*. Philadelphia: Running Press.

Climo, Liz [莉兹·克里莫]. 2015. 你今天真好看 [*The little world of Liz Climo*]. (周高逸 [Zhou Gaoyi], trans.). 天津 [Tianjin]: 天津人民出版社 [Tianjin People's Publishing House].

Lao, She [老舍]. 1994. 茶馆 [*Teahouse*] (英若诚 [Ying Ruocheng], trans.). 北京 [Beijing]: 中国对外翻译出版公司 [China Translation and Publishing Corporation].

Lao, She [老舍]. 2004. 茶馆 [*Teahouse*] (John Howard-Gibbon, trans.). 香港 [Hong Kong]: 中文大学出版社 [Chinese University Press].

Lawrence, D.H. 1959. *Lady Chatterley's lover*. New York: Grove.

Lawrence, D.H. [劳伦斯]. 2004. 查特莱夫人的情人 [*Lady Chatterley's lover*] (赵苏苏 [Zhao Susu], trans.). 北京 [Beijing]: 人民文学出版社 [People's Literature Publishing House].

Lawrence, D.H. [劳伦斯]. 2014. 查泰莱夫人的情人 [*Lady Chatterley's lover*] (黑马 [Hei Ma], trans.). 南京 [Nanjing]: 译林出版社 [Yilin Press].

Li, Shude [李树德] & Feng Qi [冯奇]. 2003. 英语修辞简明教程 [*A concise course of English rhetoric*]. 上海 [Shanghai]: 复旦大学出版社 [Fudan University Press].

Matthiessen, Christian M.I.M. & M.A.K. Halliday. 2009. *Systemic functional grammar: A first step into the theory*. Bilingual edition, with introduction by Huang Guowen. Beijing: Higher Education Press.

Munday, Jeremy. 2001. *Introducing translation studies: Theories and applications*. London & New York: Routledge.

Munday, Jeremy [杰里米·芒迪]. 2007. 翻译学导论——理论与实践 [*Introducing translation studies: Theories and applications*] (李德凤等 [Li Defeng et al.], trans.). 北京 [Beijing]: 商务印书馆 [The Commercial Press].

Pu, Songling [蒲松龄]. 1988. 聊斋志异 [*Strange tales from a Chinese studio*]. 长沙 [Changsha]: 岳麓书社 [Yuelu Publishing House].

Pu, Songling. 2006. *Strange tales from a Chinese studio* (John Minford, trans.). London: Penguin Books.

Pu, Songling. 2010. *Strange tales from a Chinese studio* (Herbert A. Giles, trans.). North Clarendon: Tuttle Publishing.

Schlepp, Wayne. 1970. *San-ch'ü: Its technique and imagery.* Madison: University of Wisconsin Press.

Tagore, Rabindranath [泰戈尔]. 1921. 五言飞鸟集 [Stray birds in the form of five-character poetry] (姚华 [Yao Hua], trans.). 上海 [Shanghai]: 中华书局 [Zhonghua Book Company].

Tagore, Rabindranath [泰戈尔]. 2015. 飞鸟集 [Stray birds] (冯唐 [Feng Tang], trans.). 杭州 [Hangzhou]: 浙江文艺出版社 [Zhejiang Literature and Art Press].

Index

Alves, Fabio 38, 90, 127–130, 145
appliable linguistics 9, 136
appraisal 26, 66–68, 91, 93, 94, 136
axis 19, 21–23, 29, 31, 54–56, 110, 137, 147

Baker, Mona 14, 23, 25, 64, 110, 142, 143
Bell, Roger 12, 14, 16, 25
Bühler, Karl 8, 9, 25, 30, 79

Catford, J.C. 4, 5, 12–14, 19, 25, 30, 31, 79, 82, 107
cohesion 15, 17, 24, 61, 73, 90, 111, 116–119, 146
comparative linguistics 5, 139, 140
context 4–6, 8, 9, 11–13, 15, 17–19, 21–24, 29, 31–33, 35–41, 48, 49, 58, 60, 66, 79–85, 94, 99, 103, 105–107, 110, 120, 123–127, 135–137, 139–141, 143, 146, 147
corpus (corpora) 19, 23, 24, 27, 82, 88, 91, 105, 109–125, 127, 128, 131, 133, 134, 143–145
critical discourse analysis (CDA) 68, 136
CroCo 24, 105, 111–116

delicacy 19, 21, 22, 29, 33, 51–54, 78, 84, 110
descriptive translation studies (DTS) 123, 124, 126
doing (field) 83, 85, 86, 97, 100

enabling (field) 40, 83, 85, 86, 97, 100
environments of translation 18, 19, 29, 31, 33, 56, 77, 107, 141, 147
equivalence 8, 13–15, 18–20, 22–26, 30–34, 48, 50, 51, 53, 60, 64, 79, 80, 106, 107, 111, 147
exploring (field) 40, 83, 84, 86, 89, 96, 100, 102, 103

expounding (field) 83, 84, 86, 95, 100
Eurotra 23, 108, 131
Even-Zohar, Itamar 124, 126
experiential (metafunction) 19, 20, 25, 41, 44, 45, 54, 59, 60, 69, 77, 109, 115, 142
eye tracking 126–128, 131, 144, 146, 147

field (contextual parameter) 14, 15, 35, 77, 82–87, 89, 92, 95, 97, 103, 119, 135, 137, 141
Fairclough, Norman 68
Firth, J.R. 9, 11, 12, 81, 82, 106, 126

GECCo 24, 105, 116–119
genre 15, 17, 82, 87, 90, 92, 99, 109, 119–121, 124, 136–138, 144
Grace, George 141, 144
grammatical metaphor 24, 41, 45, 115, 128
graphology 13, 17, 32, 33, 82

Halliday, Michael A.K. 3, 4, 6–16, 18, 19, 24, 25, 29, 30, 32, 33, 35, 37–41, 48, 49, 53, 56–61, 63, 64, 69, 78, 79, 82, 105–107, 111, 126, 131, 135–138, 142
Hansen-Schirra, Silvia 24, 82, 111–113, 115, 116, 143, 145
Hasan, Ruqaiya 8, 15, 61, 79, 82, 84, 85, 111, 136
Hatim, Basil 12, 14, 17, 25, 99
Holmes, James S. 6, 10
House, Juliane 4, 5, 12, 14, 15, 18, 25, 26, 32, 80, 87, 88, 105, 111, 116, 119–123, 126, 127, 134, 143, 144
Huang, Guowen 12, 24, 25, 65, 75, 88, 100

ideational (metafunction) 4, 8, 14, 20, 27, 40–42, 59, 60, 77, 95, 115, 142

information 17, 19, 29, 41, 59, 6164, 68, 79, 80, 92, 108, 112, 116, 122
instantiation 11, 18, 19, 22, 23, 26, 27, 29, 33, 35, 37–39, 81, 82, 103, 110, 111, 124, 136, 137, 139–143, 147
interpersonal (metafunction) 4, 8, 14, 19, 20, 24–27, 40, 41, 45, 53, 56, 57, 59–61, 64–66, 77, 84, 88, 98, 115

Jakobsen, Arnt Lykke 38, 127
Jakobson, Roman 8

keystroke logging 126, 127, 129–131, 144, 146, 147
Kim, Mira 60–64
Kunz, Kerstin 23, 115–118, 138, 145

language description 11, 78, 85, 106, 138, 145
language pair 64, 108, 111, 112, 141, 143, 144
language typology 10, 11, 138, 140, 147
Lapshinova-Koltunski, Ekaterina 109, 117, 118, 145
lexicogrammar 9, 17, 21–24, 29, 31, 31–33, 35, 39, 40, 48, 49, 59, 73, 82, 85, 107, 134, 138, 140
logical (metafunction) 19, 20, 24, 25, 41, 42, 44, 45, 59, 60, 63, 72, 73, 75, 77, 80, 91, 115, 142
logico-semantic type 42, 45, 72, 73, 75, 135, 143

machine translation 52, 53, 104–110, 119, 131, 147
Malinowski, Bronisław 11, 12, 23, 32, 126
Malmkjær, Kirsten 6
Martin, James R. 8, 26, 27, 67, 82, 85, 91, 93, 135–137, 142
Mason, Ian 12, 14, 17, 25, 69, 70, 99
Matthiessen, Christian M.I.M. 3, 4, 6, 7, 9, 11, 12, 18–21, 25, 26, 29–33, 37, 38, 40, 41, 46, 49, 52, 53, 55–62, 64, 69, 77–79, 81–86, 100, 103, 106–108, 126, 127, 133–136, 138–140, 142, 144, 146, 147

metafunction 4, 8, 14, 18–21, 25, 27, 29, 40–42, 45, 52, 58–62, 73, 76, 77, 92, 110, 115, 124, 137, 142, 147
mode (contextual parameter) 4, 15, 35, 82–84, 87, 92, 99, 119
mood 7, 17, 20, 40, 41, 45, 47, 52–58, 61, 64–66, 88, 89, 115, 135, 143–146
modality 20, 45, 46, 64, 65, 88, 90, 98, 115, 143, 146
multimodal (multimodality) 81, 89
Ma, Yuanyi 6, 7, 21, 32, 35, 40, 41, 45, 72–74, 77, 82, 89, 126, 134–136, 143, 144
Munday, Jeremy 3, 12, 24, 26, 42, 66, 67, 81, 96, 105, 111, 123–126, 137, 138

Neumann, Stella 12, 23, 24, 82, 111–113, 115, 143, 145
Newmark, Peter 12, 15, 32, 138
Nida, Eugene 5, 32
Nord, Christiane 9, 25, 64, 80

Pagano, Adriana 127, 145
Pawley, Andrew 141, 142, 144,
phonology 13, 17, 29, 31–33, 35, 48, 49, 82, 136, 137, 140
polarity 45, 47, 48, 111
polysystem theory 124, 126
Prague School 8, 25, 64
process type 20, 40, 45, 54, 56, 69, 70–72, 77, 95, 99, 128, 143, 145
projection 9, 20, 75, 76

rank 5, 6, 13, 18, 19, 21–26, 29, 31, 33, 48–52, 72, 80, 107, 108, 118, 134, 137, 147
recommending (field) 24, 83, 85, 93, 94
recreating (field) 83, 84, 86–89, 94
register 9, 10, 12, 14, 15, 17, 22–27, 37–40, 63, 64, 67, 77, 79, 81, 82, 85, 92, 100, 103, 104, 109, 111–120, 128, 130, 136–144
registerial cartography 79, 81–83, 85
Reiss, Katarina 8, 25, 30, 79–81, 103
reporting (field) 83, 84, 86, 89, 90, 100, 102
Rheme 41, 42, 57, 61–63, 97
Rhetorical Structure Theory (RST) 77, 90

scale and category theory 13, 19, 107
semantics 10, 17, 21, 22, 29, 31–33, 39, 40, 48, 49, 80, 82, 85, 108, 109, 136–138, 140, 142
sharing (field) 83, 84, 86, 89, 98, 99, 140
shift 13, 19–21, 25, 26, 30–33, 35, 40–42, 44, 45, 47,48, 50–54, 56, 60, 67–69, 71–73, 77, 90, 94, 98, 99, 124, 125, 127, 128, 143, 144
skopos 8, 9
speech function 17, 45, 47, 66, 135, 140
Steiner, Erich 4, 6, 11, 12, 18, 19, 23, 24, 30, 82, 93, 105, 107, 108, 111–116, 118, 127, 138, 143, 145
stratification 13, 18, 19, 21–23, 26, 29–33, 39, 77, 80, 82, 107, 110, 124, 136, 137, 139–141, 147
SysAm 145
SysConc 145
SysFan 145

taxis 42, 45, 72, 115, 135, 143
Taylor, Christopher 17, 18, 89, 138, 141
technology 38, 105, 107, 108, 110, 131, 144
Teich, Elke 12, 18, 21–23, 32, 56, 111, 134, 138
tenor (contextual parameter) 14, 15, 24, 35, 36, 77, 82–84, 87, 92, 93, 98–100, 119, 135, 137

Teruya, Kazuhiro 11, 49, 78, 84, 85, 100, 138–140, 144, 147
textual (metafunction) 8, 14, 16, 19, 20, 25, 40–42, 56, 57, 59–62, 73, 77, 115, 143
text type 6, 9, 17, 22, 23, 30, 37, 39, 79–82, 85, 92, 96, 97, 100, 102, 103, 111, 139
Theme 8, 17, 20, 35, 40–42, 56, 57, 60–64, 66, 89, 97, 115, 135, 143–145
transitivity 17, 41, 45, 69, 71, 77, 96, 115, 125
translation universal 116, 126, 142–144
translation unit 114, 127–130
Translog 127, 129
Toury, Gideon 6, 123, 124, 126, 143

Vermeer, Hans 8, 9, 25

Wang, Bo 6, 7, 21, 32, 35, 41, 61, 72, 73, 77, 82, 89, 126, 134–136, 143, 144
Wang, Peng 88
Wang, Yan 77, 98
Wilcock, Graham 108
Wu, Canzhong 11, 35, 65, 73, 75, 85, 100, 101, 111, 134, 138–140, 144–147

Zhang, Meifang 25, 26, 66, 100, 102, 103

Printed and bound by CPI Group (UK) Ltd, Croydon, CR0 4YY
01/04/2026

14854246-0001